DATE DUE

MY 23'00			
JE 14'00			
FE 3'00			
OC 31 01			
DE 17 01			
AP 20'03			
DE 17'04			

About the editors

Anita Hardon, MSc, PhD, received her degree in medical biology from the University of Amsterdam in 1984. She continued to do research in the field of medical anthropology on problems concerning the misuse and uncontrolled distribution of pharmaceuticals in developing countries. Her research appears in *Confronting Ill-Health: Medicines, Self-Care and the Poor in Manila* (1991) and in *Drug Policy in Developing Countries* which she co-authored (Zed Books, 1992). She worked for the Dutch NGO Wemos from 1985 to 1991 as the action research coordinator of the Women and Pharmaceuticals project. This work formed the foundation of the Women's Health Action Foundation, which initiated the studies on which this book is based.

Anita Hardon is currently associate professor at the Medical Anthropology Unit of the University of Amsterdam, where she also coordinates the international action-research network on Gender, Reproductive Health and Population Policies (GRHPP). Her work has been published in *Social Science and Medicine, Health Policy and Planning, Current Anthropology* and other journals in the field of health and development.

Elizabeth Hayes was born in New York in 1964. She received her BA in literature from the College of the Holy Cross (1986) and her MA in journalism from Columbia University in 1989. Formerly a researcher and reporter on consumer health issues, she moved into the European consumers' rights field by joining the International Organization of Consumers' Unions in 1991. From 1994 to 1996, she was the coordinator of the Women's Health Action Foundation and became involved in the project leading to this book. During that time, she edited the publication *Women and Pharmaceuticals: A Healthy Balance?* which was released at the UN Fourth World Conference on Women. Currently, she is a staff member at Health Action International, an NGO that campaigns for rational drug use, in Amsterdam. In addition, she edits and writes for a number of health institutes in the Netherlands.

Reproductive Rights in Practice: A feminist report on quality of care

edited by
ANITA HARDON AND
ELIZABETH HAYES

Zed Books Ltd
LONDON & NEW YORK

This collaborative study was carried out with the financial
support of the Netherlands Ministry of Foreign Affairs.

Reproductive Rights in Practice: A feminist report on quality of care
was first published by Zed Books Ltd, 7 Cynthia Street,
London N1 9JF, UK, and Room 400, 175 Fifth Avenue,
New York, NY 10010, USA, in 1997.

Cover designed by Andrew Corbett
Set in Monotype Garamond by Ewan Smith
Printed and bound in the United Kingdom
by Biddles Ltd, Guildford and King's Lynn

A catalogue record for this book is available from the
British Library

US CIP data is available from the Library of Congress

Distributed exclusively in the USA by St Martin's Press Inc.,
175 Fifth Avenue, New York, NY 10010, USA

ISBN 1 85649 451 9 cased
ISBN 1 85649 452 7 limp

Contents

Tables

Acknowledgements

Writing and editing such a book requires a great deal of work. The editors would like to thank the many people who have given a tremendous amount of their time to make this book a reality. To begin, we would like to thank all members of the teams who carried out the research for the collaborative study on which this book is based. Without their energy and commitment to the project, it would not have been possible to complete the research or compile this book.

The Women's Health Action Foundation (WHAF) organized the collaborative study described here and has provided formal and personal support for the project for the past two and a half years. Specifically, we would like to thank its staff members Annemarie Jurg, Connie López and Jannemieke Hanhart for their support and advice throughout the years of the original collaborative study and the book-writing period. Nicolien Wieringa, WHAF's former action research coordinator, also wrote the initial policy review for the collaborative study. The members of WHAF's advisory committee, Jessika van Kammen, Gunilla Kleiverda, Barbara Mintzes, Floor Rikken and Prisca Zwanikken, read through the final drafts and provided many helpful comments on the text from a women's health perspective. Members of WHAF's executive board, Nelly Oudshoorn, Christianne den Houting and Rita Loupias, are also thanked for their continued support for the project despite setbacks and delays.

As co-project leader of the collaborative study with Anita Hardon, Elly Engelkes was involved in the research project throughout its development and completion and has contributed significantly to the formulation of the methodology used for the study. Anita Hardon is indebted to the University of Amsterdam for the time she was given to spend on the writing of this book. Trudie Gerrits and Theresa Klerkx are thanked for taking over tasks, allowing her to concentrate on the editing and writing.

A number of people created the computer checklists that made the eight country surveys possible. The editors are indebted to Wienecke Icke and Ellen Storm who carried out this work at the Department of Social Sciences at the University of Amsterdam.

Louise Murray and Robert Molteno at Zed Books have offered a great deal of constructive criticism on the various drafts of this book and are thanked for their commitment to this project.

A special mention must be made of those who made it possible for the editors to keep working late into the night and on weekends without a complaint. Elizabeth Hayes would like to thank her husband, Nout Waller, without whose constant support and patience this book would never have reached the publisher. Anita Hardon would like to thank Pieter Streefland who encouraged her to propose the study to WHAF and the Ministry of Foreign Affairs and who has inspired the work since.

This book was made possible through funding from the Netherlands Ministry of Foreign Affairs. Special thanks must be given to Johanna Spreeuwenberg of the Special Programme Women and Development who provided constant encouragement and support for this work.

Abbreviations

ABUTH	Ahmadu Bello University Teaching Hospital (Nigeria)
AIDS	Acquired immune deficiency syndrome
AWBZ	Algemene Wet Bijzondere Ziektekosten (Netherlands' basic government health insurance fund)
BWHC	Bangladesh Women's Health Coalition
CEDAW	United Nations Convention on the Elimination of All Forms of Discrimination Against Women
DHS	Demographic and health survey
FFF	Family Federation of Finland
FGD	Focus group discussion
FPHP	Fourth Population Programme and Health Project (Bangladesh)
FWA	Family welfare assistant (Bangladesh)
GP	General practitioner
HIV	Human immunodeficiency virus
ICPD	United Nations International Conference on Population and Development (1994, often referred to as the 'Cairo Conference')
IEC	Information, education and communication
IPPF	International Planned Parenthood Federation
IUD	Intrauterine device
IVF	In vitro fertilization
LAM	Lactational amenorrhoea method
MCH	Maternal and child health
MR	Menstrual regulation
NCPD	National Council for Population and Development (Kenya)
NHG	Nederlands Huisarts-Genootschap (Dutch Association of General Practitioners)
PPFN	Planned Parenthood Federation of Nigeria
SAP	Structural adjustment programme
STD	Sexually-transmitted disease
UNFPA	United Nations Program on Human Reproduction
USAID	United States Agency for International Development
WHO	World Health Organization

PART ONE

Introduction

CHAPTER I

Reproductive Rights in Practice

Anita Hardon

Providing women and men with access to safe, effective, affordable and acceptable methods of fertility regulation is the aim of family planning programmes worldwide, at least on paper. In fact, assertions about the need for a free and informed choice of contraceptive methods have been made in international declarations for more than twenty-five years. They were first put forward at the 1968 Human Rights Conference held in Tehran, Iran, where UN member states agreed: 'Parents have a basic human right to determine freely and responsibly on the number and spacing of their children and a right to adequate education and information in this respect.'[1]

Adherence to reproductive rights was also called for in the UN Convention on the Elimination of All Forms of Discrimination Against Women (CEDAW) which was adopted by the United Nations in 1979. By June 1995, an overall majority of UN member states (140 out of 159) had ratified it. For the first time, the CEDAW document declared that reproductive rights should be exerted on the basis of *equality* between men and women.[2] Specifically, it recommends that: 'State Parties ... shall ensure, on a basis of equality of men and women ... [t]he same rights to decide freely and responsibly on the number and the spacing of their children and to have access to the information, education and means to enable them to exercise these rights.'[3]

Reproductive rights have been reiterated at UN population conferences, the first of which was held in Bucharest in 1974. This World Population Conference rephrased the 1968 formulation of reproductive rights slightly by assigning *couples and individuals*, and not just parents, the basic right to decide freely and responsibly on the number and spacing of their children. It also added the necessity of providing them with the *means to do so.*[4] It is important to note that in this formulation of reproductive rights, in keeping with the earlier formulations quoted above, people are not only granted the right to decide freely, but also the right to decide 'responsibly'. The 1984 *World Population Plan of Action* further clarified this responsibility:

'Any recognition of rights also implies responsibilities: in this case, it implies that couples and individuals should exercise this right, taking into consideration their own situation, as well as the implications of their decisions for the balanced development of their children, and of the community and society in which they live.'[5]

In practice, the provision of the 'means' to exercise reproductive rights, especially the provision of contraceptives, has been seen by many governments primarily as an effective way to reduce fertility rates and curtail population growth instead of as a means to enhance free and informed choice. This emphasis on population control is reflected in targets set to increase contraceptive prevalence rates and reduce fertility rates. It is further found in the incentives and disincentives used to motivate people to accept contraception. Social marketing campaigns urge people to assist development by limiting family size. Such messages emphasize societal responsibility, not individual rights.

As a result of the population programmes that have been implemented worldwide, the past two decades have seen a rapid expansion of family planning services around the world. While contraceptive use has increased dramatically, the emphasis remains on coverage, not care.

During the 1980s and early 1990s, the international women's health movement challenged the rationale behind population programmes aimed at reducing fertility in developing countries. They took issue with the belief that limiting family size is a societal responsibility that takes precedence over individual well-being and individual rights. This international movement comprises diverse participants ranging from radical feminist groups who view most fertility-regulating technologies as oppressive products of patriarchy to community groups involved in consciousness-raising projects and health-care provision. Their common goal became empowering women to control their own fertility and sexuality with maximal choice and minimal health problems. The movement strongly criticized population programmes' emphasis on the delivery of modern contraceptives (primarily to married women) as a means to reduce fertility and the targets used to achieve those aims.[6] Women's health advocates particularly opposed incentives and disincentives for women and family planning providers as a way to increase contraceptive use. They stressed that such manipulation of demand is not in line with the principle of free choice that is embedded in the reproductive rights declarations discussed earlier.[7] A frequently cited example is the provision of food and clothing to poor women who undergo sterilization in Bangladesh.[8] In addition, the movement has called for more male responsibility regarding fertility regulation and increased attention to the needs of adolescents.

More specifically, the movement questioned the appropriateness of longer-acting contraceptives such as Norplant® (six hormonal rods that are implanted in a woman's upper arm) and the injectable Depo-Provera®.

These two methods are increasingly promoted in programmes to overcome problems related to incorrect use of the contraceptive pill.[9] The lack of user control involved in these methods (both must be administered by health-care providers) has been put forward as an issue of concern, as have the menstrual disturbances caused by these methods.[10] The movement has emphasized the merits of barrier methods such as condoms and diaphragms, that are user-controlled and do not cause side effects.

In addition, international women's health advocates emphasized the importance of providing abortion services to protect a woman's health when an unwanted pregnancy occurs due to contraceptive failure or another reason.

During the preparatory meetings leading to the 1994 UN International Conference on Population and Development (ICPD), women's health advocates demanded that family planning services respect women's and men's reproductive and sexual rights. To succeed, in their view, services must include balanced, objective information about method options. They must grant clients a free and informed choice without any incentives, if and when a method is selected. They believe fertility regulation needs to be found within services that aim at enhancing reproductive health, not at reducing fertility. Such services should also provide women with access to safe abortion services.[11]

For the first time, the *Program of Action* adopted at the 1994 ICPD placed reproductive rights and reproductive and sexual health at the heart of plans to address population growth. In this way it decreased the importance of the demographic objectives of population programmes. This change in emphasis can largely be credited to the activism of women working at the grassroots level and non-governmental organizations (NGOs) that raised these issues during the three-year preparatory phase. The consensus document resulting from the conference moved beyond a narrow focus on family planning to enhance reproductive health, which is defined as follows:[12]

> Reproductive health is a state of complete physical, mental and social well-being and not merely the absence of infirmity, in all matters relating to the reproductive system and to its functions and processes. Reproductive health therefore implies that people are able to have a satisfying and safe sex life and that they have the capability to reproduce and the freedom to decide if, when and how often to do so. Implicit in this last condition are the rights of men and women to be informed and to have access to safe, effective, affordable and acceptable methods of fertility regulation of their choice, as well as other methods of their choice for regulation of fertility which are not against the law, and the right of access to appropriate health-care services that will enable women to go safely through pregnancy and childbirth and provide couples with the best chance of having a healthy infant.[13]

Implementation of the reproductive health approach endorsed at the

1994 ICPD requires family planning and health administrators to plan jointly the implementation of the programmes. It also calls on them to define cost-effective packages of high-quality, integrated services shaped to the specific needs of diverse clients in different settings and available to all who need them.[14]

The *Program of Action* approved during the ICPD actually sets a target for the implementation of reproductive health programmes: 'All countries should strive to make accessible through the primary health-care system, reproductive health to all individuals of appropriate ages as soon as possible and no later than the year 2015.'[15]

There was one important issue that was not resolved at the 1994 ICPD: access to abortion. While access to contraceptives and a free and informed choice of methods have been accepted worldwide as fundamental human rights, the same is not true for access to abortion services. Even though, from a human rights perspective, one can argue that prohibition of abortion prevents women from *not* having children by forcing them to continue an unwanted pregnancy.[16] The ICPD *Program of Action* states: 'In no case should abortion be promoted as a method of family planning. All Governments and relevant intergovernmental and nongovernmental organizations are urged to strengthen their commitment to women's health, to deal with the health impact of unsafe abortion as a major health concern and to reduce the recourse to abortion through expanded and improved family-planning services.'[17]

Reproductive rights in practice

This book is written in the wake of the 1994 ICPD which set ambitious targets on the adoption of reproductive health programmes. That conference's *Program of Action* is now setting the stage for international discussions on how family planning can be expanded to cover the whole area of reproductive health and sexuality. In contrast, this book examines whether or not governments are actually providing men and women today with access to the information, education and means to enable them to exert the basic right to decide freely and responsibly on the number and spacing of their children. It sets out to answer the question: Are women and men who seek family planning services now reaping the benefits of the reproductive rights principles which have been set out on paper for more than twenty-five years?

Whether or not women are able to assert their rights has much to do with gender relations, women's cultural and economic roles and their autonomy, bodily integrity and personhood.[18] Recently, a seven-country study carried out by the International Reproductive Rights Research Action Group (IRRRAG) examined how low-income women in diverse settings make reproductive decisions and how they negotiate the real or perceived opposition of parents, husbands, religious authorities and medical providers.[19] Such a study is complementary to the research described in this book. For, unlike the IRRRAG project, the material included here does not primarily describe the social and cultural context within which women negotiate reproductive rights. Instead, it focuses on the quality of care provided by family planning services as an essential prerequisite for reproductive rights to be respected.

Focusing on quality of care The quality of care given to clients in family planning services has emerged as a priority among women's health advocates and family planning administrators during the 1990s. As discussed earlier, women's health advocates have criticized the quality of care provided, saying that services are too target-oriented and over-emphasize provider-dependent methods. They demand that services adhere to women's reproductive rights and provide them with a free and informed choice of methods. Family planning administrators have become interested in quality of care for other reasons. They have increasingly come to realize that enhancing contraceptive prevalence has a limited effect on fertility rates if quality of care is lacking. That is, programmes would have greater impact if, rather than putting undue emphasis on recruitment, they took better care of the users they already had. The researcher A. K. Jain has stated:

> If a program's mission statement is clarified and defined in terms of *helping individuals meet their reproductive needs* and its impact is measured in terms of *the extent to which services are helping individuals to meet their reproductive needs*, then program strategies adopted by the managers would lead to improvements not only in the quality of care provided through health and family planning services but also in achieving the societal goals of fertility reduction because of such improvements.[20]

When quality of care is found to be lacking, research has shown that clients receiving family planning services often do not continue using methods and fertility rates are not reduced.[21] A study conducted in East Java revealed that the majority of clients (85 per cent) who did not get the method they requested in family planning clinics discontinued use within one year. In contrast, only 25 per cent of the women who did get the method they wanted discontinued using it.[22]

The innovative quality of care framework developed by Judith Bruce and her colleagues at the Population Council has been extremely influential in the 1990s.[23] This framework has been used in operational research by the Population Council and in guidelines for quality of care developed by various US agencies involved in family planning. This framework also forms the basis for an increasing number of studies on quality of care, including the one presented in this book. Building on work done by A. Donabedian[24] and R. Simmons,[25] the Bruce framework emphasizes patient–

provider interactions and informed choice. It consists of six core elements (see also the box opposite):

- Choice of methods: the number of methods available as well as the types of methods for various groups such as men and women who wish to space births.
- Information given to clients: such information includes how appropriate a method is for a potential user, details on how to use the method and its possible effects.
- Technical competence: maintaining aseptic conditions, observing protocols and having staff who are competent in performing clinical techniques.
- Interpersonal relations: how the client perceives interaction with providers, including issues such as the degree of empathy shown in the provider's manner and the amount of time spent with a client.
- Follow-up/continuity mechanisms: ways in which clients are encouraged to continue effective contraceptive use, including means such as reminder cards and home visits.
- Appropriate constellation of services: this includes the extent to which the family planning services are integrated with maternal and child health, postpartum services or other reproductive health services.

Reflecting the Bruce framework, the 1994 ICPD's *Program of Action* recommends that all family planning programmes should:

- ensure information and access to the widest possible range of safe and effective family planning methods appropriate to the individual's age, parity, family size preference and other factors, to enable men and women to exercise free and informed choice;
- provide accessible, complete and accurate information about various family planning methods, including their health risks and benefits, side effects and their effectiveness in the prevention of HIV/AIDS and other sexually transmitted diseases;
- ensure safe, affordable and convenient services for the user;
- ensure privacy and confidentiality;
- ensure a continuous supply of high-quality contraceptives;
- expand and improve formal and informal training in sexual and reproductive health care and family planning including training in interpersonal communications and counselling;
- ensure adequate follow-up care, including that for side effects related to contraceptive use.[26]

However, neither the quality of care framework developed by Bruce nor the recommendations adopted in Cairo touch on the use of incentives and disincentives in family planning programmes. This is despite the fact that the provision of incentives and disincentives to users and to family

---

The quality of the service experience: its origins and impacts

Programme effort	Elements in the unit of services received	Impacts
Policy/political support	Choice of methods	Client knowledge
Resources allocated	Information given clients Technical competence	Client satisfaction
Programme management/ structure	Interpersonal relations Follow-up/continuity mechanisms Appropriate constellation of services	Client health Contraceptive use: • acceptance • continuation

Source: J. Bruce (1990) 'Fundamental Elements of the Quality of Care: A Simple Framework', *Studies in Family Planning* 21(2): 63.

---

planning providers has been a major criticism by women's health advocates.[27] The only acceptable type of incentive, from their perspective, is reimbursement of the actual costs incurred to obtain the family planning method.

Though a strength of the Bruce framework is its emphasis on the process of providing family planning services, a limitation is that it pays less attention to the health care structures necessary for quality of care. Structural factors are included in the framework as programme efforts, but are not included in the six core elements. The need to consider a health-care infrastructure that enables safe use of fertility-regulating methods has been put forward by women's health advocates as an important criterion for quality of care in response to the introduction of more complex contraceptive technologies such as Norplant®. A study on the use of Norplant® in family planning programmes, for example, highlighted problems of unhygienic insertion and difficulties in removal[28] related to health centres' deficiencies in water supply and the equipment used.

Incentives and disincentives and the quality of the health-care infrastructure were included in a set of guidelines for the safe and ethical provision of fertility-regulating methods that was developed in 1991 by the Women and Pharmaceuticals project of the Dutch NGO Wemos which later became the Women's Health Action Foundation. These guidelines were developed in cooperation with women's health groups in developing countries. They were seen as a tool to evaluate adherence to reproductive rights in practice. The four basic criteria included in these guidelines for safe and ethical care are:

- The need for a free and informed choice of contraceptive methods. Such choice includes the number of methods offered to clients on a reliable basis. Free choice also means that clients must make their own decision about their method of choice without undue influence from a provider based upon the provider's own preference.
- Balanced provision of information. In order to make an informed choice, clients have a right to accurate, objective and complete information on all possible contraceptive methods available.
- Avoidance of incentives and disincentives. No client should be pressured to use a particular method because of any incentive or sanction tied to its use (for the client or the provider).
- A health-care infrastructure that enables safe fertility regulation. Family planning services should be seen within a broader context of reproductive and sexual health services available to clients. Providers must be adequately trained to offer services and ensure that they are carried out safely. Water supply has to be guaranteed, room for private consultations should be available, and blood-pressure cuffs and speculums should also be present in the facilities.

Table 1.1 shows how the criteria put forward by women's health advocates and the elements included in the Bruce framework are related.

For each of the four criteria put forward by women's health advocates, indicators have been developed.[29] These indicators balance interpersonal and technical aspects of quality of care, process and structure. The indicators form the basis of the data that are presented in the country chapters of this book.

The contents of this book

This book aims to reveal where reproductive rights are being respected in family planning services and, just as importantly, where, how and why they are being denied. This is done by highlighting current trends in eight different countries which have each ratified the CEDAW declaration and thus, at least on paper, are committed to reproductive rights.

The following chapter first reviews each of the participating countries' population policies and assesses to what extent they aim at respecting people's reproductive rights. Chapter 3 summarizes health and fertility statistics from the selected countries. It attempts to determine the extent to which unmet need for fertility regulation is a problem in the countries and, if so, its causes.

Table 1.1 Criteria for safe and ethical provision of fertility-regulation technologies *vis-à-vis* the more operational elements of care put forward by Bruce

Criteria for safe and ethical care put forward by women's health advocates	Elements in the Bruce framework
The need for a free and informed choice of methods.	Choice of methods: the number of the methods available as well as the types of methods for various groups such as men and women who wish to space births.
The provision of balanced and objective information on contraceptives and other fertility-regulating methods.	Information given to clients: such information includes how appropriate a method is for a potential user; details on how to use the method and its possible side effects.
	Interpersonal relations: how the client perceives interaction with providers, including issues such as the degree of empathy in the provider's manner and the amount of time spent with a client.
The avoidance of incentives and disincentives.	(Not included in the framework)
A health-care infrastructure which enables fertility-regulating methods to be used safely.	Follow-up/continuity mechanisms: ways in which clients are encouraged to continue effective contraceptive use, including means such as reminder cards and home visits.
	Appropriate constellation of services: integration of family planning with e.g. maternal and child health, postpartum services or other reproductive health services.
	Technical competence: maintaining aseptic conditions, observing protocols and having staff who are competent in performing clinical techniques.

Source: A. Hardon.

In the second part of this book, eight country case studies are presented which describe the quality of the family planning services. The countries examined are Bangladesh, Bolivia, Finland, Kenya, Mexico, the Netherlands, Nigeria and Thailand. The book thus includes information from quite different economic, health and cultural settings in order to provide assorted examples on the current status of quality of care and adherence to reproductive rights. Each country chapter assesses the extent to which people are provided with a free and informed choice of methods; whether this choice is restricted in practice; if incentives and disincentives are used; and if the family planning services are integrated within other health services in practice. Only by knowing the actual way in which clients attending family planning clinics experience their care and how providers view their own role can an assessment be made of how closely everyday practice reflects policy ideals.

Finally, the concluding section of the book reviews the relationship between the way reproductive rights are set out in policy and followed in practice.

Limitations Quality of care varies from time to time; from region to region within countries; and from health centre to health centre. Because the empirical data reported in this book have only been collected in selected areas of each of the countries mentioned, the data included in the country studies do not give an adequate view of quality of care in the entire country. In fact, the data collected in the eight countries should be seen as 'snapshots' of quality of care. The appraisals were done between November 1994 and March 1995. Since that time, changes may have taken place in the quality of care given in the studied regions. New guidelines may have been drawn up addressing the provision of contraceptives in family planning services; new methods may have been introduced; or alternately, methods found to be in common use may now be stocked in smaller amounts leading to different shortages than the ones this book records. Economies may have surged or developed crises affecting the provision of contraceptives and people's ability to pay for them. Also, donors may have decided not to renew funding to some programmes, or to call for changes in the programmes studied following the ICPD meeting where integrated reproductive health care was endorsed as the way forward.

Therefore, the data presented in the following chapters can only be indicative of elements in quality of care that require attention. When summaries are made of the data collected, it should be clear that the authors are not putting forward judgements about the *current* conduct in family planning programmes in the countries where the research took place. Still, the contributions made by the authors of this volume are extremely important.[30] This is true, first, because all the authors are researchers who view quality of care from the perspective of women's health and needs, not with a demographic objective in mind. Second, it is important as most of the countries included here have had very little information published on the quality of care provided by their family planning services.

This book sets out to provide findings, views and recommendations on quality of care from a women's health perspective. It is hoped that the points raised can provide important input for national policy discussions on the implementation of high-quality, reproductive health care as put forward as a priority in the ICPD *Program of Action*. It is hoped that this book and its companion methodology handbook[31] will encourage those interested in this issue to continue examining quality of care in their own region. Continued vigilance and advocacy are needed to ensure that family planning and reproductive health services worldwide respect women's and men's reproductive and sexual rights, first and foremost.

Notes

1. United Nations General Assembly (UNGA) (1969) *Teheran Proclamation on Human Rights*, Res. 2545 [xxiv] (New York: UN). Note that at the time it was parents who had rights, not individual men and women.

2. United Nations (1979) *UN Convention on the Elimination of All Forms of Discrimination Against Women (CEDAW)*, UN Doc. A/Res/34/180 (New York: UN).

3. United Nations (1979) *CEDAW*, art. 16(1), para. 4. GAOR Supplement, No. 21 (A/34/46).

4. United Nations (1974) *Report of the United Nations World Population Conference* (New York: UN), para. 14(f) (A/Conf. 60.19).

5. United Nations (1984) *Report of the International Conference on Population* (New York: UN), recommendation 26 (E/Conf 76.19).

6. C. Garcia-Morena and A. Claro (1994) 'Challenges from the Women's Health Movement: Women's Rights Versus Population Control', in G. Sen et al. (eds), *Population Policies Reconsidered: Health, Empowerment and Rights*, Harvard Series on Population and International Health (Boston, MA: Harvard University Press).

7. B. Hartmann and H. Standing (1985) *Food, Saris and Sterilization. Population Control in Bangladesh* (London: Bangladesh International Action Group).

8. Ibid.

9. B. Hartmann (1987) *Reproductive Rights and Wrongs: The Global Politics of Population Control and Contraceptive Choice* (New York: Harper and Row); C. Garcia-Moreno and A. Claro, 'Challenges from the Women's Health Movement'.

10. A. P. Hardon (1992) 'The Needs of Women Versus the Interests of Family Planning Personnel, Policy-makers and Researchers: Conflicting Views on Safety and Acceptability of Contraceptives', *Social Science and Medicine*, 35(6): 753–66.

11. A. Germain and R. Kyte (1995) *The Cairo Consensus: The Right Agenda at the Right Time* (New York: International Women's Health Coalition).

12. United Nations ICPD (1994) *Program of Action* (UN International Conference on Population and Development; text dated 19 September 1994) (New York: ICPD Secretariat).

13. United Nations (1994) ICPD *Program of Action*, para. 7.2.

14. I. Aitken and L. Reichenbach (1994) 'Reproductive and Sexual Health Services: Expanding Access and Enhancing Quality', in G. Sen et al. (eds), *Population Policies Reconsidered*.

15. UN (1994) ICPD *Program of Action*, para. 7.6.

16. Laws prohibiting abortion often invoke the protection of the unborn child's life and treat abortion as homicide, though international human rights laws do not recognize the foetus's right to life. The Council of Europe's Commission on Human Rights articulated its views on the primacy of women's rights regarding abortion as early as 1980. It stated that a foetus's 'right to life' could not be constructed so as

to jeopardize that of the mother and added, 'this would mean that the "unborn life" of the fetus would be regarded as being of higher value than the life of the pregnant woman'. See European Commission on Human Rights, 'Decision in the Case of X. v. The United Kingdom of 13 May 1980', Application 8416/79, D.R. 19: 244. Cited in K. Tomaševski (1994) *Human Rights in Population Policies: A Study for SIDA* (Lund, Sweden: SIDA).

17. United Nations (1994) ICPD *Program of Action*, para. 8.25.

18. See also S. Corrêa (1994) *Population and Reproductive Rights: Feminist Perspectives from the South* (London: Zed Books), for an excellent book on feminist perspectives from the South on reproductive rights. The book outlines how DAWN (Development Alternatives with Women for a New Era), a network of Southern women activists and researchers, views reproductive rights.

19. International Reproductive Rights Research Action Group (IRRRAG) (1996) *Negotiating Reproductive Rights: A Seven Country Study of Women's Views and Practices* (New York: IRRRAG).

20. A. K. Jain (ed.) (1992) *Managing Quality of Care in Population Programs*, 18 (West Hartford, CT: Kumarian Press).

21. Ibid.

22. S. Pariani (1989) *Continued Use of Contraceptives Among Clients in East Java, Indonesia.* PhD dissertation. Department of Sociology, University of California, Los Angeles.

23. J. Bruce (1990) 'Fundamental Elements of the Quality of Care: A Simple Framework', in *Studies in Family Planning* 21(2): 61–91.

24. A. Donabedian (1988) 'The Quality of Care: How Can It be Assessed?', *Journal of the American Medical Association* 260(12): 1743–8.

25. R. Simmons et al. (1986) 'Client Relations in South Asia: Programmatic and Societal Determinants', *Studies in Family Planning* 17(6): 257–68; and R. Simmons (1991) 'Methodologies for Studying Clients' Interactions'. Paper presented at the Seminar on Client Relations and Quality of Care (New York: Population Council).

26. As summarized in M. Alcala (1994) *Action for the 21st Century. Reproductive Health and Rights for All: Summary Report of Recommended Actions on Reproductive Health and Rights in the Cairo ICPD Program of Action* (New York: Family Care International), based on the ICPD *Program of Action* (1994) paras 7.5a, 7.21, 7.23a–g, and 11.21.

27. B. Hartmann and H. Standing (1985) *Food, Saris and Sterilization*.

28. B. Mintzes et al. (1993) *Norplant: Under Her Skin* (Delft: Women's Health Action Foundation and Eburon).

29. More information about the criteria and the indicators developed from them can be found in this book's accompanying methodology handbook (see note 31).

30. This collaborative study was done under stringent budget constraints. In fact, without the commitment and endurance of the researchers, who did much more than they were paid for, this book would have never appeared.

31. At the request of the Women's Health Action Foundation, Anita Hardon and a number of the researchers contributing to this book have written an accompanying methodology handbook which explains how such an assessment can be done. Copies of *Monitoring Family Planning and Reproductive Rights: A manual for empowerment* can be obtained through WHAF and Zed Books, London.

CHAPTER 2

A Review of National Family Planning Policies

Anita Hardon

The quality of family planning services finds its roots in national health and population policies. Assessing the quality of care of services therefore starts with an evaluation of national policies in the light of globally endorsed reproductive rights. In the countries participating in this study, the researchers reviewed government policies and those of other institutions involved in the provision of family planning services. Central to the policy review were the objectives of the policies and programmes, the targets set and any restrictions placed on the provision of family planning methods.

The individual countries' policy reviews are presented in the following chapters together with the results of the field work. This chapter provides an introduction to relevant policy and programme issues.

Balancing demographic and health objectives

To begin, one must first review the overall objectives of the countries' population policies in the wake of the 1994 ICPD when the quality of care appraisals were done. Of course, the official population policies of the eight countries described in this book do not yet reflect the radical changes in policy made at the global level. Some of the policies still emphasize demographic objectives, others include health targets, and still others do not have a population policy because population is not considered an issue.

Bangladesh was found to be the country with a population control programme most strongly tied to demographic goals. The Bangladesh government accords top priority to population control and family planning and is strengthening appropriate legislation to help national policies succeed. Efforts to control the population are strongly encouraged by incentives and disincentives, a policy that continued in Bangladesh's fourth *Five Year Plan for Population Control (1990–1995)*. At the lowest level of health care in Bangladesh, family welfare assistants trained specifically in family planning provide contraceptives to households. However, even the current Bangladesh plan includes health-related objectives, such as the reduction of infant and maternal mortality rates.

In Kenya, the population programme was also found to be predominantly demographically oriented. The 1989–1993 Development Plan listed only demographic goals for its population policy, no health goals. In its *1991 Program Review and Strategy Development Report*, the UN's Program on Human Reproduction (UNFPA) in fact noted that the policy underrepresented the value of fertility moderation for personal health and family welfare reasons, instead placing too much emphasis on the need to curtail population growth.[1] In practice, family planning services in Kenya are embedded in primary health-care services, and no incentives or sanctions are used to persuade people to use contraceptives.

In countries such as Mexico, Nigeria and Thailand, population policies aim to reduce fertility rates but the policies include health objectives as well. As is the case in Kenya, the family planning programmes are embedded in primary health-care services and no incentives or disincentives are used to persuade people to use contraceptives. Mexico's population policy aims to control population growth but also tries to accomplish balanced development and improvement in the quality of life of all Mexicans. In Nigeria, the *National Policy for Development, Unity, Progress and Self-Reliance* mentions demographic objectives, aiming to delay the age at which women have their first child for example, as well as lowering infant mortality. In Thailand, the official population policy emphasizes the reduction of population growth and crude death rates. Services are provided in government health clinics.

Bolivia, Finland and the Netherlands are the three countries studied that do not have a formal population policy aimed at reducing population growth. Bolivia has a high fertility rate, whereas Finland and the Netherlands both have near-zero population growth. According to its National Population Council, Bolivia needs a larger population (despite high fertility rates, its population is relatively small) and an improvement in health standards, especially for women and girls. The official policy states that birth control is not a goal in itself. Individual rights are recognized with regard to choosing the number of children to have and when to have them. In Bolivia, providing basic education for women has also been recognized as a national priority. Campaigns to promote equal distribution of domestic responsibilities between men and women are planned.

In Finland, family planning is a part of health care that has traditionally been regarded as a primary responsibility of the state. In 1977, the Dutch government officially adopted the principle of respecting the right of each couple to decide freely and responsibly on the number and spacing of their children. This decision implies that the task of the government is to create conditions which allow couples to make informed choices.

There are no demographic objectives and there is no formal population policy.

As shown, the national population policies of Mexico, Nigeria and Thailand have explicit health objectives. Does this indicate a shift to a more integrated reproductive health approach? One must realize, however, that mentioning the aim of reducing infant, maternal and/or crude birth rates does not mean that the implemented programmes are in fact aimed at improving reproductive health. Lowering mortality rates can be mentioned simply as an added rationale for the implementation of family planning programmes. Moreover, reduction of maternal and infant mortality is the objective of mother and child care programmes that exist in most developing countries. Integrated reproductive health care was not yet adopted in national policies at the time of this collaborative, eight-country study.

Promoting individual rights

To assess if reproductive rights are being met in family planning services, one should review whether or not the governments aim to enable men and women to decide freely on the number of the children they want and if they provide them with the means to do so.

The policy review shows that access to contraceptives is often still restricted. In order to respect people's reproductive rights, governments should make contraceptives accessible to individual men and women, and adolescents. Restrictions in terms of marital status, age or spousal consent violate people's individual rights.

Restrictions were found to be official government policy in Kenya, Nigeria, Bolivia, Mexico and Bangladesh. Kenya's policy requires spousal consent in the provision of all contraceptives. In Bolivia, Mexico, Bangladesh and Nigeria spousal consent is required in the case of sterilization. Only in the Netherlands, Finland and Thailand is the provision of contraceptives not officially restricted in such a way.[2]

A number of the selected countries do recognize the specific needs of adolescents and are developing policies to respond to them. One example is Nigeria, where a target has been formulated to provide suitable family life education, family planning information and to make services available to all adolescents by the year 2000. In a similar way, special family planning clinics for adolescents have been set up in Finland.

Existing gender bias in policies can lead to inequalities in the provision of contraceptives that are not in line with the CEDAW declaration which emphasizes gender equality in access to services. For example, Nigeria's policy includes double standards on the 'ideal' number of children and marriage age for men and women. It requests women not to have more than four children while it only encourages men to limit their wives and children to a number they can support. It also proposes that the ideal marriage age for women is nineteen while it is twenty-five for men. In the same way, in Mexico's guidelines on contraceptive provision, men's dissatisfaction with certain methods is stressed, while issues that affect women's dissatisfaction are ignored.

Free choice is especially important in the case of non-reversible methods such as sterilization. The national population policy of Kenya notes that all forms of surgical sterilization must be voluntary after the client has been given all relevant information. This policy reflects the need to respect individuals' reproductive rights and is a response to existing coercive practices which have been documented. The recent Bolivian policy has as one of its objectives the rejection of involuntary sterilization, a reaction to sterilizations conducted in the past without appropriate informed consent procedures.

Access to abortion services

In all of the developing countries included in this book – Nigeria, Kenya, Thailand, Bangladesh, Bolivia and Mexico – access to abortion is restricted. The limited grounds on which abortion is allowed by law are to protect the health of the mother, if there is reason to believe the child will be deformed or if the pregnancy is the result of rape or incest. In the Netherlands and Finland, abortion is available on broad socio-medical grounds.

In Kenya, Nigeria and Bangladesh the penal code permits abortion only to save the life of a pregnant woman. Despite the restrictive nature of the law in Bangladesh, 'menstrual regulation' services are available in the government's family planning programme. Menstrual regulation is allowed up to ten weeks from the last menstrual period. When performing menstrual regulation, no pregnancy test is done. Because the penal code requires pregnancy to be established for prosecution to take place, menstrual regulation makes it virtually impossible for the prosecutor to obtain the required proof. In Bangladesh, the penalty facing a person convicted of performing an abortion for non-therapeutic reasons is three to ten years in prison. In Kenya and Nigeria, a person performing an abortion risks up to thirteen years imprisonment.[3]

In Bolivia, Mexico and Thailand, the conditions under which abortion is allowed are broader. In Bolivia, it can be done to save the pregnant woman's life, to preserve her health or when the pregnancy results from incest or rape. In Mexico, exceptions include when the woman fails to take proper care of the foetus, if continuation of the pregnancy will endanger the life of the woman, or if the pregnancy is the result of rape. Persons regularly performing abortions can be sentenced to one to six years in prison in Bolivia and up to eight years in Mexico. A woman wilfully inducing her own miscarriage in Mexico may be imprisoned from six months to five years.[4]

In Finland and the Netherlands, women generally have access to safe abortion facilities. In Finland, the abortion law was liberalized in 1970. Abortion at the woman's request is allowed on the grounds of broad social and health conditions. These include when the living conditions or other circumstances of a woman and those of her family, or the delivery and care of a child would place a significant strain on her. In 1981, a far-reaching abortion law was adopted in the Netherlands. Abortion is now permitted when the woman attests to a state of distress due to the pregnancy. A five-day waiting period between the initial consultation and the procedure is required.[5]

Male responsibility

While many countries have policies that allow men to veto the use of contraceptives by their wives, few countries have formulated population policies to enhance men's responsibility for fertility-regulation matters. The population policy of Kenya aims at motivating Kenyan males to adopt and practise family planning. However, it remains unclear whether this should result in men using contraceptives themselves or allowing their partners or spouses to practise family planning. The Mexican population policy also states that it promotes men's participation in the programme. Condoms and male sterilization are the only male contraceptive methods widely available. But, as already said, in family planning guidelines, the disadvantages of these methods for men are highlighted.

Quality of care ignored

It is remarkable that the quality of care of family planning services is rarely stated as a goal in policy documents. An exception is the Kenyan policy where clinic service goals have been formulated that, when implemented, can be expected to enhance quality of care (see box on page 20).

In Mexico, a specific objective is formulated 'to raise the service quality level' without further specification of what that means.

An important aspect of quality of care is the training of family planning personnel. In Thailand, the national population policy explicitly includes the training of public health personnel to carry out family planning services. It also mentions special training for health and medical workers to enable them to provide more highly technical services, such as female and male sterilization. The clinic service goals formulated in Kenya and cited in the box overleaf include adequate counselling, examination and follow-up of contraceptive users. Also, they recognize the need to promote community-based distribution and the training of community-based

---

Clinic service goals included in the 1989–1993 Development Plan of Kenya

- To ensure availability of contraceptive services for those women and men who are ready for them and need them.
- To ensure adequate counselling, examination and follow-up of contraceptive users.
- To strengthen the Ministry of Health's capacity to collect data on births and deaths in order to give it the ability to relate provision of health and health-related services to mortality and fertility.
- To strengthen the community-based dissemination of population-related information.
- To promote the community-based distribution of contraceptives and the training of community-based distributors.
- To train, retrain and supervise health and other contraceptive workers in the provision of contraceptive services.
- To be vigilant about the type and quality of contraceptives provided in the service delivery points.

Source: 1989–1993 Development Plan of Kenya.

---

distributors as well as the training, retraining and supervision of health and family planning workers. The Mexican population policy also explicitly mentions the need to train health assistants and drugstore employees.

In the Netherlands where services are largely provided by general practitioners, training in family planning services is mainly organized by professional associations. Based on consensus meetings, national, professional guidelines on prescribing oral contraceptive pills and IUDs have been developed. Although free and informed choice is included within these standards, the focus is on medical/technical aspects (hygienic insertion and contraindications). Within the country's specialized reproductive health clinics (run by an organization called the Rutgers Foundation), service providers are generally trained to address women's reproductive health needs.

In conclusion

Apart from the Netherlands, Finland and Bolivia, the policies of the countries studied have the setting of demographic targets in common. It can be hypothesized that the setting of such targets has a negative effect on quality of care and adherence to reproductive rights. The target orientation may lead to biased information provision: an emphasis on methods' benefits while disregarding side effects that can have detrimental effects on people's health. Targets can also result in the unbalanced promotion of permanent and semi-permanent methods such as sterilization, IUDs, and longer-acting hormonal injections and implants over methods that are more user-controlled such as contraceptive pills and condoms.

In terms of access to contraception, the policies reviewed show that governments, despite aims to enhance contraceptive prevalence, tend to restrict access to contraceptives to married women. The country case studies will show to what extent such restrictions are adhered to in practice and thereby how they violate people's individual reproductive rights.

Notes

1. United Nations Program on Human Reproduction (UNFPA) (1991) *1991 Program Review and Strategy Development Report* (New York: UN).
2. International Planned Parenthood Federation (IPPF)/IWRAW (1995) Reproductive Rights Wall Chart (London: IPPF Distribution Unit).
3. United Nations (1993) *Abortion Policies: A Global Review*, Vol. 2 (New York: UN Department for Economic and Social Information and Policy Analysis); United Nations (1992) *Abortion Policies: A Global Review*, Vol. 1 (New York: UN Department for Economic and Social Information and Policy Analysis).
4. United Nations (1993; 1992) *Abortion Policies.*
5. United Nations (1993) *Abortion Policies.*

CHAPTER 3

Setting the Stage: Health, Fertility and Unmet Need in Eight Countries

Anita Hardon

In terms of economic development, the countries included in this book vary extensively. The Netherlands and Finland are considered 'highly developed' countries. Thailand and Mexico are so-called 'upper middle-income economies'. The other countries included are described as 'lower middle-income' and 'low-income' countries.

Table 3.1 presents their health and fertility statistics. It shows that the lower middle- and low-income countries included in this collaborative study (i.e. Kenya, Nigeria and Bolivia) have high mortality and fertility rates.[1] The situation in Bangladesh is unique: it has undergone a remarkable decline in fertility despite a low level of economic development and continuing high mortality.

In the high- and upper middle-income countries of Finland, the Netherlands and Thailand, relatively low maternal and infant mortality and fertility rates are found. One could characterize Mexico as a country in transition. Its mortality figures are relatively low, but it has an intermediate-level fertility rate.[2]

Unmet need

An indicator for the extent to which the existing family planning services are meeting reproductive needs in these diverse health and development settings is unmet need. This is defined as the gap between the total fertility rates found and the desired fertility rates. Table 3.2 provides data on this aspect from the six developing countries.

Table 3.2 shows that unmet need is relatively high in Kenya, Bolivia and Mexico. Here, women's desired number of children is much lower than the average actual family size. Unmet need is at an intermediate level in Nigeria and Bangladesh and low in Thailand. Strikingly, in Nigeria, desired family size is still high, indicating a limited need for family planning. In Bangladesh and Thailand, desired family size is lower and it

Table 3.1 Demographic figures 1995

Level of economic development	Nigeria	Kenya	Bolivia	Mexico	Bangladesh	Thailand	Finland	Netherlands
	Low	Low	Lower middle	Upper middle	Low	Upper middle	High	High
Population (in millions) (1993)	105.3	25.3	7.1	90.0	115.2	58.1	5.1	15.3
Maternal mortality[1] (1993)	800 (1993)	498[2] (1994)	600 (1993)	65 (1986)	600 (1993)	37 (1987)	11	10
Infant mortality (1993)	83	61	73	35	106	36	5	7
Total fertility rate (1993)	6.4	5.2	4.7	3.1	4.3	2.1	1.9	1.6
Population growth rate (1993–2000)	2.9	2.5	2.4	1.8	2.1[3]	0.9	0.4	0.6
Female illiteracy rate (%) (1990)	61	42	29	15	78	10	<5	<5
Life expectancy at birth (1993)	51	58	60	71	56	69	76	78

Notes: [1] Data on rates for Mexico, Thailand, Finland and the Netherlands obtained from *Maternal Mortality: A Global Fact Book* (Geneva: World Health Organization, 1991). [2] Data from *Kenya Maternal Mortality Baseline Study* (UNICEF, 1994). [3] This covers the period 1980–93.
Source: World Development Report 1995: Workers in an Integrated World (Oxford: OUP and World Development Indicators, 1995).

Table 3.2 Gap between total fertility rate and total desired fertility as reported by the Demographic and Health Surveys

	Nigeria (1990)	Kenya (1993)	Bolivia (1994)	Mexico (1987)	Bangladesh (1993–94)	Thailand (1987)
Total fertility rate	6.0	5.4	4.8	4.8	3.4	2.2
Total *desired* fertility rate	5.0	3.4	2.7	2.8	2.1	1.8

Sources: Demographic and Health Surveys (DHS): Nigeria 1990; Kenya 1993; Bolivia 1994; Mexico 1987; Bangladesh 1993–94; and Thailand 1987. (Data not available for Finland and the Netherlands.)

could be hypothesized that the services are doing quite well in meeting needs in these countries. No data on unmet need are available for the Netherlands and Finland. From the low incidence of abortion in these countries where abortion is legal, one can assume that unmet need is very limited.

Overall, it has been calculated that unmet need for contraception is highest in Sub-Saharan Africa. It is estimated that approximately four out of every ten women in this region who need contraception are actually using it.[3] In Asia and Latin America, higher percentages of reproductive-age women are using contraception and unmet need is lower. On average in these areas, seven out of ten women in need of contraception are actually using it.[4]

Abortion   Unmet need is a major public health problem because it leads to unwanted pregnancies and, in countries where access to safe abortion is limited, unsafe abortions. Women who are pregnant against their will resort to unauthorized facilities and providers who are not trained in performing aseptic abortions. The 1990s have shown an increase of attention on the consequences of unsafe abortion worldwide. Globally, it is estimated that 20 million unsafe abortions take place annually in developing countries.[5] Latin America has the highest estimated number of unsafe abortions: 40 out of every 1,000 women of reproductive age undergo such a procedure each year. In Africa, it is estimated that nearly 30 out of 1,000 women undergo an unsafe abortion each year. In Asia, the rate is only 12 per 1,000. For Europe as a whole, it is estimated that two women in every 1,000 women have an unsafe abortion each year, though in Western and Northern Europe the incidence is said to be negligible. In other words, these figures suggest that, depending on the developing region, between 1 and 4 per cent of reproductive-age women have an unsafe abortion each year. In Europe, this incidence is ten times lower, at around 0.2 per cent. The high incidence of unsafe abortion in developing countries leads to excessive reproductive morbidity and mortality. The risk of death due to these unsafe procedures has been calculated by the WHO. It is highest in Africa where it is estimated that one out of every 150 unsafe procedures leads to maternal death. In Asia, the figure is 250 and in Latin America only one in 800. Overall, unsafe abortions account for approximately one in eight maternal deaths.[6]

Non-use of contraceptives

In light of the severe consequences of unwanted pregnancy in countries where access to safe abortion is limited, why is it that women who do not want more children do not use contraceptives? Table 3.3 shows the extent to which women are using contraceptives in the eight countries studied

Table 3.3 Distribution of contraceptive methods (%)

	Nigeria	Kenya	Bolivia	Mexico	Bangladesh	Thailand	Finland	Netherlands
Any methods	7.5	25.9	30.1	52.7	46.6	65.5	75	–
Modern methods	3.7	20.7	11.8	44.6	36.2	63.6	74	70
Pill	1.4	7.5	1.9	9.7	17.4	18.6	29	43
IUD	0.7	2.8	5.2	10.2	2.2	6.9	17	5
Injection	0.7	5.5	0.5	2.8	4.5	8.5	0	not available
Condom	0.5	0.9	1.0	1.9	3.0	1.1	18	7
Female sterilization	0.2	3.9	3.1	18.6	8.1	22.8	8	3
Male sterilization	0[1]	0[1]	0[1]	0.8	1.1	5.7	1	7
Diaphragm/jelly	0.2[2]	0.1	0.1	0.6	not available	0	0	not available
Traditional methods	3.8	5.2	18.3	8.1	8.4	1.9	1	5[3]
No use	92.5	74.1	69.9	47.3	53.4	34.5	25	30
Total	100	100	100	100	100	100	100	100

Notes: [1] Data not included in DHS survey. [2] Exclusively foaming tablets. [3] Other methods.
Sources: Demographic and Health Surveys (DHS): Nigeria 1990; Kenya 1993; Bolivia 1994; Mexico 1987; Bangladesh 1993–94; and Thailand 1987. Finland data taken from the National Research and Development Centre for Welfare and Health (S. Sihvo et al. [1995] *Contraception and Use of Health Services: Results of a Population-based Study 1994*, STAKES series: 27/1995). The Netherlands' data taken from *Social Atlas of Women*, Part I (Rijswijk: Social and Cultural Plan Bureau, 1991).

while Table 3.4 gives the most important reasons for non-use of contraceptives in these countries.

Table 3.3 shows that contraceptive prevalence is extremely low in Bolivia and Nigeria, the countries where population growth and total fertility rates are still relatively high. Contraceptive use is remarkably high in Bangladesh. It further shows that the contraceptive pill is the most commonly used method in the studied countries, except for Bolivia and Mexico where the IUD is used more often. The question that these figures raise for the quality of care assessment is whether or not the differences in contraceptive use are related to differences in choice. That is, do women in Bolivia and Mexico actually *prefer* the IUD or is its use due to differences in service provision?

Table 3.4 lists the main reasons women gave the Demographic and Health Surveys (DHS) of the selected countries for not using contraceptives even though they did not want more children. It shows that indeed in Nigeria most women who do not use contraceptives want to have children. In the other countries, they usually do not want children. Important reasons for not using contraceptives include notions of infertility, the belief that one is experiencing menopause or health concerns.

If one excludes fertility-related reasons for non-use – i.e. those women who have had a hysterectomy or have passed through menopause – it becomes apparent that the main reasons cited differ. Religion is an important factor in Bangladesh (a predominantly Muslim country) and Nigeria (where approximately half of the population is Muslim and the other half Christian). Lack of knowledge about family planning scores high in Nigeria, Bolivia and Mexico and health concerns are mentioned as important reasons in Kenya, Bolivia, Mexico and Thailand.

Lack of knowledge about family planning is a factor that involves the coverage of family planning services, information provision from the service providers and the promotion of family planning in the media. Nigeria and Bolivia have relatively young family planning programmes and the reported lack of knowledge could be attributed to this factor. Bolivia and Mexico have large indigenous populations that do not speak Spanish and therefore cannot be easily reached by the media which predominantly provide information in Spanish. Female illiteracy is another factor that is related to lack of knowledge on family planning as most information materials on family planning are usually written ones. However, in Bangladesh, a country with high female illiteracy, this situation has not resulted in a lack of knowledge about family planning. The reason for this is probably Bangladesh's chosen method of 'doorstep delivery' of contraceptives by means of family welfare assistants. These family planning promoters talk with women and men in their homes. This greatly enhances access to contraceptives and knowledge about contraceptive options.

Health concerns can be related to a lack of appropriate counselling. If

Table 3.4 Reasons for non-use of contraceptives by women of reproductive age (15–49 years) (%)

Reasons for non-use	Nigeria (1990)	Kenya (1993)	Bolivia (1994)	Mexico (1987)[1]	Bangladesh (1993–94)	Thailand (1987)[2]
Wants children	47.1	22.1	9.4	0	13.1	2.1
Health concerns or side effects	4	15.7	15.9	15.9	6	14.3
Lack of knowledge	11.7	5.3	16.8	18.5	2.8	1.9
Hard to get methods and/or methods cost too much	0.5	0.2	2.0	n/i	0.1	1.1
Religion	12.2	6.6	7.1	n/i	10.5	1.1
Husband opposed	2.5	3.9	1.4	13.3[3]	7.8	–
Difficulty becoming pregnant/infertility	4.2	22	10.5	–	24.9	34.4[4]
Menopausal and/or had hysterectomy	3.2	12	24.7	–	16.4	–

Notes: n/i: not included in study. [1] In Mexico, the reasons for non-use are presented only for the group of reproductive-age women who do not wish to have children. [2] For Thailand, the question of why contraceptives are not used was asked to non-pregnant, non-abstaining, currently married women not using contraceptives who would be unhappy if they became pregnant. The figures for the other countries regarding reasons for non-use are based on the total group of reproductive-age women not using contraceptives and therefore they present higher percentages of women who don't use contraceptives because they *want* children. [3] This figure includes situations where the wife opposes use. [4] This figure combines menopausal women and infertile women.

Sources: Demographic and Health Surveys (DHS); Nigeria 1990; Kenya 1993; Bolivia 1994; Mexico 1987; Bangladesh 1993–94; and Thailand 1987. (Data not available for the Netherlands and Finland.)

women and men are adequately informed about possible effects related to the contraceptive method they select, they are less likely to become concerned when they experience physical changes such as weight gain or changes in menstrual patterns. Counselling needs to be culturally sensitive. One study aimed at more fully understanding contraceptive pill use in Sri Lanka, for example, found that respondents held a pervasive notion that the pill causes side effects because of its heating effect.[7] Informants noted that taking pills 'every day raised the heat level of the body to such an extent that male and female *dhatu*, a substance associated with vitality and strength, was burned up … Other informants explained that extreme heat in the body caused by taking the pill diluted *dhatu*, *dhatu direvenava*, to the point where it was no longer strong enough to create a fetus.'

Most available contraceptives can cause changes in the users' menstrual patterns. IUDs are known to cause heavy bleeding in some women; the contraceptive pill often leads to diminished bleeding; and progestin-only contraceptives lead to a variety of menstrual disturbances including amenorrhoea (lack of menstrual bleeding) and spotting.

The consequences of such menstrual disturbances are far-reaching. Menstruation is an important event in any woman's life. The meaning that is attributed to this event or its loss varies. It can affect, among other things, a woman's cooking procedures, sexual interaction and religious practices.[8] Women in many different societies perceive the delay or absence of menstruation, as often caused by progestin-only contraceptives, as unhealthy.[9] For example, a researcher working in Columbia found that the stopping of expected blood flow is perceived as an illness.[10] In Malaysia, another researcher reported a prevailing perception among Chinese Malays that irregular menstruation is unclean and bad for a woman's health and that remedies should be taken to ensure the expected onset.[11] Another study on women in East Malaysia reported that women there are encouraged to eat sweet things to increase the flow of scanty menstruation.[12] In this research area, menstruating women cannot pray during menses and men are not supposed to have sexual intercourse with their wives at this time.

Amenorrhoea also means that a woman could be unsure if she is pregnant or not. If women are insufficiently warned about this effect caused by some methods, the absence of menstruation can lead to great anxiety about a possible, unwanted pregnancy. Lack of knowledge is a relatively important reason in Bolivia and Mexico.

That lack of knowledge and health concerns are such important reasons for non-use of contraceptives among women who want to limit fertility or space their children is a result of family planning programmes that emphasize coverage over care. In a review of the worldwide statistics on unmet need, Bongaarts and Bruce emphasize the 'social failure' of family planning programmes.[13] They are social failures because they do not actively engage prospective clients in necessary dialogue about health fears and misinformation, nor have they facilitated couples' communication about disease avoidance, contraception and sexuality.

The following case studies explore the actual quality of family planning services in each of the eight countries studied and determine if they are indeed failing to inform people appropriately about fertility regulation.

Notes

1. As is evident from this attempt to categorize the countries, the demographic transition theory does not necessarily apply in practice. Indeed, demographers have come to realize that countries do not necessarily pass through all three phases in

the transition. Declines in fertility rates and increases in demand for fertility regulation services are not only determined by socio-economic progress but also by other large-scale factors such as the volume of donor support to family planning programmes. Small-scale elements also play a role, i.e. cultural ideas about the acceptability of contraception (see J. Cleland [1985] 'Marital Fertility Decline in Developing Countries: Theories and Evidence', in J. Cleland and J. Hobcraft (eds), *Reproductive Change in Developing Countries: Insights from the World Fertility Survey* [Oxford: OUP], pp. 223–52), and improvements in women's status (see K. Mason [1987] 'The Impact of Women's Social Position on Fertility in Developing Countries', *Sociological Forum* 2(4): 718–45.

2. This rough classification of the countries in terms of their economic, health and fertility status cannot help to predict what level of quality of care one should expect to find in those countries. This is due to the large volume of donor support to family planning programmes in poorer countries.

3. J. Bongaarts and J. Bruce (1995) 'The Causes of Unmet Need for Contraception and the Social Content of Services', *Studies in Family Planning* 26(2): 57–75.

4. Ibid. Note that in such estimates indigenous forms of fertility regulation are not considered. Women may resort to menstrual regulation by means of herbs to regulate their fertility or seek an abortion when confronted with an unwanted pregnancy.

5. World Health Organization (WHO) (1993) *Abortion: A Tabulation of Available Data on the Frequency and Mortality of Unsafe Abortions* (Geneva: WHO/Division of Family Health).

6. Ibid.

7. M. Nichter and M. Nichter (1989) 'Modern Methods of Fertility: When and for Whom are They Appropriate?' in M. Nichter (ed.), *Anthropology and International Health: South Asian Case Studies* (Dordrecht: Kluwer).

8. T. Buckley and A. Gottlieb (eds) (1988) *Blood Magic: The Anthropology of Menstruation* (Berkeley, CA: University of California Press); WHO Task Force on Psychological Research in Family Planning (1981), 'A Cross-cultural Study of Menstruation: Implications for Contraceptive Development and Use', *Studies in Family Planning* 12: 3–16; M. Del Vecchio Good (1977) 'Of Blood and Babies: The Relationship of Popular Islamic Physiology to Fertility', *Science and Medicine* 14B: 147–56.

9. L. F. Newman (ed.) (1985) *Women's Medicine: A Cross-Cultural Study of Indigenous Fertility Regulation* (New Brunswick, NJ: Rutgers University Press).

10. C. H. Browner (1985) 'Traditional Techniques for Diagnosis, Treatment and Control of Pregnancy in Cali, Colombia', in L. F. Newman (ed.), *Women's Medicine*, pp. 99–124.

11. C. Ngin (1985) 'Indigenous Fertility Regulating Methods Among Two Chinese Communities in Malaysia', in L. F. Newman (ed.), *Women's Medicine.*

12. C. Laderman (1983) *Wives and Midwives: Childbirth and Nutrition in Rural Malaysia* (Berkeley, CA: University of California Press).

13. J. Bongaarts and J. Bruce (1995) 'The Causes of Unmet Need …'.

PART TWO

Country Case Studies: Quality of Care

CHAPTER 4

Who Wants Family Planning? Three Areas of Kaduna State, Nigeria

Mere Nakateregga Kisekka and Folashade Bosede Okeshola

Nigeria is home to at least 250 ethnic groups and a population of 88.5 million people according to the most recent national census (1991). It is the most populous country in Africa and ranks among the world's ten largest in terms of population size. Until the recent rebirth of the Republic of South Africa, Nigeria dominated the continent in economic and political leadership. However, within the last three to five years, Nigeria has been characterized by political and civil strife and poor management of its oil wealth, all of which have stagnated its economic, academic and social development.

The social demographic situation of Nigeria is equally unsatisfactory. For example, according to the 1990 Demographic and Health Survey (DHS), there is a high maternal mortality rate of 15 in 1,000 women and an infant mortality rate of 105 in 1,000. Women, who comprise 49.5 per cent of the population, are marked by 61 per cent adult illiteracy compared to men's 37.7 per cent. Only 30 per cent of the population resides in urban areas. The country's growth rate is 2.7 per cent per year and total fertility is 6.3 births per woman.[1]

Contraceptive prevalence is remarkably low. According to the 1990 DHS, only 9 per cent of Nigerian women have ever used a modern contraceptive and only 3.5 per cent were currently using one. In such a situation, high rates of abortion (which is illegal in Nigeria) are to be expected. The Federal Ministry of Health and Human Services revealed in 1990 that 50 per cent of all maternal deaths were caused by induced abortion while 61 per cent of non-spontaneous abortions involved teenage pregnancies.[2]

Family planning services have only recently been provided by the Nigerian government. A national population policy was approved in 1988 and formally launched the following year. During the 1960s and 1970s, the Planned Parenthood Federation of Nigeria (PPFN) and a few university hospitals took the lead on this issue by educating certain sectors of the public, promoting modern family planning methods and meeting the limited demand that existed for contraceptives. Since 1983, donor agencies such as USAID, UNFPA and the World Bank have increased the technical and financial assistance they give the government for family planning training, health facility equipment, supplying and distributing contraceptives and developing policy.

The findings presented in this chapter are reinforced by a 1994 UNFPA mission report[3] which listed the major constraints to family planning acceptance in Nigeria as follows:

- Geographical inaccessibility: only 19.3 per cent of public health facilities provide any form of family planning services. They are usually located in urban centres where only 30 per cent of the population lives.
- Poor IEC materials: insufficient and sometimes inappropriate information, education and communication messages focusing explicitly on a 'small family norm' in a pro-natalistic society rather than emphasizing health benefits.
- Limited services and training: technical unavailability of services as many health workers currently in the field have not had any training in family planning delivery skills.

National population policy

In the mid-1980s, the fall of petrol prices led to a severe economic recession which brought about the introduction of a Structural Adjustment Programme (SAP). At this juncture, the country started expressing concern and awareness about the high population growth's effect on development. As a result, in April 1989, Nigeria formally launched its first population policy entitled the *National Policy on Population for Development, Unity, Progress and Self-Reliance*. This title was broad enough to depoliticize the policy and create space for a wide range of information, education and communication (IEC) activities on population issues. The policy provides an institutional framework for demographic data and development and planning, plus ways to increase the provision of family services, enhance the status of women, bring about continued decline in maternal and infant mortality, reduce fertility and slow the rapid rate of migration to cities among other objectives. A selection of the targets is given in the box on page 35.

The policy document raises several feminist concerns. For instance, women's associations were not involved in its formulation. Secondly, women are requested to adhere to the four-child limit whereas men are merely 'encouraged to have the limited number of wives and optimum number of children they can foster within their resources'. The policy also reinforces patriarchal ideas in family organization and reproductive choice, stating: 'In our society, men are considered the head of the family and they take far-reaching decisions including the family size, substance

---

Selected national population policy targets, Nigeria

- Reduce the proportion of women marrying before age eighteen by 50 per cent as of 1995.
- Reduce the proportion of women who bear more than four children by 80 per cent in the year 2000.
- Reduce infant mortality to 50 in 1,000 by 1995 and 30 in 1,000 by the year 2000.
- Reduce the number of pregnancies to mothers below age eighteen and above thirty-five by fifty per cent in 1995 and 90 per cent by the year 2000.
- Make family planning services available to 50 per cent of women of child-bearing age by 1995 and 80 per cent by the year 2000.
- Reduce the present rate of population growth from 3.3 to 2.5 per cent by 1995 and 2.0 per cent in the year 2000.
- Provide suitable family life education, family planning information and services to all adolescents by the year 2000.

The document also strategically identifies target areas, including:

- providing family planning services and private outlets;
- promoting responsible parenthood among men; and
- promoting improved economic and social status for women including the expansion of women's education.

Source: Federal Republic of Nigeria (1988), *National Policy on Population for Development, Unity, Progress and Self-Reliance*.

---

and social relations. The patriarchal family system in the country shall be recognized for the stability of the home.'[4] This statement suggests that obtaining spousal approval to receive contraceptives might be required in public health services as is the current practice in some parts of the country. Yet in other sections, the policy appears to sanction reproductive choice, saying, 'Government shall ensure the availability of family planning services to all couples and individuals seeking such services at affordable prices.'[5]

Moreover, the different ideal marriage ages (nineteen for women and twenty-five for men) implicitly legitimize a double standard which could have an effect in areas of career achievement. It should also be emphasized that despite all the controversy raised over the four-child target per woman and the marriage ages, there is no compulsion or legal mechanism to enforce them.

Family planning service delivery

These days family planning has become almost a household word among both its proponents and opponents thanks to the extensive information campaigns undertaken by state and federal television and radio organizations. Posters, booklets, soap operas, jingles and newspaper advertisements advocating child spacing are seen and heard daily. In the public sector, almost every facility offers family planning services including primary health-care centres, clinics and hospitals. Nevertheless, in 1991, of the 17,725 public health facilities, family planning services were only delivered in 1,492 of them. In the private sector, the PPFN continues to dominate with about ninety urban-based vertical family planning services. It is complemented by an estimated 4,342 private health facilities in addition to community-based distributors who dispense non-prescription contraceptives.

The national population policy is not oriented towards population control; rather it stresses the medical, social and emotional well-being of the mother, child and family. Accordingly, the health sector has taken the lead in coordinating population matters within the Ministry of Health and Human Services. Except for abortion, almost all other forms of contraception (i.e. hormonal, IUDs, barrier methods and implants) are available at one service delivery point or another.

In the past, family planning has not been sufficiently well integrated with other reproductive health services such as the prevention and control of sexually transmitted diseases and antenatal care. While family planning is provided at the same location as maternal and child health (MCH) services, this does not imply integration. Only PPFN clinics attempt to combine services by offering expert advice and counselling to infertile and sub-fertile couples and carrying out Pap smears and pregnancy tests as part of their list of services.

A mid-1992 Situational Analysis study of family planning facilities in six Nigerian states found serious problems, including frequent shortages of methods favoured by clients, inadequate storage of supplies, spousal consent requirements, equipment shortages and, in some cases, provider bias against certain contraceptives resulting in their being withdrawn from the methods offered.[6]

Escalating costs have also made contraceptive accessibility a large problem. Although many contraceptives are given for free or at a nominal fee, patients at government clinics often have to pay for equipment upkeep or supply and the drugs needed for the smooth operation of family planning services.

The government has, however, started the process of reviewing the national population policy in order to bring it more closely into line with the 1994 ICDP's *Program of Action* and other recent international consensus documents on development. For example, the review plans to address such issues as abortion, sexually transmitted diseases, AIDS, sexual harassment and rape. It will also involve a cross-section of influential groups such as NGOs, women, religious and traditional leaders in all deliberations.

Study design

To complement other studies conducted in Nigeria, research was carried out in Kaduna State between November 1994 and February 1995. Three research sites which are fairly representative of the population of Kaduna State and which were also easily accessible in view of the then prevailing petrol crisis were chosen for examination.

Kaduna State falls within the savannah region and is characterized by an annual wet season between May and October at which time the bulk of crops is grown. From November to February the area experiences *harmattan*, a dry, dusty season with cold nights and mornings. The area's manufacturing consists of blacksmith products, iron work, cotton-spinning, pottery, hide-tanning, weaving, embroidery and calabash-carving.

The Kaduna metropolitan region is ethnically heterogeneous although the majority of the population consists of the Hausa people, who are Muslim, and other mainly Christian ethnic groups from Southern Kaduna. In Zaria, the researchers looked at service delivery points in Zaria City (where historically a majority of Hausa people live) and other areas such as Sabon Gari where a majority of non-Hausa people reside. The Makarfi area was selected to represent an agricultural rural area. It has a hospital which is 54km from Zaria. This region is inhabited by the Hausa and a sub-ethnic group called the Maguzawa. The area hospital is complemented by four other health districts, a number of privately-owned medicine stores, dispensaries and clinics.

The field work for this research involved two methodologies. One was the collection of qualitative data through focus group discussions (FGDs) with men and women, boys and girls and commercial sex-workers. The second used structured interviews and observations at the service delivery points, community-based distributors and pharmacies in all the study areas.

Conducting research in metropolitan Kaduna proved most taxing as service delivery providers had little time to spare for interviews and usually cancelled or postponed interviews for hours or days. Many clients also declined to take part in exit interviews on the grounds that their privacy was being invaded. Others demanded payment and when that was denied, they terminated the interview. These problems were most pronounced in the private service delivery points, notably in Kaduna Town where providers claimed that the results of most (previous) studies invariably favoured government service delivery points. As such, they did not want to waste their time on an exercise they deemed would be of no benefit to them. In addition, exit clients attending private service delivery points tended to be middle-class and many charged that the researchers merely wanted to exploit them.

Community-based distributors were extremely difficult to locate. The study revealed a general perception that they take family planning supplies (i.e. pills and condoms) and equipment for their own use instead of offering free services to clients. For this reason, community-based distributors were thought to hide as they suspected that the researchers were government agents sent to question them or spy on their activities.

At the same time, access to providers in commercial outlets was difficult as owners often do not work there. Instead, the outlets are run by assistants who understandably refuse any interview not approved by the owner. These assistants proved reluctant to cooperate with the researchers as well. Locating commercial outlet clients was the most daunting task since none of them was specialized in the sale of family planning supplies. As most of the drugs are sold over the counter without a prescription, it took a great deal of effort to identify buyers of family planning drugs.

Most of the service delivery points visited did not have any specific days scheduled for family planning appointments. Hence, several trips had to be made to a delivery point in the hope that a family planning client might turn up. Some of the government service delivery points explained that designating particular days for family planning would drive away many of their clients who practised family planning without their husbands' or families' knowledge. They often came to get family planning services under the guise of bringing children for treatment or other health grounds. In Zaria City, for example, the turnout of family planning clients had decreased dramatically during the last two years as a result of Islamic anti-family planning propaganda broadcast on the radio.

Only the Ahmadu Bello University Teaching Hospital (ABUTH) clinics, the PPFN and some well-established private hospitals in Kaduna Town designated days and times to provide family planning services. The clients of these service delivery points were generally educated and middle-class. These clients had a tendency to engage in discussions among themselves on their experiences and the different types of contraceptives while waiting to see a provider. They did not mind being identified as family planning users although they were not necessarily more willing to be interviewed.

It should be mentioned that Norplant® insertion is only offered at ABUTH clinics. Therefore all patients requiring this method are referred there. Female sterilization was widely performed in both private and public service delivery points mainly on health grounds. However, the researchers were told that even on health grounds many, particularly uneducated clients or their close relatives, resisted having their 'wombs turned out'. One medical practitioner (a Hausa man) at a private service delivery point confided that under those circumstances he feels obliged to do the sterilization and later talks to the husband who then accepts the decision as a *fait accompli* or Allah's will.

The field work proceeded most smoothly in the rural area, namely in Makarfi. Here, no resistance or hostility from either providers or clients was experienced. Informational material promoting the virtues of child-spacing was evident all over the town. In Zaria City the atmosphere was quite charged against family planning.

Service delivery point results

The study of service delivery points involved Zaria, Makarfi and three zones in metropolitan Kaduna. Table 4.1 shows the types of service delivery points included in the study. In total, forty-four delivery points, twelve commercial outlets and twelve community- based distributors were included.

Table 4.1 Location and type of family planning service delivery points visited

	Kaduna	Zaria	Makarfi	Total
Government				
Hospital	4	2	1	7
Clinic	3	3	5	11
Private				
Hospital	4	2	–	6
Clinic	6	5	4	15
Missionary				
Hospital	1	1	–	2
Clinic	–	–	–	–
NGO				
Clinic	1	–	–	1
Other				
Military clinic	1	1	–	2
Commercial outlets	6	3	3	12
Community-based distributors	6	3	3	12
Total	32	20	16	68

Source: Field work data; M. Kisekka and F. Okeshola.

Most service delivery points, aside from government clinics, operated daily, six days a week, from 8 a.m. until 9 p.m. In the forty-four service delivery points surveyed there were six medical doctors (all male except one) and thirty-eight female providers (four nurses, three midwives, eighteen registered nurses, twelve registered midwives and one nursing aide).

Providers' technical competence Most of the providers had between two and three years' experience in family planning. About 70 per cent of the providers had received family planning training as part of their original curriculum. Only 30 per cent did not have basic family planning training in their original curriculum. The majority had taken a family planning course. For about half (54 per cent), the last family planning training had been done within the past five years. Most respondents did not regard the family planning training they had received as adequate.

When surveyed, most community-based distributors indicated that they were trained. More than half (58 per cent) said that community-based distributors were supervised. Everyone interviewed said they kept records. Of the twelve community-based distributors, nine were female and three were male, aged between twenty-seven and sixty years. Eleven of the community-based distributors had received basic training of varied duration lasting between three months and two years. These distributors were volunteers interested in propagating the importance of family planning in their communities. They were not paid for providing this service to their community. In fact, all twelve of the community distributors interviewed had another permanent job such as trader, teacher, leader of commercial sex-workers or community nurse. Their number of clients was not known.

The commercial outlets were mostly comprised of pharmacists and nurses. Their working experience ranged from two to ten years, with 50 per cent of the providers having received secondary school training. About 17 per cent had diploma-level or vocational training. Of the total, 66 per cent received additional training in family planning methods.

Profile of clients A total of eighty-eight clients were interviewed at the forty-four service delivery points surveyed. Of these, 80 per cent (71) were between the ages of twenty-five and forty-four years. Ninety per cent (79) of the clients attending family planning services at various types of service delivery points were married. Fifty-seven per cent (50) of the clients said they were in monogamous marriages and 33 per cent (29) were in polygamous marriages.

Of the eighty-eight clients interviewed, 54.5 per cent (48) had received secondary education, 19.3 per cent (17) had attended post-secondary institutions. Only 26.2 per cent (35) attended primary school or had no schooling. Therefore, 73.8 per cent of the clients interviewed had been to school. Looking at literacy levels, only 51 per cent (45) could read and write easily, while 23 per cent (20) could read and write with difficulty. Twenty-six per cent (35) could neither read nor write. Only 58 per cent (51) said they had the ability to speak and read English, the official language, while 42 per cent (37) said they could not. Of the 88 clients interviewed at the forty-four service delivery points, 72.7 per cent (64) were female and only 27.3 per cent (24) were male.

Table 4.2 Types and number of focus group discussions in the research areas

	Total
Men	
Maguzawa educated men	1
Hausa educated men	3
Hausa uneducated men	3
Maguzawa uneducated men	1
Women	
Maguzawa educated women	1
Hausa educated women	3
Maguzawa uneducated women	1
Hausa uneducated women	3
Hausa commercial sex-workers	3
Maguzawa commercial sex-workers	1
Youth	
15–19-year-old Hausa girls	3
17–20-year-old Maguzawa girls	1
15–17-year-old Hausa boys	3
15–19-year-old Maguzawa boys	1
Total	28

Source: Focus group discussions; M. Kisekka and F. Okeshola.

Twenty-eight focus group discussions were carried out with various age, sex and educational groups as shown in Table 4.2. In the Makarfi area, commercial sex-workers were included as they featured prominently in social activities including drama and NGO projects, whereas women in purdah, the majority of area Hausa women, were not represented. Purdah is the practice of secluding married women in their compounds or homes so that they are not seen in public. This practice is rationalized on Islamic principle. Where it is practised among the Muslim Hausa, these women cannot move outside of their homes without the explicit permission of their husbands and when they do so during the day, it is restricted to such occasions as going to the hospital, voting or attending marriage ceremonies or literacy or religious classes.

Free and informed choice of methods The researchers found that methods requiring minor surgery such as vasectomy and Norplant® were usually referred to the general or teaching hospitals. Commercial outlets and community-based distributors specialized in supplying pills, condoms and injectables, and often referred clients to the teaching hospitals. The methods most widely available at all service delivery points were pills. These were

Table 4.3 Type of contraceptives, availability during the survey and actual provision in the past three months

Type of contraceptive	Availability (%)			Provided in last three months (%)	
	SDP	CBD	COs	SDP	COs
Combined pill	59	33	83	86	92
Progestin-only pill	11	25	42		
Condoms	71	83	75	50	92
Diaphragms	18	8	25	11	8
Spermicides	27	50	36	23	50
IUDs	27	–	21	66	17
Injectables	39	67	71	84	50
Female sterilization	12	–	–	0	
Vasectomy	9	–	–	3	–
Norplant®	2	–	–	0	–
Others	8	8	25	36	–
N =	44	12	12	44	12

Source: Field data; M. Kisekka and F. Okeshola.

evenly distributed among the private, government and non-government clinics. Table 4.3 shows the type of methods available during the survey.

As seen in the table, combined pills were available in 59 per cent of the service delivery points, 33 per cent of the community-based distributors and 83 per cent of the commercial outlets. However, progestin-only pills were relatively scarce with only 11 per cent availability at all service delivery points. Condoms were found in 71 per cent of the service delivery points, 83 per cent of the community-based distributors and 75 per cent of commercial outlets. The diaphragm was not a popular method and was available only in 18 per cent of the delivery points and 25 per cent of the commercial outlets. Spermicides could be found at 27 per cent of the service delivery points, 50 per cent of the community-based distributors and 36 per cent of the commercial outlets. The IUD was available in 27 per cent of the service delivery points surveyed and 21 per cent of commercial outlets. This was most often the Copper T 380A®.

Injectables, Noristerat® to be specific, were available in 39 per cent of the delivery points, 67 per cent of community-based distributors and 71 per cent of commercial outlets. Female sterilization was found in only 12 per cent of the delivery points. It was closely followed by vasectomy which was provided only in 9 per cent of government hospitals. Norplant® was also found at the teaching hospital. In general, natural family planning methods were not encouraged.

When researchers investigated which methods had been provided during the last three months, it was found that the pill had been provided at 86 per cent of service delivery points and 91 per cent of community outlets. The condom was provided more often in commercial outlets than at service delivery points. The diaphragm could be found at very few delivery points and commercial outlets. IUDs were mainly provided at service delivery points and only rarely in commercial outlets. Injectables were available at 84 per cent of service delivery points and 50 per cent of outlets (Noristerat® only).

As mentioned, Norplant® is provided only at the ABUTH in Zaria where there are providers trained in this method. Its unpopularity among clients is reflected in the fact that within the last three months of the survey period, no client had been provided with it. This response pattern was also seen with female sterilization. Vasectomy was provided only by 3 per cent of the service delivery points. Natural family planning was also not applied in either the service delivery points or commercial outlets. As pointed out earlier, this method was generally not recommended by any of the providers in the delivery points. There was no record of their usage by the commercial outlets. When specific unavailable methods were requested, 83 per cent of providers referred clients to general hospitals or other, better-equipped service delivery points.

When comparing availability during the survey to the methods provided during the past three months, one discovers that what was provided in the last three months was more than was available during the survey. With regards to the different availability of methods between the study locations, the most commonly available methods at service delivery points, community-based distributors and commercial outlets were condoms, pills and injectables (especially Noristerat®). Vasectomy was performed in a private clinic and maternity centre in Makarfi which is part of the rural area. However, it appears that the sterilization that was done was not technically a vasectomy but rather a resection of the prostate gland due to enlargement. Therefore, it was not motivated by family planning need but, rather, medical reasons. IUD insertions were carried out only in private and government service delivery points in Kaduna (north and south) and Zaria, both urban centres. It is probable that Makarfi, which is a rural area, does not have a trained provider to insert IUDs.

Private clinics, missionary hospitals and military hospitals were able to refer clients to the ABUTH. Rural health clinics referred to the area general hospital, missionary, private hospital or private clinics.

The methods which were sometimes out of stock were injectables, combined pills and condoms. This was thought to be caused by the fact that they are in high demand and often preferred by clients. The distance necessary to travel from rural areas to procure these contraceptives and the high cost of transportation as occasioned by extreme petrol scarcity often contributed to some of these methods not being replaced on time.

Cost of methods Cost did not seem to be a determining factor in choosing a method. During interviews, clients were more concerned with the safety and reversibility of methods. Clients using family planning services were not reimbursed for any contraceptive method given. Generally, pills were dispensed at twenty-eight-day duration cost. Thus, pills were sold per sachet at service delivery points and commercial outlets. The cost per sachet ranged between US$0.18 and US$1.45 with the average being US$0.43. Condoms could be obtained in packets or as single pieces. The cost ranged between US$0.09 to US$0.10 per condom. The IUD sold for US$2.10 to US$2.80. Most injectables cost US$1.20. Vasectomy and female sterilization were services provided only by doctors whose charges depended on the circumstances. No actual cost records were obtained for these two methods.

Costs in commercial outlets were similar. A sachet of pills was found to cost US$1. Condoms could be obtained for US$0.60 (a packet of three). Injectables could be obtained for US$1.50 every three months. Post-coital pills sold for US$1.

Restrictions All contraceptives are legally approved in Nigeria, with the exception of abortion which is allowed only for medical reasons when the mother's life is threatened. In theory, government services are limited to married people and usually a consent form signed by the husband must be shown to allow the wife to receive contraceptives. However, the data indicate that these rules are not strictly adhered to in practice in Kaduna State. The research did reveal that access to contraceptives is restricted in some service delivery points on grounds of age, number of children, marital status and spousal consent as shown in Table 4.4.

Sterilization methods have the greatest restrictions followed by pills, injectables and the IUD. Nearly 50 per cent of the service delivery points applied an age restriction for providing pills. Commercial outlets' restrictions were found to be based on age and number of children.

However, the study revealed that many single women patronize local community-based distributors and commercial outlets. In Nigeria, any female under the age of eighteen is still considered a child medically. For this reason, medical regulations forbid giving contraceptives to any woman below the age of eighteen. Yet, in the northern part of Nigeria, i.e. Kaduna State, children are often given in marriage between the ages of ten and fifteen. Thus, they become mothers at a very young age.

The restriction on age and pill use is still upheld in private and government service delivery points. The reverse is true for commercial outlets which have a profit motive. For them, a client's age is no hindrance. Community-based distributors also show little or no regard for an age restriction on pill use. Many of the community-based distributors are even unaware that there is a formal age restriction for pill use.

Table 4.4 Percentage of service delivery points implementing non-medical restrictions on contraception (n = 44)

Method	Age	No. of children	Marital status	Spousal consent
Combined pill	46	34	28	30
Condom	7	9	2	2
IUD	18	23	21	36
Injectables	25	30	25	23
Sterilization (tubal ligation)	50	48	32	50
Sterilization (vasectomy)	36	34	16	9
Norplant®	21	21	16	16

Source: Field data; M. Kisekka and F. Okeshola.

Quality of the provider–client interactions Most service delivery points and commercial outlets (91 and 100 per cent respectively) encouraged clients to decide for themselves which method they preferred. Clients who chose methods other than those available were referred to other clinics. Providers were found to interact with clients during consultations to enhance information. Commercial providers' interaction with clients was suspected to be money-driven rather than motivated by concern for the welfare of the clients. When clients reported problems with their current method, providers usually encouraged them to switch methods. Most breastfeeding clients were advised by providers to use combined pills. Exit interviews revealed that 46 per cent of the visits were for resupply. Only 27 per cent were new users and 28 per cent had a problem with the current method and probably wanted to discontinue use.

Of the providers, around 60 per cent said that they consulted with clients about their reproductive goals and that they inquired if the client was breastfeeding; but only 33 per cent said that they discussed possible method side effects with clients. During exit interviews, most of the clients, 81 per cent (71), reported that the clinic staff were friendly.

When asked about method/service satisfaction, the majority (74 per cent) of the interviewed clients claimed that they were satisfied with the service provided. A majority of interviewed clients (65 per cent) said they always had to wait an hour before the consultation. Only 24 per cent said they waited less time and 11 per cent waited longer. This relatively long waiting time could dissuade clients from using the family planning services, especially in light of the accompanying transportation costs and difficulties. Only 47 per cent of the eighty-eight clients interviewed were informed about when they should return for their next medical check-up.

Community-based distributors' interactions with new clients were found to be of good quality. Both new and existing clients were encouraged to decide on their own which method they preferred. Eleven of the twelve providers said they encouraged clients to decide for themselves. Observations proved that clients received a friendly greeting from seven of the community-based distributors. About half of the community distributors informed clients of their next appointment or visit, though only five asked clients if they had any questions. People were found to use community-based distributors as if they were doctors.

Recommendations given for specific conditions While service delivery points allowed clients to decide what method they wanted, they also gave advice on contraceptive methods depending on the client's wish to delay or prevent pregnancy. Asked what they would recommend to clients who desired no more children, providers at delivery points mostly recommended female sterilization. Injectables topped the list (41 per cent) of methods providers would never recommend, followed by the IUD, mentioned by 36 per cent of providers.

Providers at commercial outlets recommended condoms (42 per cent) and injectables (42 per cent) for child-spacing above all other methods available during the survey. When commercial outlet clients expressed the desire to have no more children, outlet providers recommended female sterilization (42 per cent) and, to a lesser degree, vasectomy (25 per cent). When asked which methods they would never recommend, the IUD (25 per cent) ranked the highest.

Clients' knowledge of contraception The majority of the focus group members had heard about pills, injectables, IUDs, condoms and spermicides although they did not necessarily know how they worked. Only a small number had ever heard of diaphragms, vasectomy, tubal ligation or Norplant®. The participants pointed out the possible side effects associated with pills such as weight gain or loss, dizziness and infertility; excessive bleeding with injectables; and IUD failure and 'disappearance' which could call for surgery. Condoms were widely described as interfering with sexual pleasure and causing a slippery and artificial sensation in the vagina. Similarly, the natural or calendar method was seen as creating tension by continually having to count days.

On the positive side, some housewives praised Norplant® and injectables for their long-acting duration and clandestine nature. Sex-workers reported that they liked using foaming tablets to prevent pregnancy and enhance sexual enjoyment (through lubrication). This group also reported using Ampiclox® tablets (amoxicillin, an antibiotic) to prevent pregnancy and sexually transmitted diseases. They used condoms if the client did not object. However, they reported that if they insisted on using condoms, they would lose some clients.

The minority of men who were familiar with vasectomy described it as tantamount to castration. At the same time, several participants in Makarfi alleged that many women in their community had undergone tubal ligations because of their number of children.

Government hospitals and clinics were described by some discussants as having qualified staff and providing a full range of contraceptives. In addition, these facilities were praised particularly by educated women for proper patient screening, medical history-taking, treating side effects and monitoring gynaecological conditions. However, school-age girls in rural Makarfi asserted that providers in these same facilities were harsh with them, asked too many questions and insisted on parental consent before giving contraceptives. Similarly, male discussants were irritated by the bureaucratic procedures which they regarded as interfering with one's privacy.

At Makarfi service delivery points, women reported that they were routinely asked to bring a letter of consent from their husbands in order to receive contraceptive services. Hence, they expressed bitterness towards the health workers for not helping them when they knew that many husbands opposed family planning. Not surprisingly, the client turnout at such service delivery points was quite low.

Commercial sex-workers reported that they felt uncomfortable in government facilities because the providers were hostile towards them and discriminated against them by levying charges for commodities which should be free. Similarly, uneducated women reported that staff at government service delivery points shouted at them and used derogatory language. In contrast, they felt the staff treated educated women with courtesy and served them first.

Group participants expressed the view that commercial outlets' staff (i.e. chemists, pharmacists, medicine stores) were friendly, attentive and ready to offer help at any time. They said they found them accessible because they did not ask 'unnecessary' or 'embarrassing' questions about spousal or parental authority. In addition, they were accessible in terms of proximity and did not waste time on bureaucratic procedures. However, participants claimed that their drugs were expensive and of unknown quality since they were sometimes expired, adulterated or simply fake. At the same time, many of the attendants at small outlets were regarded as unqualified. For example, a group of girls in Makarfi complained that in some chemist shops, the staff 'always gives injections on the wrong side', and did not examine clients before prescribing drugs.

Community-based distributors were not mentioned by many focus group participants. Commercial sex-workers described their community-based distributor as their madam (*magajiya*) or head prostitute who supplied them with condoms. A group of educated women in Kaduna Town was vehemently opposed to community-based distributors whom they regarded as appropriate only for villagers who are commonly sceptical about family

Table 4.5 Traditional methods of birth control mentioned by respondents

Method	Description	Uses
Madaci	Bitter leaves.	Prevents pregnancy, also used as abortifacient.
Guru	Charm wrapped in leather piece and worn around waist before having sex.	Prevents pregnancy.
Layar	A verse from the Qur'an written on a piece of cloth or pure leather and pinned to underwear.	Prevents pregnancy.
Sauyar lalle	A leaf to be eaten.	Prevents pregnancy and causes abortion.
Vigorous sex		Prevents pregnancy and causes abortion.
Samiyar	Tamarind soaked in water and eaten.	Prevents pregnancy.
Kanwan	Potash soaked and eaten.	Prevents pregnancy.
Yayan garahuni	Nut powder inserted into the vagina.	Serves as a spermicide.
Abortion belt	A girdle tightened around the stomach.	Expels pregnancy.
Toilet broom	Water rinsed from a broom used to clean toilets. The water is drunk.	Prevents pregnancy.
Hot drink	Brandy and gin are drunk with incantations by traditional healer buried in a calabash.	Prevents pregnancy and causes abortion.

Source: Focus group discussions; M. Kisekka and F. Okeshola.

planning or reluctant to visit hospitals. They also argued that such distributors were unsafe as they were not properly trained and did not possess the needed family planning equipment.

Knowledge of traditional family planning methods was widely discussed during the focus group discussions, particularly the postpartum taboo on sex for the duration of one to two years during breastfeeding. The belief is that during breastfeeding, semen can mix with the mother's milk and harm the infant. Other traditional birth-control methods mentioned included herbs, charms and a variety of other concoctions as shown in Table 4.5.

Although most of the participants said that these traditional methods were cheap and easily accessible, they had little confidence in their efficacy.

Claims were also made that some traditional herbs (i.e. *Madaci* and *Sauyar lalle*) could lead to excessive bleeding and even death if too much was given. Others complained of the unhygienic manner in which these herbs were prepared. As for the postpartum sex taboo, some women said that it often encouraged marital infidelity because during the interim the husband found other sexual partners and the wife was also tempted to seek sexual outlets.

Traditional healers and herbalists were judged to be the friendliest, most attentive and cheapest of all categories of providers. Nevertheless, some reservations were expressed about them. Young, unmarried girls in Makarfi complained that traditional healers insisted on parental consent before providing birth-control methods. Other groups of women also alleged that they were required to give proof of spousal consent to the traditional healer unless one bribed them with a lot of money.

Other reservations concerned the efficacy, hygiene and safety of traditional medicine. It was alleged that due to the rivalry among traditional healers and also the insincerity of some of them, the efficacy or potency of their drugs was reduced. Some participants referred to unhygienic preparations or overdoses which could lead to complications or death. Young girls claimed that they sometimes found it difficult to locate such a healer and complained at the same time that some of the local herbs were seasonal and, therefore, sometimes unavailable. Other complaints centred on the 'demonic means' used by some healers which ran counter to the Christian or Islamic beliefs of clients.

Men's attitudes   The dominant attitude of the interviewed men towards family planning was condemnatory. Some of the antagonistic views were premised on the grounds that family planning is against Islam, while the Christian Maguzawa farming community expressed the desire for many children to work on the farm. The overwhelming majority of participants supported the traditional postpartum sex taboo method of family planning. There was strong feeling that some methods of family planning such as condoms and tubal ligation would encourage immorality.

Men also argued that family planning had nothing to do with poverty alleviation since, according to Islamic beliefs, Allah takes care of both rich and poor and everything is predestined. One group of educated men supported the idea that the government should spend money on children's welfare rather than fertility control. They argued that if the economy was good, there would be no poverty and therefore no need to worry about large families. Even among the minority of men who revealed that their wives were currently using a modern contraceptive, this was done for child-spacing or to allow 'rest', not to limit family size.

On the contrary, the women's groups reflected no pronounced pro- or anti-family planning attitude. The discussion centred mostly on fears regarding side effects and the logistical problems related to availability and accessibility. For some groups, the issue of spousal or parental authorization was singled out as the most acute reason regarding the accessibility of family planning services.

Balanced and objective information   Clients interviewed at various service delivery points received information about family planning services from the radio, discussions at delivery points, posters, pamphlets and television.

Participants in focus group discussions indicated that they were aware of a variety of information sources on modern contraceptives. These included the radio, health discussions at service delivery points, posters, pamphlets and television. They mentioned several radio and TV programmes, dramas, advertisements, discussions and songs which featured family planning. Friends and relatives were also named as useful sources of information.

Before people decided to go for a consultation, they had information on the advantages of child-spacing. For a client to take the bold step of visiting a family planning service, it was assumed that she or he had prior knowledge and already knew which method she or he really wanted. Posters on child-spacing, written in both Hausa and English, could be found in almost all forty-four service delivery points surveyed. They were seen to a lesser extent at commercial outlets. Table 4.6 shows the percentage of service delivery points and commercial outlets which actually provided various types of information.

As shown in this table, commercial outlets lack most of the necessary

Table 4.6 Percentage of service delivery points/commercial outlets providing adequate general information

Indicator	SDP	CO
Written materials are available	80	42
Information is understandable	66	33
Information is in local language	77	42
Materials provide balanced information	18	8
IEC materials are used (observation)	90	8
Flip chart is used	–	8
Brochures/pamphlets are used	23	17
Instruction sheet is used	81	42
Examples of contraceptives are used	11	42
Other informational materials are used	31	–
N =	44	12

Source: Field data; M. Kisekka and F. Okeshola.

informational materials needed for their work. Service delivery points are better equipped with this type of informational materials.

Discussion with women from different socio-economic and educational groups showed that clients received differential treatment. It was observed that providers accorded educated women respect and always gave them preferential treatment over illiterate women. Illiterate women were treated with disdain, especially in rural areas, and were often addressed in derogatory language. These women felt this was dehumanizing and said that it discouraged them from using modern family planning services. The negative attitude towards uneducated women was quite common in government clinics and hospitals. This was not found to be the case in private clinics and hospitals.

Of the eighty-eight clients interviewed when leaving the service delivery point, only 35 per cent claimed they received written information. Among those who had received it, only 55 per cent said that the information given was understood. Thirteen per cent stated that the written information was printed in the local language. Usually, the clients who could not understand the written material were illiterate women. The discriminatory attitude of the clinic staff was also found to contribute to clients' lack of understanding of the material given. Exit interviews showed that 43 per cent of the clients said that the clinic staff were easy to understand, while 25 per cent thought they were difficult to understand. The others failed to respond to this question.

Adequate counselling Providers were asked what specific method information they would discuss with new clients. They mentioned information about pills, IUD and injectables. The extent to which they would discuss effectiveness, use and corresponding side effects is shown in Table 4.7.

When providers were asked what information they would give on the contraceptive pill, they were found more likely to discuss side effects than effectiveness. However, this was not true for injections and IUDs, in which case, information on effectiveness and side effects was reportedly provided in similar percentages. These findings raise questions on the attitude of the providers towards the pill. They seem to be promoting IUDs and injectables in a more balanced way.

Of the eighty-eight clients interviewed when leaving the service delivery points, only 2.3 per cent (2) said that they had actually received a clear explanation by the clinic staff on how the method works. This could be explained by the fact that most of the clients interviewed were not new users. A high percentage of clients mentioned that side effects were discussed.

The written educational materials available for family planning have been pre-tested and adapted to the people's culture and language. During

Table 4.7 Percentage of providers who reportedly give specific information on selected methods to new users in service delivery points (n = 44)

Selected methods	SDP
Combined pill	
Effectiveness	14
How-to-use	18
Side effects	38
IUD	
Effectiveness	32
How-to-use	0
Side effects	29
Injectables	
Effectiveness	43
How-to-use	0
Side effects	39

Source: Provider interviews; M. Kisekka and F. Okeshola.

the pre-test, it was found that men would prefer that family planning be called child-spacing. They said that child-spacing had always existed traditionally. They rejected the idea of family planning or, more precisely, limiting the number of children.

Television and poster advertisements promoting family planning normally portray two couples. The first has two children. They look well-groomed, healthy and neat, the result of proper child-spacing. The second couple is shown with seven children including a toddler who is on the back of the again-pregnant mother. The couple and their children look wretched, malnourished and older than their age due to poor child-spacing. Based upon the two portrayals in these advertisements, it is assumed that the public can decide what is best for them. These commercials are made in both the English and Hausa languages.

Use of incentives and disincentives Nigeria's family planning policy contains no sanctions for users or non-users of the services. In the same way, no incentives were given to acceptors at the forty-four service delivery points surveyed with the exception of two which gave free condoms and spermicides. Family planning providers receive a monthly salary. Their payment is not dependent on the number of method acceptors. None of the twelve community-based distributors interviewed gave incentives to their clients and also had no sanctions for non-users.

A health-care infrastructure that enables safe use Table 4.8 shows that

Table 4.8 Adequacy of facilities and materials in service delivery points (n = 44)

Type of facilities	Percentage
Separate room	86
Clean examination area	84
Water	91
Blood-pressure cuff	89
Vaginal speculum	86
Examination table	84
Needles/syringes sterilized	84
Other equipment clean	41
Inventory kept	82
Records kept	80
Written guidelines	80

Source: Field data; M. Kisekka and F. Okeshola.

while the infrastructure was available in the forty-four service delivery points surveyed, it was often not in good condition.

Among community-based distributors, 25 per cent had blood-pressure cuffs, 17 per cent had stethoscopes, 75 per cent had record books and 42 per cent had a procedures manual. Only 5 per cent had a flip chart while 50 per cent had a contraceptive sample kit. About 33 per cent had a pill checklist and 42 per cent had referral slips. Condom instruction sheets were found with approximately 50 per cent of the community-based distributors interviewed.

About 33 per cent of community-based distributors reportedly took the client's medical history. This was done at 42 per cent of the service delivery points. A contraindication checklist was used by 67 per cent of community-based distributors and 89 per cent of service delivery points.

Of the ninety observation interviews conducted in the forty-four surveyed service delivery points, only 11 per cent involved Norplant® or an IUD insertion. In approximately 50 per cent of the cases, sterilized equipment was not used for the procedure. Gloves were generally not used. For these reasons, it can be said that there is a relatively low level of hygienic procedure followed for IUD insertion at the service delivery points covered. This implies that clients using these methods are at risk of infection.

Breastfeeding advice The responses that various service providers gave regarding contraceptive options while breastfeeding show confusion on what the correct response should be. At service delivery points, 11.4 per cent felt that contraception was unnecessary while breastfeeding. About 31.8 per cent of service delivery points recommended pills.

The most common method suggested to breastfeeding clients was the combined pill (i.e. Lofemenal®). Apparently, providers are not aware of the medical fact that estrogens can reduce milk supply and, therefore, if pills are used, progestin-only pills are the best choice. Clients were found to be advised to choose the method they liked the most.

Managing side effects When providers were asked to specify how they managed side effects related to IUD users with severe abdominal pain, 85 per cent said they would want to know the date of insertion and would advise treatment after performing a pelvic examination. However, 15 per cent disclosed that they would advise their clients to switch methods and would remove the IUD.

If confronted with a pill user reporting headache, nearly all said that they would take the client's blood pressure and would advise the client to stop using the method for some time to check whether or not the headache was related to pill use.

Other health services provided As shown in Table 4.9, about 80 per cent of the service delivery points provided services for sexually transmitted diseases (STDs). Approximately 35.6 per cent said clients with HIV/AIDS were cared for in their units. Infertility was treated at 72.2 per cent of the service delivery points covered. Of the total, 88.9 per cent said they had facilities providing maternal and child health services.

The observations noted that STDs were treated as common diseases. However, HIV/AIDS was regarded with dismay. The providers did not seem well acquainted with the disease. The researchers who interviewed the providers doubted that they treated HIV/AIDS patients. It should be noted that these providers are regarded as doctors in most of their areas of operation due to the community's level of education.

Table 4.9 Appropriate prevention and treatment services at service delivery points (%) (n = 44)

STD care	80.0
HIV/AIDS care	35.6
Infertility	72.2
Maternal/child health care	88.9

Source: Field data; M. Kisekka and F. Okeshola.

Conclusion

Nigeria has a population policy that is embedded in the Ministry of Health's maternal and child health programme. Consequently, one could characterize the programme as being focused on health rather than fertility control. Clients are provided with information on a range of methods and no incentives or sanctions are used to persuade them to use contraceptives.

The focus group discussions revealed that awareness of contraceptive pills, injectables, IUDs, condoms and spermicides is relatively high in the study areas. These methods are the most easily accessible in the service delivery points and the commercial outlets. Pills are available in approximately six out of ten and condoms in seven out of ten commercial outlets. People were found to be less aware of Norplant®, the diaphragm and male and female sterilization as contraceptive methods. The Situational Analysis study previously conducted by the Population Council in 1992 resulted in slightly different findings. That study, conducted in six states of Nigeria (excluding Kaduna), indicated a higher availability of the pill, not in six out of ten service delivery points as found in this study, but in eight out of ten. The reason for lower availability in Kaduna State could be due to the fuel crisis which occurred during the study. On the other hand, Kaduna State could also have lower than average availability. Also, it is important to note that the Situational Analysis was not able to cover a representative sample of delivery points. It aimed at covering a representative sample of 181 family planning service delivery points (out of the approximately 1,400 delivery points in the country) in six states. Due to the lack of family planning clients on the day of the visit, it was possible to observe interactions between providers and clients and to interview clients at only ninety-four service delivery points, representing possibly a positive bias (service delivery points with a better quality of care attract more clients; those with no clients during the visit might have a low quality of care).

The material presented in this chapter shows access to sterilization is restricted by age, number of children and spousal consent in approximately half of the service delivery points. About one-fourth of the delivery points restrict availability of IUDs, injectables and the pill on these grounds. Fewer restrictions are placed on men who might request sterilization.

However, service delivery point clients were found to be concerned about these methods' side effects as also reflected in the finding that 86 per cent of the clients interviewed when leaving delivery points indicated that they had discussed the side effects of the contraceptives with the provider.

The quality of the provider–client interaction was found to be especially problematic for uneducated clients. Nearly 50 per cent of the clients interviewed when leaving a clinic indicated that they had not understood the information provided by the provider. Only 35 per cent of the clients had received written information. The focus group discussions revealed that people tended to prefer the private clinics and commercial outlets because they were treated in a more friendly way there. These services are also less likely to ask a woman to obtain consent from her husband. A lack of quality client counselling was also found in the 1992 Situational Analysis. In this study, it was observed that the providers asked clients about their goals and plans only in one-half of the cases observed. Virtually all clients were greeted in a friendly manner upon entry, but only one-third were asked at the end of the consultation whether they had any questions. It should be noted that a lack of information, education and communication materials inhibits providers' ability to communicate. Of the eighty-three patients for whom a particular method preference was observed at the beginning of the counselling session, only 54 per cent obtained the method they had indicated.[7]

With respect to the health-care infrastructure, the researchers in Nigeria were especially concerned about the unhygienic insertion of IUDs.

While the Nigerian government devotes a large part of its annual budget to health care so that staff members at government clinics are qualified, the shortage of staff in rural areas poses a problem. This situation is also responsible for the fact that clients for family planning services tend to wait for a long period. It is often very difficult for the clinic staff to cope with the huge numbers as they must also attend to the antenatal patients. This makes them overlook the importance of information, education and communication materials in some cases.

Recommendations

Sensitize men and decision-makers   The researchers suggest that information, education and communication, and advocacy strategies be intensified and extended to all vulnerable groups including men, youth, religious and traditional leaders and communities at the grassroots level. In light of the cultural norms, very little can be achieved on this topic without the cooperation of these groups.

Do away with restrictions   Women should have total control of their bodies. The need for a husband's consent for family planning has significantly inhibited the programme's progress and has been detrimental to women's health. Lack of contraceptive usage leads to high maternal mortality in Kaduna State where the study was done and throughout Nigeria.

Improve provider interaction skills   Providers at government hospitals need to be trained in interpersonal skills as some of them tend to discriminate between educated and illiterate clients. This behaviour jeopardizes the effective utilization of the available family planning services.

Boost provider training for all areas   The Ministry of Health should, as a matter of urgency, provide the opportunity for family planning providers to attend refresher courses to update their techniques and boost overall effectiveness. This should be carried out without any discrimination between providers in urban and rural areas, as this is often the current practice. The ministry should also ensure the availability of contraceptives at various service delivery points, at affordable prices.

Require minimum training All community-based distributors and commercial outlets should be mandated to have the required minimum family planning training before they are allowed to provide such services. Since these outlets are the most accessible to people in rural communities, training will enhance their credibility and efficacy as well.

Integrate family planning into other health services Family planning services should be of sufficient quality to ensure that clients receive safe and effective services which enable them to meet their reproductive health needs. Family planning should be widely understood as a basic human right and an enhancement of women's health and social development. In this regard, family planning services should now champion the treatment of STDs, infertility, reproductive tract infections, and other gynaecological conditions as an integral part of their reproductive health care and management.

Define quality standards Definitions and measurements of quality standards must be made to enable researchers to examine the relationship between programme quality and output. This will also assist policy-makers in setting programme standards and evaluating their progress towards meeting those standards.

About the authors

Mere Nakateregga Kisekka, PhD, coordinated this study while working at the Center for Social and Economic Research, Ahmadu Bello University, Zaria, Nigeria. *Folashade Bosede Okeshola*, MSc, has a position at the Department of Sociology, Ahmadu Bello University, Zaria, Nigeria.

The researchers wish to acknowledge the assistance and cooperation received during the course of this investigation. Dr Hanatu H. Shehu, Director of the Preventive Health Services in Kaduna State Ministry of Health and Social Development expressed great enthusiasm and gave prompt permission for the research. Mal. Muhammad S. Ladan, principal nursing officer, and Hadiza Abubakar Sambo, Makarfi nursing officer, both of Makarfi General Hospital, as well as Mathew Yaji, head of the Department of Medical Social Welfare at Ahmadu Bello University Teaching Hospital, Zaria, played an active role in mobilizing the community for the research. Members of the Women's Health Research Network in Nigeria (WHERNIN) participated in various ways in this research. They include Ladi Yakubu, Christy Akau and Patience Mudiare. Essien Ndon, Mallam Lawal and Uduak Eduok handled both the administrative and secretarial aspects with a great deal of patience and commitment. The researchers would also like to acknowledge the institutional support given by Ahmadu Bello University which also made this investigation possible.

Notes

1. Federal Office of Statistics (1992) *Nigeria Demographic and Health Survey 1990* (Lagos: Institute for Resource Development and Columbia, OH: Macro Systems, Inc.).

2. Federal Ministry of Health (1990) *State Profiles* (Lagos: Department of Population Activities, Family Health Services).

3. L. Monoja *Mission Report to Nigeria*, UNFPA/CSTAA (29 May–26 June 1994), p. 8.

4. Federal Republic of Nigeria (1988) *National Policy on Population for Development, Unity, Progress and Self-Reliance*, Section 5.3.

5. Ibid., Section 5.1.5.

6. Population Council (1992) *Nigeria: The Family Planning Situational Analysis Study*, Africa Operations Research and Technical Assistance Project.

7. Ibid.

Additional references

Kisekka, M. N. (1990) 'Family Planning Services: Access to Contraceptives', *World Bank Report 1992*.

— (1992) 'Women's Organized Health Struggles: The Challenge to Women's Associations', in M. N. Kisekka (ed.), *Women's Health Issues In Nigeria* (Zaria: Tamaza Publishing Co.).

World Bank (1992) *Federal Republic of Nigeria: Implementing the National Policy on Population Sector*, Report, Vol. 2.

CHAPTER 5

A Wide Range of Methods to Reduce Population: Two Rural Regions and One Urban Area in Kenya

Ann Ndinda Mutua, Ochieng Ondolo,
Eunice Munanie and Kisuke Ndiku

Kenya's family planning programme has long been considered weak by international family planning policy-makers. However, the programme's image has greatly improved since the Population Council concluded in its 1991 Situation Analysis study that the programme was doing fairly well. Indeed, a 1993 Demographic and Health Survey showed that a remarkable increase in contraceptive prevalence had occurred: 27 per cent of married women of reproductive age were found to be using modern contraception; in 1984 this number was only 9 per cent.[1]

The country's population is still increasing rapidly. By the year 2000, it is expected to reach 30 million, up from 10.9 million in 1969. Fertility rates are declining gradually. At current fertility levels, the average Kenyan woman will give birth to 5.4 children during her reproductive years. This rate is significantly lower than the level of 6.7 births reported for the late 1980s.[2] Although it is difficult to determine the cause of this drop in fertility rates, the provision of family planning services can be cited as one of its contributing factors.

Family planning policy in Kenya

In 1957, the non-governmental organization, the Family Planning Association of Kenya, was formed to coordinate policy formulation on birth control for the Kenyan government. Ten years later, it launched a focused family planning programme. Systematic action was prompted by alarming data included in the 1969 population census. As a consequence, the government put mechanisms in place to reduce the high population growth rate and improve maternal and child health within five years. This decision marked the first practical policy act aimed at population control in Kenya. Family planning was integrated into maternal and children services at the operational level.

It took another ten years for the government to discover that its policy had been based on the wrong premise. The forecasting used to set the population growth rate was skewed and the capacity of service delivery systems had been overestimated. At the same time, the policy had placed more emphasis on supply rather than on social and family value systems as a starting point to change families' attitudes towards fertility control. It is not surprising that the 1979 census results recorded no change in the population growth rate compared to that of 1969, remaining at 3.8 per cent.

This fact led to policy reformulation which resulted in the establishment of the National Council for Population and Development in 1982. The country's current family planning policy is based upon this council's work.

The government's policy on family planning can be divided into broad and specific policy items. In general, the policy aims at reducing the high population growth rate by encouraging Kenyans to have small families, in this way reducing fertility rates that sustain population growth. At the same time, the policy emphasizes that family planning is a matter of free choice. That is, the family should choose whether or not to accept the idea and the different techniques associated with it. For those choosing family planning, the policy states that adequate information and education should be provided. It also suggests that such education should be targeted at less-educated groups as they have the highest fertility levels.

Current government policy also attempts to motivate men to practise family planning as a way of reducing the high population growth rate. At the same time, while the policy encourages Kenyans to have small families, it is also meant to help those families who want children but are unable to have them.

The government's policy is to cooperate with NGOs when providing family planning services in order to reach rural areas effectively. Through such cooperation, services for rural areas are expected to be decentralized and the health facilities and trained personnel needed to provide the services are also assumed to be easily available.

Regarding ethics, the policy states that family planning activities should safeguard the rights, health and welfare of their beneficiaries. When providing surgical sterilization to a woman, the client's full consent as well as that of her husband must be sought and full information about the effects of this type of contraception must be given. Abortion is illegal in Kenya.

In light of the fact that women make up the majority of family planning recipients, Kenya's population policy sets out to improve their status through equal access to higher education and training. At the educational level, government policy has also targeted education for youth on population control issues. The sex education programme to be introduced in Kenyan schools reflects this policy concern.

At the operational level, government policy is now formulated to ensure that:

- contraception is available to all those who want it;
- adequate counselling, examinations and follow-up for contraceptive users are available;
- relevant data on births and deaths are collected and related to mortality and fertility;
- information related to population is disseminated at the community level;
- community-based distribution of contraceptives and the training of distributors is promoted;
- contraceptive distributors are trained, retrained and supervised;
- oversight on the type and quality of contraceptives provided at service delivery points is given.

The government's policy on family planning is well designed in practice. In collaboration with NGOs and other private institutions, it has provided a service delivery system that spans from the community level, through service delivery points to referral levels at the district, provincial and national levels.

Approximately two-thirds of family planning services in Kenya are provided by the government. Private medical facilities and NGOs provide approximately 20 per cent while only an estimated 4 per cent is provided by private doctors and pharmacies. Community-based health workers supply only 2 per cent of total family planning services.

In Kenya, many different NGOs play a role in family planning. These include secular organizations such as the Family Planning Association of Kenya and Marie Stopes which provide a wide range of services including sexual health care and adolescent counselling and religious groups such as the Kenya Catholic Secretariat, the Family Life Counselling Association (also Catholic), the Christian Health Association of Kenya (Protestant), and Crescent Medical Aid (Muslim). Each one supports the government's family planning programme in a different way. In addition, one women's group called the Maendeleo Ya Wanawake organization provides services through community-based distributors.

Constraints in the implementation of family planning

Today, one out of every three women of reproductive age in Kenya uses a family planning method. Approximately 50 per cent of non-users say that they do not use one either because they want to become pregnant or because they think they cannot become pregnant due to menopause or other reasons. The other half say that they do not use family planning for various reasons: their partner opposes it, they fear side effects or other health problems, religious reasons, lack of knowledge or difficulty in obtaining a method.[3]

A number of factors have acted as constraints on the implementation of the family planning policy in practice.

Religious opposition to free choice Family planning services provided through the Catholic Church and the Family Life Counselling Association discriminate on the basis of age, spousal consent and marital status. These institutions promote dogmatically the use of natural family planning methods while stressing the contraindications of what they call 'artificial' methods. In this way, some organizations limit their clients' access to free and informed choice and contribute to rumours and fears about the adverse effects of modern contraceptives.

The three natural family planning methods advocated by the Catholic Church (especially the 'sympto-thermal' method) require a certain level of literacy on the part of the user to be completely effective. Illiterate clients can therefore use only some of the methods. At the same time, other religious institutions – such as the Protestant-run Christian Health Association of Kenya and the Muslim organization Crescent Medical Aid – do promote modern contraceptives with minimal restrictions.

Legal issues Single adolescents have no legal right to receive contraceptives. This fact has resulted in unwanted pregnancies and unsafe abortions. At the same time, the government does not allow abortion as a method of fertility regulation.

Cultural factors Many communities still practise early, forced marriages for girls, exposing them to early motherhood and its associated risks. Some parents' preference for a child of a particular sex makes it difficult for couples to decide on the ideal number of children to have. Plus, polygamy and wife inheritance are still rampant in many communities. These practices increase women's risk of contracting sexually transmitted diseases including AIDS.

Socio-economic factors Studies have established a link between fertility and a woman's educational level. In light of the economic hardship which prevails in many rural areas, families often opt to educate boys rather than girls. Girls' meagre education further limits their chances for paid employment. This sometimes leads to prostitution and its related health risks.

Institutional factors Many NGOs lack adequate, trained personnel to run their facilities while they also oversee the quality of services provided by community-based distributors. Such supervision is constrained by financial and logistical factors. The Ministry of Health's supervisory role is also limited by budgetary constraints. In addition, only two organizations have the capacity to do outreach services on voluntary, surgical contraception.

Even these are organized on an ad hoc basis, making it difficult for prospective clients to have access to them.

Study design

In order to appraise the quality of care and adherence to reproductive rights in selected sites in the country, the researchers visited service delivery points and the community-based contraceptive distributors working at these points. Interviews with service providers and their clients were held and clinic interactions were observed. The study covered two of Kenya's rural regions, namely Embu District in Eastern Province and Homa Bay District in Nyanza Province, and one urban area, the capital city, Nairobi. In all of these areas, a sample of NGO and governmental services were visited (see Table 5.1 for the number of different service points visited).

The study's findings are not representative for Kenya. They should be seen as indicative for the country's situation. Important findings are related to a larger survey conducted by the Population Council in 1989 which was done in a random sample of ninety-nine government service delivery points. The findings of this larger survey are also not representative for Kenya, because data could not be collected at approximately 50 per cent of the selected service delivery points due to the fact that there were no new clients available on the day of the visit.[4]

Table 5.1 Number of targets covered by the study

Method used	Embu	Homa Bay	Nairobi	Number covered
Interviews with service delivery points/ providers	13	9	10	32
Interviews with community-based distributors	2	1	8	11
Service delivery point clients interviewed	17	15	13	45
Service delivery point clients observed	13	6	13	32
Community-based distributors' clients interviewed	8	6	10	24

Source: Field data; A. Mutua.

Profile of the service delivery points

A total of thirty-two service delivery points were visited and interviews were held with family planning service providers. Organizations whose service delivery points were visited include the Ministry of Health, mission services and the services of other NGOs such as the Family Planning

Association of Kenya. Most of these service delivery points provided family planning services from 8 a.m. until 5 p.m. with a one-hour lunch break.

In Kenya, service delivery points do not serve a specific geographical area with a defined population. Some of them are located very close to one another and therefore have overlapping geographic areas and populations served. Clients are also free to choose health-care services, depending on availability, quality and costs.

In this country, family planning services are generally integrated with other maternal and child health services such as antenatal and postnatal care and child welfare clinics. The majority of service delivery points visited were dispensaries and health centres. Two hospitals, a nursing home and a mobile clinic run jointly by the Ministry of Health and an NGO were also visited.

All of the service providers interviewed were full-time workers with organizations providing family planning services. They were paid monthly salaries instead of per acceptor. Virtually all of them were nurses. Only two of the interviewed service providers were doctors and one was a midwife.

According to the study's respondents, the basic training course for service providers did not include family planning. Only 28 per cent had learned about family planning during their basic training. However, while working in family planning services, 8 per cent had attended in-service courses on family planning. Lack of training on family planning was also found in the Situation Analysis study. Here, only 54 per cent of the nursing staff in service delivery points were found to have received the core seven-week training course in family planning which makes them eligible to deliver family planning services according to Ministry of Health guidelines. In-service training had been received only by 16 per cent of the interviewed staff.[5]

Profile of community-based distributors

The community-based distributors who operate in Kenya are mostly trained by NGOs including Christian hospitals and the Family Planning Association of Kenya. Though nationally only 2 per cent of users receive their contraceptive supplies from community-based distributors, their services are well accepted in the areas where they operate.[6] Increasingly, the government's family planning programme intends to support the work of such distributors by means of supervision and training.

Community distributors were operating in all three areas visited for the study. In total, eleven community-based distributors were interviewed. The field observations revealed a lack of systematic policy on community-based delivery. It should be noted that this system is crucial as these distributors can connect the community to formal delivery systems. Those distributors covered by the study had worked in their present capacity for a period ranging from two to six years. When recruited, all of them had gone through initial basic training for a period ranging from one to six weeks. The training was provided by a wide range of institutions including the Family Planning Association of Kenya, the Family Life programme, the Ministry of Health with support from the German donor GTZ and the women's organization, Maendeleo Ya Wanawake.

Their training included the following topics:

- communication and counselling skills
- advantages and disadvantages of all methods
- possible adverse effects of the methods
- contraindications of oral contraceptives
- management of method failure and side effects.

Although the topics listed above were covered in most of the training sessions, eight of the eleven community-based distributors felt that their training was inadequate and that refresher courses were not held frequently enough to update their knowledge, skills and practices. This was said although nine of the distributors had attended refresher courses. They suggested that more refresher courses be organized regularly.

The study also found that there was no clear policy regarding payment of community-based distributors. Seven of the distributors were paid for their services, while four were not. The amounts received varied from US$6 to US$60 per month.

Another problem identified by the research team was that the distributors did not know which geographical areas they were supposed to cover.

Eight of the interviewed community distributors were female and three were male. Those interviewed indicated that gender did not affect their work. They varied in age and nearly all had received secondary education.

Study findings

Free and informed choice of methods In the research areas where the survey took place a relatively wide range of contraceptives was found to be available in the service delivery points (see Table 5.2).

The table shows that virtually all of the service delivery points have combined contraceptive pills, progestin-only pills, injectables and condoms available. Clients have less access to IUDs, spermicides and sterilization. Referral is often needed for the latter. Norplant® is available only in a limited number of service delivery points and the diaphragm is rarely supplied.

Usually if a method is not available at the service delivery point, clients

Table 5.2 Percentage of service delivery points where specified contraceptive methods were available during the survey (n = 32)

Contraceptive method	Percentage available
1. Combined pill	
Microgynon®	91
Neogynon®	76
Eugynon®	66
Nordette®	25
Logynon®	22
Trinordial®	16
2. Progestin-only pills	81
3. Norplant®	22
4. Injectables	
Depo-Provera®	91
Noristerat®	56
5. Barrier methods	
condom	91
diaphragm	6
6. Spermicides	
foaming tablets	41
jelly	9
7. Intrauterine devices	
Copper T 380A®	59
Lippes®	9
Multiload 375®	9
Multiload 250®	3
8. Sterilization	
Female sterilization	
minilap, local anaesthesia	34
minilap, general anaesthesia	6
laparotomy	3
Male sterilization	
vasectomy	16
9. Natural family planning	31

Source: Field data; A. Mutua.

are referred to another outlet. The study revealed that the distance to the nearest referral facility varied from less than 4km (28 per cent) and 4–7km (16 per cent) to more than 8km (56 per cent). Service providers interviewed revealed that it takes between four and eight hours to travel back and forth to the referral centres.

As an indication of recent use of contraceptive methods, the research team recorded which types of contraceptives were reportedly prescribed

Table 5.3 Distribution of contraceptive methods prescribed during the last three months (n = 32)

Contraceptive method distributed	Percentage service delivery points where available
Pill	97
Injectable	97
Condom	78
IUDs	56
Female sterilization	16
Norplant®	16
Spermicide	13
Diaphragm	3

Source: Field data; A. Mutua.

to family planning clients during the last three months. Table 5.3 shows the results. This table confirms that providers most often supply the pill, injectables and condoms.

The Population Council's Situation Analysis study reported a similar situation.[7] The team concluded that, in Kenya, oral contraceptives and injectables were widely available. Adequate supplies of condoms, foams and IUDs were found to be available only in less than half of the service delivery points visited.

One problem regarding contraceptive pill supply which was also noted by the Population Council team is the availability of eight different brands. This causes problems when users have to switch brands due to temporary shortages of their regular brand. Table 5.2 shows that, in the current study, one brand of contraceptive pill was found to be supplied adequately (Microgynon®), while the others were often out of stock.

Table 5.4 shows the types of contraceptive methods stocked by community distributors and those which were regularly out of stock.

Table 5.4 Availability of contraceptive methods at community-based distributors

Type of contraceptive	Regularly available
Combined pills	Yes
Progestin-only pill	Yes
Condoms	Yes
Diaphragms	No
Spermicides	No

Source: Field data; A. Mutua.

This table shows that community-based distributors generally provide contraceptive pills and condoms. The researchers were told that sometimes they were out of stock due to delay in supply; high demand for some methods; lack of transport; expiry of some methods; and lack of stock at the central government stores. The community-based distributors complained that in particular the pill brands Nordette® and Trinordial® are often out of stock. Injectables are not available from community distributors as they are not authorized to provide injections.

Provider–client interactions at service delivery points   In more than 90 per cent of the cases, service providers reported that they encourage clients to choose themselves which contraceptive method is most appropriate and convenient for them.

In total, 98 per cent of the interviewed clients (n = 45) felt that the clinic staff was friendly, easy to understand and told them when to return. In addition, 96 per cent said that they were satisfied and would encourage a friend to visit the same facility. Of these, 89 per cent felt that they received what they wanted. The remaining 11 per cent were dissatisfied because certain contraceptives were not available.

Overall assessment of the quality of family planning services, calculated using selected indicators, was generally positive. The responses are presented in Table 5.5.

Of the thirty-two interactions observed, three-quarters came for resupply of contraceptive methods, 16 per cent to discuss a problem with the method, 6 per cent to switch methods and 3 per cent for other reasons. In 91 per cent of the cases, the service providers gave the client a respectful and friendly greeting. In two-thirds of the consultations they inquired about reproductive goals. In the Situation Analysis study, client–provider interactions were also rated as relatively good.[8] In that study, 88 per cent of clients were reportedly greeted in a respectful and friendly

Table 5.5 Clients' overall assessment of the quality of family planning services and service delivery points (n = 45)

Indicators for assessing quality of care	Percentage yes
Were clinic staff friendly?	98
Were staff easy to understand?	98
Do you feel you got what you wanted?	89
Were you told when to return?	98
Would you encourage friends to visit the same facility?	96
Overall satisfaction	96

Source: Data from client exit interviews; A. Mutua.

manner. The Situation Analysis study systematically observed new client consultations to assess if information was provided on a range of methods. The researchers found that, generally, clients were indeed provided with information on a number of family planning methods. Ninety-four per cent of the clients were told about two or more methods. Nearly all clients were told about oral contraceptives and Depo-Provera®. About three-fourths were told about IUDs and only 60 per cent received information on condoms. Sterilization was discussed the least. In 17 per cent of the consultations, female sterilization was mentioned in contrast to 4 per cent which discussed vasectomy. On average, four different methods were discussed per consultation with a new user.

Accessibility of sterilization for women and men who no longer want children appears to be a problem in Kenya. Few clinics provide these services and providers apparently do not mention it often in their consultations.

Contraceptive method preference and restrictions   Although service providers indicated that clients had the freedom to choose their own method, some of them preferred particular methods in certain situations. Table 5.6 shows which contraceptive methods service providers said they would recommend to mothers wanting to space the next delivery and those not wanting any more children.

Table 5.6 Percentage of service providers who recommend a specific method for child-spacing and for those wanting no more children (n = 32)

Contraceptive method	Recommended for spacing children	Recommended for those not wanting more children
Pill	62	0
Injectables	50	19
Norplant®	65	3
Natural family planning	19	0
Condom	16	0
Spermicides	13	0
IUD	6	0
Female sterilization	0	94
Male sterilization	0	0

Source: Provider interviews; A. Mutua.

This table confirms the finding that the main methods advised for spacing are hormonal ones and that IUDs are not favoured by service providers. Contraceptive methods such as the condom, spermicides and the diaphragm received low ratings because service providers described them as 'messy'. The table shows that when it is clear no more children are desired, female sterilization is advised.

Client–provider interactions with community-based distributors   A total of twenty-four clients were interviewed about their latest visit to the community-based distributor. Of these, twenty-one (88 per cent) indicated that the distributor gave them a friendly greeting. Most (80 per cent) of the clients visited the distributor to obtain a resupply of contraceptives. The remaining 20 per cent came to receive advice on a problem she/he was having with the method being used. During these visits, the community-based distributors made several inquiries about the client's status as summarized in Table 5.7.

Table 5.7 Percentage of community-based distributors who inquired about specific issues (n = 24)

Conditions inquired about:	Percentage yes
Reproductive goals and plans	67
Breastfeeding	54
Problems with method currently used	92

Source: Client interviews; A. Mutua.

Restrictions on method provision   As pointed out earlier in this chapter, the organizations providing family planning in Kenya differ in their policies on user restrictions. Catholic services emphasize marital status and spousal consent. Government services also require spousal consent for sterilization. Protestant services do not request spousal consent or marital status, but clients cannot be younger than eighteen years old.

The actual restrictions applied in the service delivery points visited were assessed by age, number of children, marital status and spousal consent. The findings are summarized in Table 5.8.

Table 5.8 Percentage of service delivery points where restrictions are applied (n = 32)

Indicator	Tubal ligation	IUD	Injectables	Combined pill
Age	66	69	59	47
Number of children	69	69	72	0
Consent of spouse	56	0	0	0
Marital status	0	0	0	0

Source: Field data; A. Mutua.

This table shows that, in practice, age is the only major consideration for restricting a client's use of some contraceptive methods. Adolescents have difficulty obtaining contraceptives. The number of children was found to be important regarding use of injectables, IUDs and for tubal ligation. The providers apparently considered the possible delay in fertility related to injectables and the risk of pelvic inflammatory disease and infertility associated with the IUD. Spousal consent was an important consideration only for tubal ligation, which follows government policy. Still, nearly fifty per cent of the providers did not apply this restriction. It is also important to note that, in practice, marital status (though stressed by Catholic institutions) was not mentioned as an important reason to restrict contraceptive use.

Balanced and objective information   While contraceptives are generally available and clients are treated well, the survey found that insufficient information is provided on the methods. Fifty-nine per cent of the visited service delivery points had information on family planning (in the Situation Analysis study 60 per cent did *not* have information), and approximately one-half of the interviewed providers said the information they had was not balanced.

According to clients interviewed at service delivery points, written information was not commonly used during consultations. No written information was provided to the client in 75 per cent of the consultations. In the 25 per cent of cases where it was used, clients indicated that they could not understand the message. This was mostly due to the fact that it was not written in the local language. Only some of the thirty-two surveyed service delivery points had information available in the local language.

Table 5.9 shows how the forty-five clients interviewed at service delivery points rated the information they received during the consultation.

Table 5.9 Information provided by service providers (n = 45)

Activities of service provider during consultation	Yes (%)
Explained how method works	56
Showed how to use the method	85
Described possible side effects	60
Told what to do if there are side effects	76
Told where to get method	93
Asked if client had any questions	60

Source: Client exit interviews; A. Mutua.

This table shows that the information commonly given by providers is how to use the method, where to get it and what to do if side effects occur. Information on *how* the method works and possible side effects are given less often. Providers do not routinely ask clients if they have questions. The earlier Situation Analysis study found similar results. Here, in 87 per cent of the consultations clients were told how to use the method, and in only 60 per cent were they told what possible complications could occur.

Government policy supports the provision of contraceptive information to encourage people to choose for 'a small family'. Field evidence revealed that ten of the eleven community-based distributors had educational materials on family planning. Nevertheless, nine of them said that they doubted their clients understood the given information.

Use of incentives and disincentives   None of the service delivery points covered by this study used any incentives to motivate clients to accept or continue use of contraceptive methods. They also did not impose any sanctions on potential clients deciding not to accept family planning services.

A health-care infrastructure that enables safe use   In terms of the quality of the health-care infrastructure, the researchers observed that the service delivery points visited had limited working space. Evidence from the field revealed that 69 per cent of the observed delivery points did not have separate rooms for client examinations. In the same way, only 38 per cent of them had separate counselling rooms.

The researchers also found that one out of every three examination rooms was not clean. Although 81 per cent of the service delivery points had water available, most of them did not have running water in the examining rooms. Water was kept instead in buckets. While the study has shown that injectables are a commonly provided contraceptive method, disposable syringes were used only in approximately 40 per cent of the service delivery points. The lack of running water in many clinics makes it doubtful that reusable injection equipment was adequately sterilized or that other procedures such as IUD insertion could be done in a hygienic way. A recent evaluation of the Ministry of Health in-service training concluded that most clinics follow acceptable procedures for disinfecting and sterilizing equipment when supplies are available.[9] However, supplies such as disinfectants and sterile examining gloves are often lacking.

The service delivery points' storage facilities were generally found to be of good quality with record systems in place. Given the regular shortages of some brands of contraceptive pill and IUDs, it is questionable whether the recording is actually used to check inventory.

Proper storage facilities for contraceptive methods are an essential component of the community-based distribution programme. This study showed that only four (36 per cent) of the distributors had a metal or wooden box supplied by the programme specifically for storage of contraceptive methods. Others (64 per cent) kept their contraceptives in paper bags, baskets made of sisal or in another way. Most community-based distributors kept records of the contraceptive methods they received and distributed. They also maintained clear records of the clients they served and the contraceptive methods they used.

Client management The researchers assessed the providers' technical competence by observing consultations. During thirty-two observed consultations, a medical history was taken in 84 per cent of the cases; blood pressure was taken in 81 per cent and the date of the next visit was given in 66 per cent of the cases. These findings suggest that the providers are relatively competent in giving services. This is confirmed by the findings of the Situation Analysis study which found when focusing on new clients that 96 per cent of new clients observed had a gynaecological history and blood pressure taken. In Miller's Situation Analysis study, a medical history was taken for 85 per cent, weight was measured for 79 per cent and a pelvic exam was performed on 73 per cent. The Situation Analysis study found that providers told clients when next to return to the clinic in 98 per cent of the 48 new cases observed. Addresses were observed in the record-keeping system for 88 per cent of the clients.[10]

Management of breastfeeding women and complications To evaluate further service providers' technical competence they were asked to explain how they would manage clients who were breastfeeding and those with certain medical conditions such as severe abdominal pain while using an IUD and headache while using the pill. The providers' views on how to manage these situations are summarized in Tables 5.10, 5.11 and 5.12.

Table 5.10 Distribution of service providers according to how they would manage clients who are breastfeeding

Mode of management	Percentage of providers
Use progestin-only pill	75
Use pills (not specified)	11
Use combined pills	6
Use other method (not pill)	6
Ask child's age	6
Stop contraception while breastfeeding	6

Source: Provider interviews; A. Mutua.

Table 5.11 Percentage of service providers according to how they would manage clients experiencing abdominal pain while using an IUD

Mode of management	Percentage of providers
Take medical history	43
Examine for infection	25
Refer to another facility	18
Check if IUD is in place	6
Other (blood pressure, HIV test, etc.)	6

Source: Provider interviews; A. Mutua.

Table 5.12 Percentage of service providers according to how they would manage clients experiencing headache while using oral contraceptives

Mode of management	Percentage of providers
Take blood pressure	50
Take history of menses and severity	34
Refer to another facility	9
Ask to choose another method	6

Source: Provider interviews; A. Mutua.

These three tables show that providers generally know that progestin-only pills are indicated for breastfeeding women, though two women said they would suggest combined pills for breastfeeding mothers, which are contraindicated. They do not mention the LAM method. Most providers dealing with a client complaining of severe abdominal pain while using an IUD would take a medical history and/or examine her for a reproductive tract infection which is appropriate. When confronted with headaches related to the pill, most providers said they would take a history of menses and/or a blood-pressure reading suggesting that in this case as well they felt competent to act on the concerns put forward by the women. These findings seem to suggest that the providers have received some training in managing side effects and contraception for breastfeeding women.

Conclusion

The Kenyan case study provides a country context in which fertility decline has increasingly become the object of government policy. A national council has been set up to implement the policy in close collaboration with a wide range of NGOs involved in family planning.

The study, conducted in two rural areas and the capital region, shows that the government's policy seems to be making a wide range of contraceptives available. The data reveal that providers prefer hormonal methods, including the pill and injectables. IUDs are less accessible to users and while condoms are generally available at service delivery points, they are not promoted as a contraceptive method by providers. Access to sterilization services also seems to be a problem as most clinics do not provide such services and providers rarely discuss the option with clients.

Community-based distributors provide clients with access to condoms and contraceptive pills. This community service is important to clients. There appears to be a lack of policy on the community-based distributor's role and tasks *vis-à-vis* the service delivery points. This is also indicated by the fact that most of the interviewed distributors were unaware of their catchment area.

Both providers at service delivery points and community distributors were found to treat their clients with respect, inquire about their reproductive goals and provide them with a choice of contraceptive methods. Age is the main restriction for contraceptive availability in Kenya. This indicates that adolescents have difficulties getting contraception. No incentives and disincentives are further applied.

While the supply of contraceptives is good, the provision of balanced and objective information is poor. In around 40 per cent of the service delivery points no written information was available. While clients are generally told how to use the method they select and what to do if problems occur, they receive little information on how the methods work and possible side effects. This lack of information could be related to the lack of training noted among providers. Only around one-third of the nurses providing care had received initial family planning training and very few had access to continuing education courses.

Despite their limited access to training opportunities, the technical competence of providers at service delivery points appears to be relatively good.

Recommendations

The most important recommendations resulting from this study for the Kenyan family planning programme are the following suggestions.

Increase male responsibility There is a need to promote male methods of contraception (condoms and vasectomy). Currently the programme remains too focused on female clients, even though two clinics for male clients have been set up in Kenya.

Train providers Training for service providers needs to be strengthened by ensuring that the basic seven-week course is followed by all staff involved in family planning and by setting up a system of continuing education and strengthening worker supervision.

Provide more and better information to clients On a related note, there is a need to strengthen information provision to clients. Currently, there is a lack of written information materials that are understandable to clients. Other forms of communication also need to be developed.

Examine the role of community-based distributors The role of community distributors should be better defined and strengthened. Currently, there is no clear policy on their role and tasks. In addition, their financial compensation varies significantly and they have no clear guidelines on which areas they should cover.

Improve services for adolescents and single clients There is an urgent need for services for unmarried, young people who are often denied services under programmes' current rules.

About the authors

Ann Ndinda Mutua, B Ed, is a community-based health-care consultant; *Ochieng Ondolo*, MB, Ch B, MPH, works for the Kenya Medical Research Institute; *Eunice Munanie*, M Sc (Economics) specializes in population policies and programmes and works as a reproductive health consultant; and *Kisuke Ndiku* is the director of the organization LINDA and is a trainer in community development.

Notes

1. National Council for Population and Development (NCPD), Central Bureau of Statistics (CBS) (Office of the Vice President and Ministry of Planning and National Development, Kenya) and Macro International Inc. (MI) (1994) *Kenya Demographic and Health Survey, 1993* (Calverton, MD: NCPD, CBS and MI).

2. Ibid.

3. Ibid.

4. R. A. Miller et al. (1989) *A Situation Analysis of the Family Planning Program of Kenya: The Availability, Functioning, and Quality of MOH Services* (New York: Population Council).

5. Ibid.

6. UNFPA (1991) *1991 Program Review and Strategy Development Report* (New York: UN).

7. R. A. Miller et al. *A Situation Analysis of the Family Planning Program of Kenya*.

8. Ibid.

9. Ibid.

10. Ibid.

CHAPTER 6

Reproductive Rights on Paper: Four Bolivian Cities

Micaela Parras and Maria José Morales

The introduction of family planning within Bolivia's health services has been controversial. Under pressure from the Catholic Church, past government administrations followed pro-natalistic policies, presenting Bolivia as a 'dangerously uninhabited country'. Family planning has also carried the stigma of imperialism ever since Peace Corps volunteers reportedly conducted sterilizations among Indian women in the Bolivian highlands during the 1960s.

In 1977, in response to church pressure, the government introduced a decree forbidding public institutions from providing family planning services.[1] Thereafter, the few services available were provided by the private sector. This resulted in decreased access to contraceptives due to the commercial prices people had to pay at these outlets for both consultations and methods.

During the early 1980s, the government became concerned about the growing number of illegal, unsafe abortions and the resulting maternal mortality. (Abortion in Bolivia is legally permitted only to save a woman's life or in cases of rape.) Although no official data were available on the number of illegal abortions performed in Bolivia, hospital-based data and surveys suggested a very high incidence. In the capital, La Paz, one survey of women aged fifteen to forty-four reported that 20 per cent of the respondents had undergone at least one induced abortion in their life.[2] A study of maternal mortality conducted in 1980 in eight Bolivian health units found that 27 per cent of all maternal deaths were caused by septic abortion.[3]

The government's recognition of the health consequences related to unwanted pregnancy initiated a slow expansion of family planning services in Bolivia. Regulations adopted in 1982 permit the provision of family planning information and some services as part of postpartum care. Post-abortion family planning services were also included. In 1986, the Bolivian government issued a child-spacing policy, stating that it was the government's responsibility to provide family planning information and services to high-risk groups.[4]

The current government's policy on family planning is contained in the National Plan for the Reduction in Maternal, Perinatal and Infant Mortality, called *Plan Vida*, which has been in effect since 1993. The government now aims to make family planning services widely accessible: 'The policy of the plan is to allow access without restriction to maternal and child health services, to nutrition and to family planning to all citizens.'[5]

In this document, for the first time, the government formally recognizes *all* citizens' fundamental right to health care, geographic and economic accessibility to those services and the participation of rural and urban people's organizations so that the health system can truly respond to the needs of the entire population, including family planning services. Family planning is incorporated within reproductive health care which, in turn, since August 1993, has been seen as a strategic part of state health policies which support women.

In the context of Bolivian primary health care, reproductive health care includes the following:

- information, education, communication and high-quality, family planning services
- prenatal care, low-risk delivery and postnatal care
- prevention and treatment of abortion-related complications
- treatment of reproductive tract infections, sexually transmitted diseases and other reproductive health problems
- referral to additional services related to family planning, pregnancy complications, delivery and abortion, infertility, reproductive tract infections, STDs and HIV/AIDS and cancer.

The Bolivian government intends to enhance the ability of all citizens to exercise their right to adequate health care and wants to guarantee women the right to make their own decisions about sexuality and reproduction. Therefore, the government, in principle, does not have a demographic objective behind the implementation of these services. Rather, it is working to meet the population's unsatisfied need for information and services.

It is remarkable that in a country where women have been denied access to family planning services for so long that such a radical reproductive health policy has been adopted in the wake of the United Nations International Conference on Population and Development (ICPD) in 1994. Of all the countries involved in this current study, the Bolivian policy is by far the one most in agreement with the recommendations adopted at the ICPD.

Irrespective of the good policy, much remains to be done in Bolivia. As was said in Chapter 3, the country has very poor health and development indicators. At present, maternal mortality is still relatively high, estimated to be six per 1,000 live births.[6] Four in ten births take place without professional assistance and some 47 per cent of pregnant women do not receive prenatal care. Though fertility is falling, women still have more children than they consider ideal. If unwanted pregnancies could be avoided, the total fertility rate would fall to 2.7 children per woman instead of the current 4.8.[7]

Not surprisingly, contraceptive prevalence is low, only 18 per cent of reproductive-age women use modern contraceptive methods. Natural family planning, more specifically the rhythm method, remains the most popular method, with one in five women reportedly using it.

Numerous investigations in the country have shown that it is women who have already had their desired number of children who are the principal users of modern family planning services. Such clients are usually above the age of thirty.

In Bolivia, the government serves around one-third of the contraceptive users through its hospitals, health centres and health posts. It also works through community-based health promoters and *responsables populares de salud* (community health workers). Governmental services also include the *Caja Nacional*, a form of health insurance for employees that caters to approximately 7 per cent of users. The private sector (including commercial clinics and hospitals, NGO services and pharmacies) serves the remaining two-thirds. The various NGOs involved in family planning mostly focus on reproductive and sexual health services in poor communities. They are largely funded by USAID.

Study design

Data for the present appraisal were collected during interviews with family planning providers and clients and from observations of their interactions in four Bolivian cities which represent the country's cultural and ethnic diversity. The cities studied were Santa Cruz, El Alto, Oruro and Sucre. In these cities, the study was carried out in all centres offering family planning services. That is, government health centres (a total of twenty-three were visited), non-governmental health centres (N = 11) and pharmacies (N = 14) in order to reach all the institutes offering some kind of family planning service. The researchers were not able to include systematically private, for-profit clinics because the researchers were often denied entry into these clinics by the managing physicians. This is a limitation of the study as the 1994 *Demographic and Health Survey* (DHS) estimated that approximately 21 per cent of contraceptive users rely on private physicians for family planning services while another 19 per cent go to private clinics and hospitals.[8]

Apart from visiting the health centres, the researchers interviewed a total of thirty-one community-based distributors in the four regions.

Exit interviews were done with women attending family planning clinics for the first time and those who had been using the service for some time (a total of forty-nine women were interviewed). The most common characteristic found among these groups was their low economic status. This was to be expected, given the sample of service delivery points included in the study. The private for-profit services which were under-represented in the study cater to people who can afford to pay for consultations. The state and NGO services are more often used by those with lower incomes. It was further apparent that the clients had a large number of children (more than three in 90 per cent of the cases observed), that they had not spaced births and that the women did not bring their partners with them for the consultation.

The providers

The majority of the thirty-four service delivery point providers included in this study were medical doctors who had been trained in family planning services. In fact 65 per cent of the interviewed staff were trained in gynaecology. The remaining providers were general physicians. Only 70 per cent of those interviewed said they had received their last family planning course less than a year ago. More than 80 per cent of the providers described themselves as quite able to carry out their work as a family planning service provider. Because the majority of the interviewed staff members were doctors, this chapter refers to them as such. While the clients were nearly always women, men made up the majority of the family planning doctors at the state-run centres. More female doctors than male were found at NGO centres.

Of the community-based distributors interviewed, half of them said they had received complementary training to provide family planning services. Most of them were women originally trained as nurses. They are able to perform more complex procedures such as IUD insertion. The health workers categorized here as community-based distributors occupy positions in health posts, as health aides at health centres and as health promoters or community health workers.

Study findings

Free and informed choice of methods Nearly all health centres and community-based distributors had the following methods available: combination pills, condoms and IUDs. Pharmacies primarily supply condoms and pills and to a lesser extent IUDs and injectables. Rarely were other types of methods found in these first-level services. A small proportion of health centres performed sterilizations.

Progestin-only pills were not widely available and the researchers concluded that providers were not well informed about their possible benefits for lactating women. Only one pharmacist interviewed mentioned this type of pill, and Santa Cruz was the only city in which state centres provided it. The diaphragm was not found in any of the service delivery points or pharmacies visited (see Tables 6.1–6.3).

Table 6.1 Global availability of methods, by type of service delivery point (%)

Available method	State SDPs	NGO SDPs
Pill	95	90
Progestin-only pill	22	0
Condom	92	100
Diaphragm	0	0
Spermicides tablet	30	63
IUD (T 380AR)	100	100
Injectables (Depo Provera®)	7	27
Female sterilization	30	9
Vasectomy	9	18
Natural methods	40	45
Total SDPs visited	23	11

Source: Field data; M. Parras and M. J. Morales.

Table 6.2 Availability of methods at community-based distributors (n = 31)

Available method	Percentge of CBDs
Pill	94
Condom	94
Spermicides	61
Injectables	26
IUD	94
Other	
Female sterilization	10
Vasectomy	3
Natural methods	23

Source: Field data; M. Parras and M. J. Morales.

What stands out is the availability of natural methods of family planning from different channels since this is the method most used in Bolivia. While many women use the rhythm method, many do not know when they are fertile within their cycle. By obtaining information on how to use this method correctly, more unwanted pregnancies and high-risk abortions

Table 6.3 Availability of methods at pharmacies (n=14)

Availability	Percentage of pharmacies
Combination pills	100
Progestin-only pills	7
Condoms	100
Diaphragm	–
Spermicide	86
IUD	57
Injectables	57
Natural family planning methods	36

Source: Field data; M. Parras and M. J. Morales.

are now being prevented and the wishes of the majority of women and couples are being respected.

In general, centres offered clients only those methods which were available there. When a certain method was requested but unavailable, an available method was given to the client instead.

Restrictions The researchers did not observe significant restrictions in the provision of contraceptive methods by the different services. Medical contraindications were mentioned most of the time. At state centres, the client's age and the partner's consent were taken into account in all cases requesting sterilization, but civil status (married or not) was not a hindrance. All of the centres visited affirmed that partner consent was desirable in all cases but not necessary for methods to be provided.

At pharmacies, no significant restrictions were applied. These outlets provide services to young and unmarried people. In only two pharmacies were adolescents reportedly not allowed to obtain contraceptives.

The majority of family planning doctors agreed that single people and adolescents should be able to obtain family planning services. However, the percentage of adolescents reached by such services is quite low. The researchers did not see adolescents in the waiting or consulting rooms of any of the centres visited. The adolescents observed at the clinics were already mothers.

In Bolivia, adolescent sexuality is not an issue that is easily discussed, as premarital sex is strongly opposed by society, although a large proportion of Bolivian girls (45 per cent) have sexual relations before they marry.[9] Family planning is considered appropriate only for married women. Adolescents, in fact, are kept ignorant about contraception and fertility. In a survey among young urban girls it was observed that only 30 per cent of them were able spontaneously to mention one or more contraceptive methods. In a rural area, this figure dropped to 20 per cent. The pill was the best-known method followed by abstinence. Young adults said that private clinics and drugstores were their information sources.[10]

Contraceptive prices Until recently, the high cost of contraceptives restricted their availability. This trend has started to reverse now that the government is implementing a family planning programme and donor funds are used to import contraceptives. The study found that low-income clients are guaranteed a choice between a wide range of contraceptives at very low prices at state and NGO health centres. This has diminished the economic barriers that used to prevent many women and men from having access to contraceptive methods. For example, in commercial outlets, the pill costs approximately US$2.20 per strip. One condom costs US$0.30.

Quality of provider–client counselling In the majority of provider–client interactions, the researchers found that respectful treatment was given to clients. Negative value judgements were not given based upon a client's information about their sexual and reproductive lives. However, the researchers sensed that women often left the interactions with a number of unanswered questions.

Observations in health centres revealed that doctors inquired about clients' reproductive goals in two-thirds of the consultations with new users. When clients came for resupply or because of doubts or problems with their selected method, they generally did not discuss reproductive goals. In these circumstances, providers almost always inquired whether or not the client experienced problems with the method.

Doctors at health centres most often brought up the IUD and secondly the pill when discussing methods for spacing births, as can be seen in Table 6.4 which shows the types of information given to new users. At community-based distributors, clients were generally given information about the IUD, the pill and, often, natural family planning.

Table 6.4 shows that approximately half of the new clients at service delivery points were told how to use the pill and only one out of four clients was told about its effectiveness. In contrast, nearly all of the clients were told about the IUD's effectiveness. Injectables and natural family planning methods were mentioned least often in the observed consultations, in approximately one-fourth of the cases. When discussing IUDs and injectables, information on how to use the method was not given as these methods are administered by doctors. The community-based distributors provided information on a wider range of methods.

When asked about their preferences, the majority of doctors at health centres said their advice generally depended on the client's situation. They tended to discourage clients from using the pill, condoms, spermicides and injectables because they believed that 'lower'-class men and women were incapable of complying with these birth-spacing methods and also

Table 6.4 Specific information given on selected methods during consultations with new users at service delivery points and by community-based distributors (observations)

Information given	Percentage of CBDs	Percentage of SDPs
Combination pill		
effectiveness	89	23
how-to-use	100	54
side effects	78	23
IUD		
effectiveness	92	92
how-to-use	0	0
side effects	69	62
Injectables		
effectiveness	50	23
how-to-use	0	0
side effects	100	15
Natural family planning		
effectiveness	67	23
how-to-use	56	15
side effects	0	0
Number of consultations	13	13

Source: Field data; M. Parras and M. J. Morales.

because they had little time to explain their proper use. Consequently, they tended to promote methods whose effectiveness does not depend on the user. This paternalistic attitude diminishes clients' capacity to decide for themselves.

Providers pointed out a number of daily impediments they encountered while trying to adhere to quality of care and reproductive rights. These included a lack of sufficient training in communication and counselling skills; inadequate numbers of personnel and an insufficient infrastructure dedicated to family planning; inadequate information material for the country's multi-ethnic and multi-cultural society and, finally, poor co-ordination and support of their work on the part of institutional directors.

The researchers noted that many health-care centres pass along responsibility for family planning counselling through the different types of staff. For that reason, auxiliary personnel and nursing staff usually do not take client histories (being occupied with other tasks), believing that the doctor will do this. At the same time, doctors usually suppose that counselling has already been done, at least in part, by the auxiliary personnel. This results in a rushed consultation during which information about method efficacy is given, but little information on possible side effects is mentioned.

Community-based distributors said they try to encourage clients to make their own decisions. Strategies used for this include explaining the advantages and disadvantages, giving advice, discussing method reliability and alluding to the client's precarious economic situation. This may differ from doctors' more 'technical' attitude during the consultation. Some doctors spoke of using contraceptives as a woman's duty if she did not have the economic resources to support more children. Such an attitude blames poverty on people and blames women for their reproductive function (especially poor ones).

In general, clients were found to receive more respectful treatment from community-based distributors than from health-centre staff. The researchers thought this might be due to the fact that the distributors belong to the same culture as the clients and better understand their needs and fears. For that reason, they do not inspire the same mistrust or fear that doctors do during consultations.

Balanced and objective information   In nine out of ten service delivery points, written information was available. However, the observations showed that these materials were used in approximately only 20 per cent of the consultations.

Written material collected during the study was found to use stereotypes and employ language more familiar to members of the middle class, creole, white and urban sectors and so did not reflect the majority of clients actually using the services, who have low incomes and education and are generally Indian.

Ninety per cent of the interviewed community-based distributors said that they used written information but 50 per cent stated that these materials were not understood by clients. In this case, the materials most frequently used were leaflets, pamphlets and contraceptive samples. The reasons given as to why these materials could not be understood were the language problem (technical vocabulary) and difficulty in understanding the concepts involved (terminology differing from that used in popular language).

Pharmacies generally lacked information materials for clients. Some distributed leaflets which were donated with contraceptives subsidized by USAID.

The researchers noted that the majority of family planning centres visited relied on written material to inform their clients. Family planning staff stated that there is a need to adapt available material to local cultures and to carry out extensive health education campaigns. Providers spoke about the need for other forms of information (written material is not suited to the majority of clients). There was a great need to work with audio-visual methods in particular.

Adequacy of information: clients' experiences In exit interviews, clients were asked about their consultation and the information they had received (see Table 6.5).

Table 6.5 Quality of provider–client interactions from the users' perspective (from user exit interviews in health centres, n = 49)

	Percentage of clients
The client:	
wanted to use a different method than the one she received	16
was informed about how the method worked	71
was informed how to use the method	65
was told about possible side effects	45
was informed about measures to take if problem arose	57
was told where to get method	55
was asked if she had any doubts	25
The client could explain how the method worked	31
The client received written information	45
The information was written in the client's own language	77
The client understood what the provider explained to her	69
The client received information on various methods	59
The client said she received the service she wanted	74

Source: Field data; M. Parras and M. J. Morales.

The table shows that clients usually received the method they wanted. When women who had used family planning services were asked what had been explained to them about the different methods, 59 per cent said that they had been told about various methods. The majority said that they were mostly informed about how a method worked and how to use it. Less than half said they had been told about side effects. Of those who *had* been informed about side effects, fewer than half had been told what to do if they experienced them and where to get help. The provider seldom assured him- or herself that the explanations had been understood by the client (24 per cent). Around half of the clients had received written information. In approximately one-fourth of the cases where information was received, the clients said that it was not in their own language.

Avoidance of incentives and disincentives The majority of doctors interviewed received a salary from the Health Ministry or the NGO where they worked. However, this salary was not dependent upon the services they provided. Some doctors working at NGOs volunteered their services there.

In general, if incentives did exist, they were insignificant and seemed to be used to compensate clients for the impersonal nature of the medical consultation by providing a small gift, such as a school notebook or some food. This was not the general case, but rather an exception found at some health centres. The researchers found no cases where any sanctions had been taken against a client deciding not to use a contraceptive method.

A health-care infrastructure that enables safe use The surveyed centres complied with minimum facility standards. All of them had running water, a blood-pressure cuff, sterile needles and syringes (often disposable), a clean speculum, registers of all clients and manuals for providers. Hygiene conditions were adequate at the majority of visited centres (see Table 6.6).

At the same time, it must be noted that the Health Ministry's clinics were the most poorly equipped in terms of materials and infrastructure to provide family planning services in a proper way. Many clinics gave the impression of extreme austerity, with little attention being placed upon non-essential details. Few facilities were in good condition. The public clinics' waiting rooms were found to be cold and impersonal.

Table 6.6 Adequacy of facilities and materials at service delivery points (n = 34)

Characteristic	Percentage of SDPs
Separate room for examinations	14
Separate areas for examinations	70
Clean examination area	73
Water available	86
Blood-pressure cuff available	95
Vaginal speculum available	95
Examination table available	89
Needles/syringes sterile	54
Inventory kept	86
Storage adequate	89
Records kept	92
Written guidelines and manuals available for providers	89

Source: Field data; M. Parras and M. J. Morales.

The NGO centres visited seemed more concerned with giving an appearance of warmth for clients. They had more access to audio-visual equipment and graphics. The facilities also seemed more comfortable. It must be said that NGO clinics are mainly financed by USAID which considers such aspects within their budgets. However, state resources are scarce and tend to focus on salaries and providing family planning services.

The community-based distributors who were interviewed generally lacked materials, as can be seen from Table 6.7.

Table 6.7 Health-care infrastructure that enables safe fertility regulation (community-based distributors' adequacy of facilities and materials) (n = 31)

Equipment	Percentage of CBDs
Bicycle	0
Blood-pressure cuff	3
Stethoscope	3
Record book	23
Procedures manual	0
Flip chart	80
Contraceptive sample kit	35
Pill checklist	3
Referral slips	0
Condom instruction sheet	10
Diaphragms	0
Pill instruction sheet	10
Pamphlet on the benefits of family planning	61
Pamphlet on sterilization	6
Video	26
Posters	13
Other	6

Source: Field data; M. Parras and M. J. Morales.

Adequacy of medical check-up Table 6.8 shows how adequate new client check-ups were at the service delivery points.

Table 6.8 Global adequacy of check-up during consultation of new users (n = 13)

Actions taken	Percentage of consultations 'yes'
History taken	77
Contraindication checklist used	15
Blood pressure taken	62
Pregnancy excluded	46
Informed about follow-up	62

Source: Field data; M. Parras and M. J. Morales.

Table 6.8 shows that, generally, a history is taken; however, contraindication checklists are rarely used, and pregnancy is not excluded in approximately half the consultations. At government clinics researchers also observed that the provider asked about breastfeeding only in one-third of the consultations with new clients. NGO clinic staff paid more attention to breastfeeding.

The researchers found that, out of respect for local norms of privacy, clients were not required to take off their skirts for a gynaecological examination. Researchers were present at many consultations where the examination was carried out on clients still wearing them. This practice was found to be of great importance as the requirement to disrobe was a large barrier to access of reproductive health services for many native women from rural areas.

However, such respect for privacy was not guaranteed at many of the services facilities visited given the scarcity of adequate space and the generally deficient condition of the infrastructure. Normally, consulting rooms had no space reserved for undressing and dressing or a separate room for gynaecological examination, although there was a separate area. This obviously affected many clients' privacy since the separated area did not ensure total privacy in many cases. In addition to clients' fears about having a gynaecological examination performed by a male doctor, there was often added unease caused by people entering and leaving the consultation room during the exam (e.g. observing students, nurses and auxiliary workers) who did not consider the effect their presence might have.

Follow-up services Health centres operated by the Ministry of Health offer clients integrated services. In this way, family planning services are joined with prenatal care, risk-free births, postnatal care, prevention and treatment of abortion complications, screening for cervical and breast cancer and diagnosing and treating sexually transmitted diseases, among others. It is normal practice to take advantage of a woman's visit to a clinic with a sick child to discuss family planning. Many of those interviewed also said that the centres offered infertility services and treatment though, in reality, these services seemed scarce.

Management of side effects When clients came to the centre with contraceptive complaints, health workers sometimes opposed discontinuation of their method. This was based upon their assumption that women and men from indigenous groups form myths about the use of modern contraceptive methods and ask for prescriptions and stop use in an arbitrary manner. They saw reported problems as psychological rather than clinical in nature. Medical personnel were more disposed to change the method of clients using the pill as, in general, hormonal methods are regarded with suspicion by doctors.

Table 6.9 shows how family planning doctors said they would manage specific, hypothetical complaints presented to them during interviews. It shows that, indeed, providers would usually not advise clients to change their method. In the case of the IUD complaint, it is apparent that the family planning doctors do not really know what they should do.

Table 6.9 Adequate management of side effects by service delivery points (n = 34 providers)

Action reported	Percentage of providers
For IUD user with severe abdominal pain:	
Advise stopping use of method	22
Do clinical appraisal	78
Advise user to change methods	30
Advise user to have specific tests	8
Give pharmacological treatment	11
Other	14
For pill user with severe headache:	
Advise stopping use of method	30
Do clinical appraisal	49
Advise user to change method	49
Other	22
Does not know	3

Source: Field data; M. Parras and M. J. Morales.

Advice to breastfeeding clients When asked what family planning doctors would advise to breastfeeding clients, the researchers found that private clinics most often recommended the IUD or a method other than the pill. State-run centres tended to recommend natural methods combined with IUDs or barrier methods (condoms). NGO centres showed a preference for natural methods and IUDs. When natural methods were recommended, the age of the child was asked to determine effectiveness.

Community distributors most often recommended IUDs, natural methods (asking the age of the child) and barrier methods (in combination with natural methods). Pharmacists emphasized the need for a medical consultation to many women. In addition, they usually recommended non-systemic methods in combination with natural methods.

Conclusion

Today Bolivia is presented with the challenge of incorporating quality care and reproductive rights in its family planning services. This must be done despite scarce human and material resources in the public sector. These scarcities are inherited from the earlier political situation which designed a health system that did not focus on guaranteeing the entire population's right to health care. In addition, cultural obstacles regarding gender and professional and economic status remain. Bolivia's family planning system does not adequately address issues such as gender, culture and communication. These three subjects are common problem areas in light of the practice, learned values and formation of bio-medical training. As a consequence, family planning services suffer from deficiencies, one of the most prominent being the inability of some family planning doctors to understand different, cultural preferences regarding health and illness.

The researchers found that the range of methods provided showed that the state attempted to make a wide selection available to users. While the percentage of spermicides and injectables is lower than that at NGO centres, the Health Ministry does make female sterilization and vasectomy available. These methods are not offered at other centres due to their limited capacity to carry them out.

On the basis of a national survey carried out in 1994[11] the most commonly used contraceptive methods are natural ones, followed by the IUD, sterilization and the pill. Based on this data, it can be seen that the country's family planning services do offer the methods with the highest demand and preference among the population. However, the preference shown for the IUD seems based upon the family planning doctors' underestimation of women's capacity to choose the best method for their own situation.

In contrast to other countries, the amount of information provided by health centres on natural methods is remarkable. This is important as a great number of women who reported using the 'rhythm method' did not know when they were fertile.

There is a strong cultural rejection of condoms by men in stable partner relationships. The 1994 DHS found that the most discontinued methods were the condom (13.7 per cent) and withdrawal (13 per cent) because of the male partner's dissatisfaction with it. Some women interviewed mentioned how difficult it was for them to use condoms. It has been suggested that the physical manipulation required to use a condom implies a 'rationalization of sexual relations'. This goes against the common, cultural conception of sexuality as a passionate and irrational act. At the same time, men often say that condoms reduce their sexual pleasure.[12]

No significant restrictions were found regarding the supply of contraceptive methods by different services. Higher requirements were given for women seeking female sterilization (number of children, age, spousal consent) than for male sterilization. However, while consent from the partner is sought, it is not actually required.

The percentage of adolescents currently reached by services is low. Adolescents were not found at any of the observed clinics. Those who did fall within this category were already mothers. Nevertheless, community-based distributors and commercial outlets stated that condom distribution is centred on this group. The majority of commercial suppliers and promoters agreed that unmarried couples and adolescents should be able to obtain contraceptives.

A high percentage of providers interviewed said that they encourage their clients to decide themselves which method is most suited to their needs. In actual fact, information and method provision is centred on IUDs and, to a lesser extent, the pill, sterilization and natural methods. Moreover, a paternalistic approach was observed and this attitude diminishes clients' ability to make their own decisions.

At the same time, doctors often do not advise clients to stop using a particular method if problems arise. If a woman asks to change or stop, the provider most often asks why. This stems from the fact that many providers believe that women and men tend to form myths about the use of contraceptive methods and base their requests for supply or stopping use on personal whims. Therefore, many providers pay little attention to a client's request to change methods.

While all family planning personnel at public clinics have been trained to offer information on contraceptive methods, it has been observed that this responsibility is often passed on to others within the health-care hierarchy. For that reason, auxiliary personnel often do not inform clients about family planning as they assume that the doctor will do so during the consultation. At the same time, the doctors often assume that such information has already been given by auxiliary personnel. This results in only partial or hurried information being given to a client.

Respect for privacy is not always guaranteed at family planning clinics. Most often, the facility's infrastructure does not permit confidential counselling to take place. This is due to lack of time, interruptions by others and the fact that providers often offer services according to the type of user (social position, ethnic background, economic resources) and tailor their information accordingly.

In general, the researchers found that medical personnel often become demoralized because they are overworked, have few materials to work with and feel that their efforts are not valued by the responsible institutions or the population they serve.

At the same time, paramedical personnel were found to be motivated in their work due to the recognition given to them by the community. They showed dedication and the ability to disseminate information and advice. However, better economic incentives are required on the part of the institutions in order to avoid the defection of highly valuable staff. The moral benefits obtained through the work were seen only as temporary motivation. The community-based distributors' interest in clients was not highly valued and a lot of their work was in effect voluntary.

Recommendations

To address some of the issues raised in the Conclusion, the researchers suggest that the following topics receive attention.

Give more complete information to clients Health workers should take sufficient time to ask clients about their reproductive plans, rule out the possibility of pregnancy and give information about possible side effects caused by different family planning methods.

Promote male methods Providers in all facilities should work to promote the use of condoms for the prevention of sexually transmitted diseases as well as pregnancy. This should be done in spite of the fact that there is strong cultural rejection of condoms by the adult population. The researchers believe that a good strategy would be to promote women's sexual health and autonomy by giving women complete and accurate information about the transmission, prevention and treatment of sexually transmitted diseases. (STDs are one of the main reasons that women consult a reproductive health clinic.) In this way, women would develop the capacity to negotiate condom use with their partner(s).

Train providers to communicate The study found that a high percentage of the service providers have received specific and ongoing training about different technical aspects of family planning. Thus, 80 per cent of medical personnel are found to be capable of carrying out their responsibilities in this area. At the same time, providers requested training in communication and counselling not only for medical personnel but also for nurses, auxiliary workers and promoters assigned to family planning services. Further training should include communication aspects so that providers and clients can have a better understanding of each other during consultations. Such ability to communicate is essential for clients to understand the information they receive.

Put aside paternalism The interviewed family planning service providers agreed that family planning was a right for all citizens. They try to adapt their technical/professional training to the educational and cultural circumstances of the clients. However, their manner is often paternalistic. This makes it difficult for them to treat clients on an equal level. The researchers believe that aspects of gender and communication must be addressed during the training of family planning service personnel.

About the authors

Micaela Parras is trained as a sociologist and is a specialist in development co-operation at the Complutense University in Madrid, Spain. She also works as a consultant on health and development projects. *Maria José Morales* is a lawyer.

Notes

1. Presidential Resolution No. 184393, 5 August 1977.
2. E. Saldías and E. Del Castillo (1981) *Conocimientos, Actitudes y Prácticas de*

Concepción y Anticoncepción en la Ciudad de La Paz (*Knowledge, Attitudes and Conception and Contraceptive Practices in the City of La Paz*).

3. Ministry of Public Health (1989) *Seminario de Lucha Contra El Aborto* (*Seminar on the Struggle Against Abortion*) (La Paz: Ministry of Public Health).

4. Ibid.

5. Ministry of Human Development, Ministry of Health (1994) *Plan Vida Bolivia 1994–1997* (La Paz: UNFPA, USAID, UNICEF, OPS/OMS).

6. These are 1993 figures, cited in the *World Development Report 1995: Workers in an Integrated World* (1995) (Oxford: OUP and World Development Indicators).

7. M. Gutiérrez et al. (1994) *Encuesta Nacional de Demografía y Salud* (ENDSA) (*National Demographic and Health Survey*) (La Paz: National Institute of Statistics; and Calverton: Macro International).

8. Ibid.

9. According to the Ministry of Planning and Coordination's (1989) *Dos Casos de la Planificación Familiar en Bolivia* (*Two Cases of Family Planning in Bolivia*), 28 per cent of the female Bolivian population between the ages of eighteen and nineteen are already mothers. In urban areas, the figure is 23 per cent and in rural areas, 46 per cent. In addition, 38 per cent of urban adolescents first have sexual intercourse before the age of seventeen. In the rural areas, the figures differ greatly on this fact: in El Altiplano (El Alto, Oruro) 40 per cent of adolescents begin having sexual relations before they reach age seventeen; in Sucre, the figure reaches 41 per cent; and in Santa Cruz, 62 per cent. In total, 45 per cent of Bolivian women have had sexual relations before marriage (which usually occurs around age twenty).

10. Ministry of Planning and Coordination (1989) *Two Cases*. Data from ENDSA (1989) and S. Rance (1995) *Aborto, Género y Salud Reproductiva* (*Abortion, Gender and Reproductive Health*; Summary of Phase I of the Research Project) (El Alto), p. 11.

11. M. Gutiérrez et al. (1994) *National Demographic and Health Survey*.

12. Ibid.

CHAPTER 7

Fulfilling Providers' Preferences: Four Mexican States

Gloria Sayavedra H.

Mexico adopted a population policy in 1973. In it, the government's profound change in policy regarding women's sexual and reproductive health was justified as a way to bring about equal development and improvement in the quality of life and well-being of all Mexicans. Later, the policy was directed more towards the improvement of maternal and child health and health institutions were given responsibility to achieve the demographic goals drawn up by international organizations and the government.

To a certain extent, population and family planning programmes fulfil women's great need to control the number and spacing of their children. This is something they have been trying to achieve for hundreds of years in a variety of ways ranging from clandestine abortions that risked their own health to various natural contraceptives that were not always effective and carried the risk of early and multiple unwanted pregnancies. In light of these facts, the women's movement in Mexico has demanded that women be able to exercise their reproductive rights. It promotes the view that as women become a larger part of the country's paid labour force, receive more formal education and play a larger public role in society their need for contraception increases. In the same way, women's changing circumstances also increase their desire to separate their sexual and reproductive lives.

In Mexico, the most important provider of contraceptives, accounting for 67 per cent of the contraceptive users, is a social security institution called Instituto Mexicano del Seguro Social (IMSS).[1] All employees in Mexico (except civil servants) pay health-care insurance premiums to the IMSS, and this arrangement is responsible for one-third of the organization's income. The IMSS is further financed by fixed contributions from employers and the government. IMSS is a rich organization and is known in Mexico for its high quality health services. Apart from services for employees who pay fixed insurance fees, the IMSS is increasingly involved in community-based health programmes for populations that are not formally employed, such as peasant communities and the urban poor who tend to work in the informal labour market. Another similar institution responsible for a much lower percentage of contraceptive users (9 per cent) is the Instituto de Seguridad Social al Servicio de los Trabajadores del Estado (ISSSTE). Almost all civil servants are insured through this institution. The state further offers basic health services to people who are not formally employed and/or are poor through the health centres operated by the Ministry of Health (SSA). In 1992, the SSA provided services to 22 per cent of contraceptive users.[2] Thus the public and semi-public sectors account for approximately 98 per cent of contraceptive provision in Mexico. Family planning is provided as an integral part of health care through these semi-public and public services. The remaining contraceptive users obtain health services in the private sector. They go directly to pharmacies, attend private clinics or go to specialized family planning clinics run by the Mexican Family Planning Association (MEX-FAM). The wide range of services available in Mexico makes family planning accessible to the Mexican population and explains the relatively high contraceptive prevalence rates found in Mexico as compared to other Latin American countries. According to the Mexican government, by 1992, 63.1 per cent of the country's reproductive-age women were using some form of contraception.[3] In 1987, the usage rate was much lower with only 33.9 per cent of these women using a contraceptive method according to the Demographic and Health Survey.[4]

However, the rural areas appear to be under-served. Data from 1992 reveal that 88 per cent of the contraceptive acceptors live in urban areas, while only 12 per cent come from rural areas. In the rural areas in the south-eastern part of the country, in fact, only two out of every ten women were found to use any method of contraception. An additional two women out of every ten did not know of any contraceptive method.[5]

In 1989 an Interinstitutional Group on Family Planning was formed, directed by the Ministry of Health, which coordinates the activities of the various agencies involved in family planning. The general and specific objectives of the National Programme of Family Planning in the period 1990–94, the time during which the current quality of care study was undertaken, are given in the box opposite.

Thus, the objectives stress both health and fertility goals. It is remarkable that abortion's association with the incidence of unwanted pregnancies is acknowledged in the general objectives. Today, in practice, it is almost impossible for women to gain access to abortion under any condition. There have been dramatic cases in which women with many children receive permission from a medical committee to have an abortion, but by the time permission is received, she is already four or five months pregnant and it is considered too late to carry out the procedure. Further, the intention to expand coverage among rural populations, enhance quality of

---

National programme of family planning 1990–94

General objectives:

- cooperate to improve the health of the population, especially maternal and infant health
- contribute to decreases in fertility levels (the aim was to reach a total fertility rate of 2.8 by 1994, with 63.8 per cent of reproductive-age women using a contraceptive method)
- reduce the frequency of unwanted pregnancy and prevent associated problems such as abortion.

Specific objectives, among others:

- extend the coverage of services to the country's rural areas
- raise the standard of quality of the services
- increase the adolescent population's knowledge of family planning
- promote men's participation in the programme
- increase contraceptives' acceptability to the population by incorporating new methods.

Source: Mexican National Programme of Family Planning (1990–94).

---

care and promote family planning to the adolescent population are relevant specific objectives to this study.

Mexico's population policies give special attention to the promotion of post-abortion and postnatal contraception in order to enhance child-spacing and limit fertility. The IMSS has set an increased contraceptive prevalence target for these two groups of 80 per cent.

Though not commonly offered by the first-line services, female sterilization is the most common form of contraception in Mexico. It is increasingly being performed directly after childbirth, abortion or during a Caesarean section, especially at IMSS services which have set a target to achieve 80 per cent coverage of these groups. These programmes are popular with users despite the resistance of some doctors and feminists who say that such a vital decision cannot be taken under such circumstances of distress or pressure. Informed consent infers that the woman has been previously informed and that she has given her written consent before the event.

New guidelines

In 1994, the Mexican government published detailed guidelines on family planning,[6] stressing that the objective of family planning is to prevent health risks for men, women and children. In it, family planning services are projected as a means to exercise reproductive rights. However, when these guidelines were being developed, only international organizations and private institutions were consulted. In general, feminist groups, academic institutions and civil organizations were excluded from the drafting process.

The guidelines appear to pay less attention to women's health and sexuality than to men's. For example, they mention various forms of dissatisfaction men may have with certain contraceptive methods or the post-surgical care they will need after sterilization, while ignoring contraceptives' effect on women's sexual satisfaction or the care their bodies may require after surgery. The family planning programmes further show an evident preference for semi-permanent and permanent methods used by *women*. The majority of recommended methods are designed for women. These methods receive the greatest amount of explanation, distribution and accessibility, thereby emphasizing *inter alia* that contraception is the responsibility of women.

In general, the guidelines present contraception in a very positive way with emphasis placed on the qualities and use of methods. At the same time, risks, precautions, age limitations and the condition of potential women users are omitted. There is no strategy linking programmes on AIDS control with those on contraception.

The 1995 report from the Ministry of Health provided reliable estimates on the types of contraceptives actually used in Mexico (see Table 7.1).[7] These data show that in 1992 male methods were indeed hardly used in Mexico. Most men in Mexico still oppose using any method of contraception or any protective device against AIDS infection. Their masculine identity emphasizes a patriarchal attitude and the power to take risks.

Table 7.1 Contraceptive use in Mexico among reproductive-age women 1987 and 1992 (%)

Method used	1987	1992
Pill	9.7	9.8
IUD	10.2	11.1
Injection	2.8	3.1
Condom	1.9	3.2
Female sterilization	18.6	26.9
Male sterilization	0.8	0.9
Diaphragm/jelly	0	0
Traditional methods	8.1	8.1

Source: Ministry of Health (SSA) (1995) *Profile of Contraceptive Practices* (Mexico City: Cuadernos de Salud. Población y Salud. Secretaría de Salud).

Teenagers Avoidance of teenage pregnancy is a specific goal of the family planning policy in Mexico. In practice, the programme places emphasis on girls' responsibility and to a lesser extent on that of boys. This is in spite of findings from focus group discussions showing that boys are better informed about sex and are more interested in having early sexual relationships than girls.[8]

In the family planning guidelines, IUDs and hormonal contraception are recommended to teenagers and women who have never had children. It is not mentioned that a secondary effect of IUD use can be pelvic inflammatory disease (PID) and possible infertility.[9] The guidelines also do not mention that adolescents should be encouraged to use male condoms with other contraceptives because of their ability to help prevent the spread of sexually transmitted diseases and HIV infection.

MEXFAM has set up an innovative programme to reach out to adolescents that could be used as an example to private family planning clinics in Mexico. The programme called *Gente Joven* (Young People) was intended to bring information on sex education and family planning to young people living in the country's marginal urban areas. Initial need assessments showed that adolescents have sex sporadically, and that they therefore feel the need to use only barrier methods. In its initial phases it also became clear that an adolescents' programme had to go beyond the medical domain and directly address issues of sexuality in a serious and candid manner. Today, the *Gente Joven* programme reaches out to adolescents where they are found, in schools and colleges, at sport and recreational centres, at work, on the streets and in other gathering places. Promoters are trained to work with adolescents in these diverse settings. The *Gente Joven* programme does not provide adolescents with textbook information on reproductive biology and contraception. Instead, through a process of debate and analysis, it stimulates young people to make their own decisions about sexuality and acknowledges differences between young men and women in this respect. The promoters refer adolescents who actually want to use contraceptives to MEXFAM's community clinics where they can choose a contraceptive appropriate for their age, health conditions, lifestyle and preferences.

Study design

This study sampled health services in four different Mexican states. Two of them were selected because they are considered 'target states' in the family planning policy (Oaxaca and Chiapas) due to their high percentage of poor, rural populations and low contraceptive prevalence rates. The other two were included because contraceptive prevalence in these states is not perceived to be a problem (Mexico City and Tiaxcala). The fertility rates for Chiapas and Oaxaca are respectively 4.7 and 4.5, while those for

Tlaxcala and Mexico City are 3.2 and 3.0 respectively. Mexico City's rate is the lowest in the entire country.[10] In each state, the researchers aimed to cover the wide range of first-line services available. In doing so, they intended to show the quality of care found within the range of services available, from a user's perspective. However, the samples are not representative for the states' service delivery as they were not drawn randomly. The results provide a general picture and indicate each state's situation. In the study, 81 per cent of the service delivery points were semi-public or public clinics and the rest were private ones, in line with the dominance of the country's semi-public/public sector in the provision of family planning.

The research team adapted the study's checklists to the Mexican situation. The checklists asked about providers' ways of offering the different contraceptive methods and clients' experiences. Provider–client observations were also undertaken. When no permission was granted to observe consultations, the checklist designed for client exit interviews was used. While visiting service delivery points, the researchers collected a great deal of distributed material and educational brochures targeting different population groups, drawn up by the official family planning office in various states of Mexico. The material was collected to study the explicit and implicit messages they contained, as well as to judge if it lacked necessary information.

Data were collected at various levels: at the first-line health clinics (service delivery points), at community-based distributors and outreach clinics in far-away villages, in private clinics and in religious institutions.

Focus group discussions were also carried out to study more closely some aspects that did not come up during individual interviews. They included such topics as the accessibility of methods for adolescents, the practice of midwives and the views of medical professionals on family planning in comparison with their own contraceptive practices.

Because contraceptive methods are also recommended and provided to users by pharmacy employees who do not have any medical knowledge, pharmacy staff members were also interviewed.

The majority of personnel interviewed said they felt they did not have sufficient training to carry out the duties assigned to them. Although this statement was more frequently heard from community distributors and pharmacy employees, 50 per cent of the medical doctors interviewed felt the same way. This seemed due to the fact that doctors said, on average, their last refresher course had been seven years ago. They were also not familiar with the national family planning guidelines published in 1994.[11] In Mexico, community-based distributors are usually volunteers who have been trained to distribute contraceptives and to refer clients to hospitals and service delivery points for services they do not offer themselves. They are motivated individuals. Some community distributors are outreach workers from health centres providing ambulatory services to communities that are far away from health centres. Community distributors usually receive a US$8–12 donation per month. They do not offer scheduled care and were more difficult for the researchers to locate. They also do not have access to refresher courses.

Study findings

Availability of contraception   Table 7.2 shows the extent to which different contraceptives were available during visits to first-line health services, pharmacies and community-based distributors.

Table 7.2 Percentage of service delivery points with contraceptives available during visit (%)

Methods	Service delivery points	Pharmacies	Community-based distributors
Condoms	77	91	77
Combined pills	67	100	85
Natural family planning	54	0	0
Vasectomy	30	0	0
Female sterilization	19	0	0
Norplant®	12	9	0
Progestin-only pills	12	9	0
Spermicides	5	73	0
Injectables			
(Cyclofem®)	5	0	23
(Noristerat®)	26	82	14
(Depo-Provera®)	0	82	0
Diaphragm	0	0	0
IUD (Copper T)	79	30	30
Total number of SDPs	n = 43	n = 11	n = 13

Source: Field data; G. Sayavedra H.

Three methods were most often found at the studied service delivery points: IUDs, condoms and pills. Vasectomy and female sterilization are usually not performed as first-line services but are available through referral. In some of the health centres, condoms were becoming more and more scarce. For this reason, service delivery points had started referring condom users to pharmacies or other care centres. Injectables were available in approximately one-third of the centres. The most commonly available method was the quarterly, progestin-only injectable

Noristerat®. The once-a-month injectable Cyclofem® has been available in Mexico since 1992. It contains a combination of the progestin DMPA (the same progestin that is present in Depo-Provera®) and the estrogen oestradiol cypionate. In this assessment, Cyclofem® was not found to be available in pharmacies and was found in only 5 per cent of the service delivery points and with some of the community-based distributors studied. The progestin pill is rarely available and the diaphragm is not provided at all. Norplant® is available only in some specialized clinics, in this study, those of MEXFAM.

Community-based distributors generally supply condoms and pills. They refer clients who request an IUD. Three of the thirteen interviewed community-based distributors provided the monthly injectable Cyclofem® and two provided Noristerat®.

The data show that pharmacies generally stock condoms, pills, spermicides and quarterly injectables.

The availability of the monthly injectable Cyclofem® is particular to Mexico. The Human Reproduction Program of the World Health Organization in Mexico developed Cyclofem® after it had become clear that a similar injectable was very popular in Mexico and other Latin American countries in the late 1980s. The once-a-month injectables were then available in the private sector through pharmacies and manufactured by local companies. However, they were not part of the national family planning programme.[12] Still, WHO estimated that more than a million doses of the combination injection containing the progestin dihydroxy-progesterone acetophenide and the oestrogen estradiol enantate were sold every year. The advantage of the monthly combination injectables is that they result in monthly bleeding. Women reportedly preferred the once-a-month injectables over the quarterly ones because they found it easier to remember the date of their last shot. At the time of the study, monthly injectables have become part of the national family planning programme though they are not commonly available.

Out of stock Providers were asked what they do when methods are out of stock. When contraceptive pills are out of stock, medical providers reported a variety of strategies to use with clients requesting them, including: recommending that the client switch to an IUD; or writing a prescription so that the client can buy them at the pharmacy; or telling clients to change to a 'more safe and easy to obtain' method.

When no IUDs or condoms are in stock, medical personnel reported that they would recommend clients to change to a hormonal method; or go to another clinic or level of care; or return later.

The cost of different methods Currently, family planning methods are distributed free of charge to the public. This is done either through the

SSA programme or the Ministry of Health for those who are uninsured, or by the health services of the social security institutions (IMSS and ISSSTE) for clients paying insurance fees. In the private sector, a fee for services generally has to be paid. However, as said, these private services cater to only 2 per cent of the family planning clients. In some community clinics, people can pay for services by providing services to the health centre, such as painting it, keeping it clean and taking care of its garden.

Applied restrictions Providers in service delivery points were asked to what extent they placed restrictions on contraceptive availability. Their answers revealed that age is the most commonly applied restriction. Approximately four out of ten providers restrict the availability of the pill and female sterilization by age. In contrast, only one out of four providers restricts the IUD or vasectomy by age. They rarely reported restricting access due to marital status. However, in the case of sterilization, spousal consent was required by one out of four providers. One-third of the providers further restrict access to sterilization by the client's number of children. Seven of the forty-two interviewed providers restrict access to injectables according to the number of children. Researchers thought this was probably because of the delay to returned-fertility associated with these methods. Only a few doctors commented that they would not advise the IUD to women who did not yet have children, to women in unstable relations or to those with changing partners. The providers said that they would not recommend combined pills to adolescents or to women in relationships where a partner's discovery of pill use could result in physical or emotional violence.

The researchers were surprised to find that many providers restrict access to condoms in various ways. Many chose not to prescribe condoms, stressing people's ignorance in using them correctly. They also mentioned men's reluctance to use condoms. This is reflected in the relatively large percentage of providers (37 per cent) who request spousal consent when prescribing condoms. Providers tend to persuade clients to choose another method considered more 'safe' by the health establishment. Family planning policies still consider the condom to be an ineffective method for the majority of Mexican women with a low educational level or a macho spouse.

The findings on restrictions applied by family planning services suggest that women were considered unable to decide which method would best suit them. Table 7.3 shows how restrictions were applied.

In general, pharmacies do not restrict access to contraceptives. Nine out of ten pharmacy employees reported that they sell contraceptives without restriction to unmarried clients. Eight out of ten said that this was true for adolescent clients as well.

Table 7.3 Percentage of service delivery points that apply restrictions for the most commonly used contraceptive methods (n = 42 SDPs)

Methods	Age restriction	Only to married client	Only with consent of spouse	Related to number of children
Combined pills	37	14	5	12
IUD	26	9	14	10
Injectables	35	12	7	16
Vasectomy	26	0	23	23
Female sterilization	42	2	26	35

Source: Field data; G. Sayavedra H.

Recommended methods IUDs, condoms and oral contraceptives are the most commonly available methods. The study found no difference in which methods were recommended during the past three months between the different types of services. Combined oral pills, IUDs and injectables were given preference. In Oaxaca, only IUDs and combined hormonal pills were recommended by providers. When doctors were asked which method they recommended to clients not wanting any more children, all providers preferred female sterilization. In Oaxaca, for each occasion where vasectomy was mentioned, female sterilization was recommended more than twice.

In two client exit interviews, researchers learned that doctors had refused to perform a vasectomy and had instead recommended that it would be better if 'the woman would get sterilized'. In addition to the fact that providers are prejudiced against barrier methods, they also seemed to prefer 'modern methods' that call for greater medical intervention.

Barrier methods: a distant option? In this era of AIDS, it was unfortunate to find that male participation in sexual and reproductive health was still insignificant. Although this fact is due to different reasons, it mostly seemed to be based upon gender prejudice that made men see women as the only ones responsible for reproduction or family planning.

As in many other countries, the only barrier method available in Mexico is the male condom. This method assumes the cooperation of men, not only male clients but also male providers. The study found considerable resistance among service providers to incorporate men in family planning. There is a lack of free condoms at family planning services and AIDS prevention centres. At pharmacies, condoms are expensive. In addition, Catholic organizations operating in Mexico such as PROVIDA still oppose condom use and any other modern contraceptive method.

Quality of provider–client interactions In provider interviews, 84 per cent said that they encourage clients to decide for themselves what the best method would be. However, when observing consultations, the researchers did not find any indications that this is actually done in practice.

Through observations, the quality of the provider–client interaction was evaluated by checking if the provider asked the client about her reproductive goals, asked if she was breastfeeding, if she had experienced any problems with her method, and if she wanted to switch methods. Clients were divided into those coming for resupply, those wanting to change methods and new users. The results of these observations are given in Table 7.4.

Table 7.4 Quality of provider–client interaction by reason for consultation in service delivery points (n = 48 observations) (%)

Provider asked about:	Resupply clients	New users	Clients wanting to change methods
Reproductive goals	20	26	52
If the client was breastfeeding	7	0	20
Any past problems with the method	53	Not applicable	60
Total observations	n = 15	n = 8	n = 25

Source: Field data; G. Sayavedra H.

Table 7.4. shows that reproductive goals were rarely discussed with clients except when they explicitly came to switch methods. Also, the providers very rarely asked if clients were breastfeeding. This should have been brought up when consulting new clients. The providers most commonly asked if the client had experienced problems with methods in the past, suggesting that providers often are concerned about method continuation.

In the interviews, community-based distributors also mentioned their intention of encouraging clients to decide for themselves about the most appropriate contraceptive method. Most of the community-based distributors gave information about family planning during the consultation or at home visits. However, as with the service delivery point providers, problems were observed in practice. Observations of community distributors during consultations revealed that clients in only two out of ten consultations were asked about their reproductive goals. In the same way, in only an approximate one-third of the cases did they ask clients wanting resupply if they had experienced any problems with the method.

Balanced and objective information A large variety of educational material (brochures, posters, booklets, flip charts, etc.) exists in Mexico. However, the health sector encounters serious distribution problems. As a result, no informational material was found in approximately one in every four of the visited family planning clinics. When information is given it is generally understandable, although Indian communities' services lack materials in the local Indian languages.

Despite having information materials available, the researchers noted that family planning providers hardly ever used the materials during consultations. Clients received brochures on family planning in only 10 per cent of the observed consultations. This trend is similar for community-based distributors. While nine of the thirteen interviewed community distributors had information materials available, only two used them during consultations. It appeared that family planning providers and community-based distributors do not see the use of information material as a way to improve counselling by making the information easier to understand.

The information that was available was often found to be unbalanced by the researchers. While clinic posters tended to emphasize the principle of free choice, individual brochures described indications and ways to use each method, but rarely mentioned side effects, risks or contraindications.

It was difficult for the researchers to obtain information on the material used in pharmacies. Such client information hardly exists. However, employees said that they had pamphlets but never showed or used them.

Clients' perceptions about information   The lack of written information was confirmed in the exit interviews. Seventy-one per cent of the eighty-six clients interviewed after a consultation said that they did not receive written information about family planning (see Table 7.5). Most clients reported that they were satisfied by the type of information given orally by the family planning workers. Seven out of ten clients found the clinic staff easy to understand, though one-fourth of the clients said that they were difficult to understand.

Table 7.5 'Were clinic staff easy to understand?' (n = 86 exit interviews)

Answer	Percentage
Easy	70
Difficult	25
No answer	5

Source: Field data; G. Sayavedra H.

During exit interviews, clients were also asked to give more details about the information provided to them on their selected contraceptive method. An eight-point scale was designed to evaluate the information given. It was thought that each of these elements should be addressed by the provider. Providers received points for each element they brought up. If all eight were discussed, the provider would be judged as offering good information provision.

The eight elements comprised:

1. Client was told how the method works.
2. Client was shown how to use it.
3. Possible risks were discussed.
4. Client received information on what to do in case of possible adverse effects.
5. Client was told where to get the method.
6. Provider asked if the client had any doubts about the method.
7. Other methods were discussed.
8. Client was informed when to return to the clinic.

Using these criteria, as seen in Table 7.6, only 22 per cent of the clients received good quality consultations. Around half of the consultations were poor in terms of information provided, irrespective of the reason for which the clients came. One would expect resupply clients to receive less information, but this was not observed in the study.

Table 7.6 Comparison of quality of care according to reason for consultation (in exit interviews with clients at service delivery points; n = 85) (% cases)

Quality	Index (points)	New user	Re-supply	Change or discontinue	Other	Accumulated percentage
Bad	0–3	50	53	57	53	54
Average	4–5	40	40	17	17	24
Good	6–8	10	7	27	30	22
Total respondents		(10)	(15)	(30)	(30)	100

Source: Field data; G. Sayavedra H.

Incentives and disincentives Medical personnel were found to receive a monthly salary in the range US$250–300. The payment that they receive for their family planning work is generally unrelated to the number of acceptors, though in Oaxaca providers reportedly received salary rewards for improved performance. In a few private-sector cases, providers acknowledged receiving incentives in the form of a consultation payment per patient (the greater the number of patients, the higher the sum). In the public sector, reported incentives were intangible, such as praise by the management.

The use of incentives (economic or cash) to encourage clients to use contraceptives was not seen during the study. Other, more subtle incentives such as promises to clients about better well-being, an improvement in the user's economic situation, health and sexual pleasure were used to encourage clients to accept contraceptives. The fact that family planning services are offered free of charge in the semi-public or public health centres can also be seen as such an incentive.

Sanctions against non-users were reported by a few providers. For example, some providers said that their clinics provide health care during pregnancy and birth to women who already have two children only if they agree to be sterilized. Some clients reported that providers refused to provide them with milk for their children or scolded them for not planning and 'being irresponsible'. These sanctions were reported in Oaxaca, where contraceptive prevalence is still relatively low and where the government has set strict goals and targets to be achieved through rigorous implementation of the family planning programme.

Half of the community-based distributors involved in the study said that they don't receive any payment for their work, since it is strictly voluntary. Those who are paid said that they receive approximately US$8–12 per month. However, this is seen as more of a scholarship than a payment, and it is not related to the number of acceptors they bring in. These distributors further reported that incentives and disincentives targeted at potential clients regarding method choice did not exist.

A health-care infrastructure that enables safe use The quality of the health-care infrastructure offering family planning in Mexico is relatively good. In approximately 80 per cent of the service delivery points the researchers found the examination area to be clean. Water was available in three out of four centres, and the overall majority of centres had a speculum, blood-pressure cuff and needles and syringes available. The service delivery points generally offer a broad range of services for women's health, such as preventive screening for cervical and uterine cancer, sexually transmitted diseases, AIDS, and maternal and child care. Approximately half also offer infertility services.

Despite the good medical infrastructure, the medical check-up given to new users was found to be inadequate. In the majority of cases, service providers gave a method without performing an adequate check-up and without asking about breastfeeding. This could be related to the fact that only 50 per cent of the service delivery points had written guidelines on family planning.

Paradoxically, the management of clients' side effects was generally found to be adequate. The majority of community distributors referred clients with side effects to another level. The service delivery points would, in most cases, carry out a differential diagnostic test before stopping a method's use. In most cases, they would first draw up a good clinical history. In the case of a client complaining of severe headache while using hormonal contraceptives, providers would discuss possible circulatory problems. Again, it seems that providers are more concerned with users who want to change methods or who have problems with their method than with new users.

Conclusions

The study's researchers expected to find differences between family planning centres due to the fact that in some states government policy is especially targeted at reducing fertility rates and increasing contraceptive prevalence. The survey did find differences in the way in which the policy was applied. The researchers, in fact, found more incentives and sanctions being used in Chiapas and Oaxaca.

One of the most important findings of the study was the observed emphasis that services gave to contraceptives designed to be used by women and the absolute lack of attention given to barrier methods. Also the poor quality of counselling, which was given within an otherwise adequate health-care setting, is remarkable. Family planning workers are not providing women with sufficient oral and written information for them to make informed choices. In the same way, providers are not only paying little attention to men in family planning, they are actively discouraging male contraception. The low quality of counselling could be related to the lack of written guidelines for family planning.

Much needs to be done for these services to support men and women as they decide themselves how to control their pregnancies and prevent sexually transmitted diseases. Their choice should not be limited to the so-called 'secure' methods, which exclude condoms and diaphragms. Otherwise, while trying to provide protection against 'the risk of pregnancy', such health care leaves couples, and women in particular, unprotected against the risk of sexually transmitted diseases including AIDS. Studies have shown that Mexican women's health has not improved during the past few years. Figures of sickness and mortality remain the same, especially for those women who receive no health services. Maternal deaths caused by toxaemia and illegal abortions are still the order of the day.[13]

Recommendations

Based upon the findings of this study, the researchers urge Mexican health authorities and service providers to integrate the following suggestions.

Widen method choice Providers and programme administrators should broaden the diversity of methods available to clients by introducing female barrier methods such as the diaphragm and female condom. These methods increase women's ability to protect themselves against pregnancy and sexually transmitted diseases. Medical personnel should be trained not to discourage clients interested in using barrier or natural family planning methods.

Involve men in family planning Media campaigns need to be launched which emphasize partners' shared responsibility for family planning. Male methods should be promoted and more research should be carried out on new male methods. The national campaign launched in 1995 to raise awareness of vasectomy should be strongly supported.

Support male condom use Campaigns must be started to increase the public's and family planning providers' awareness about the condom's role in preventing the transmission of HIV and other sexually transmitted organisms, as well as pregnancy.

Promote national standards Programmes should disseminate the guidelines on family planning among medical family planning personnel. However, any sexist or racist bias should be pointed out and corrected by women's health advocates and NGOs, as these groups were left out of the guidelines' development.

Provide adequate and frequent training Training for family planning personnel should incorporate a gender perspective, as well as that of human, sexual and reproductive rights. Any macho or racist bias that is still present among some service providers and reflected during consultations and in some educational material should be discussed and changed.

Produce independent information materials Sufficient information needs to be given to clients and providers about each method's possible side effects and contraindications. There is a need to produce material on the advantages and disadvantages of surgical methods and those mainly used by the health sector, hormonal methods and IUDs. Such information should take into account not only the medical aspects influencing their use, but also social, psychological and cultural ones. Groups should also devise ways to deal with undesired problems found with these methods.

Ensure informed consent The practice of performing female sterilization after any obstetric event (birth, abortion, Caesarean section) should be stopped if the decision has not been made with sufficient thought. Free choice cannot be made under duress without violating reproductive rights.

Implement integrated women's health care These services should emphasize women's health and not solely demographic goals. They should meet the health needs of women who want to be mothers as well as those who do not wish to become pregnant. Such services should focus on female health problems that are important causes of mortality, such as cervical and breast cancer. They should also take into account broader issues such as violence against women and their lack of power to take decisions on controlling their own fertility.

Promote joint action by women's groups and NGOs Women's health organizations and NGO, community-based health organizations can play a role in improving the quality of care and adherence to reproductive rights in Mexico by carrying out a campaign on sexual and reproductive rights, emphasizing free and informed choice for both women and men as well as access to abortion services; and emphasizing the advantages of breast-feeding and its possible contraceptive qualities in health education.

Notes

The author would like to thank those who carried out the field work for this project: Barbara Cadenas, MD, a member of Chiltak and Women's Network/Produsem; Judith Cid, MD, coordinator of the TB programme in Oaxaca; Georgina Sánchez, a social worker working towards her Master's degree in population; and Margarita Romero, a social worker specializing in the family.

1. Ministry of Health (SSA) (1992) *Report of the Interinstitutional Programme of Family Planning* (Mexico City: SSA).

2. Ibid.

3. Ministry of Health (SSA) (1995) *El Perfil de la Práctica Anticonceptiva (Profile of Contraceptive Practices)* (Mexico City: Cuadernos de Salud. Población y Salud, Secretaría de Salud).

4. Y. Cabrera et al. (1987) *Encuesta Nacional sobre Fecundidad y Salud (Demographic and Health Survey)* (Mexico City: Director General for Family Planning, Subsecretariat for Health Services, Ministry of Health; and Columbia, OH: Institute for Resource Development/Macro Systems, Inc.).

5. A. Langer and Mariana Romero (1995) 'Diagnóstico de la Salud Reproductiva en México' ('Diagnosis of Reproductive Health in Mexico') *Reflexiones* 1(11).

6. Ministry of Health (SSA) (1994) *Norma Oficial Mexicana de los Servicios de Planificación Familiar (Official Mexican Standards of Family Planning Services)* Mexico City: SSA).

7. Ministry of Health (1995) *Profile of Contraceptive Practices.*

8. These findings are taken from focus group discussions with eighty adolescent boys and girls between thirteen and eighteen years of age in Mexico City.

9. *British National Formulary* (1995), p. 324.

10. In the official presentation of the demographic transition, eight states are mentioned as priority targets in demographic policy. These are the poorest states that have a rather high fertility rate. See, PROLAP/UNAM (1993) *Demographic Transition in Latin America and the Caribbean* (Mexico).

11. Mexican Ministry of Health (1994) *Official Mexican Standard of Family Planning Services.*

12. Anon. (1984) 'One-month Injectables are Popular Choice in Mexico', *Network* 5(3): 4–5.

13. G. Sayavedra-Herrerías (1995) 'Mexico: The Difference Between Policy and Practice', in E. Hayes (ed.), *A Healthy Balance? Women and Pharmaceuticals* (Amsterdam: Women's Health Action Foundation).

CHAPTER 8

Contraceptives at Your Doorstep: Two Urban and Two Rural Areas of Bangladesh

Sandra Mostafa Kabir and Hasina Chaklader

Bangladesh's family planning programme has had a chequered history. Reports on the programme's target orientation and use of incentives for clients and providers have stirred debate nationally and internationally about its ethical conduct. Most controversial were the reports in the mid-1980s of local officials withholding food aid from destitute women unless they agreed to be sterilized.[1] Such reports have affected the image of the Bangladesh family planning programme for the past decade.

Bangladesh is one of the world's most densely populated countries with an estimated population of 111 million. Due to past high fertility and decreasing mortality, Bangladesh's population has doubled since 1961. Its fast population growth is tied to extraordinary levels of poverty and illiteracy. With a per capita income of US$210 in 1990 and more than half of its population living below the poverty threshold, Bangladesh remains among the countries with the shortest life expectancy (57.1 years at birth in 1992) and high maternal and infant mortality.[2] Though educational levels of the Bangladeshi population have increased tremendously during the past few decades, approximately 50 per cent of females aged six years and above included in the recent *Demographic and Health Survey*[3] had not received any form of formal education. This figure was lower (35 per cent) for men.

The state is secular with 90 per cent of the population being Muslim and the remainder divided among Hindus, Christians, Buddhists and animists. The Constitution states that women shall have equal rights with men in all spheres of state and public life. Conspicuously absent is the provision for equality in the private sphere. In practice, private life is governed by traditional Islamic law. Under it, women are subordinate to men. Rules regarding their seclusion (purdah) also limit their mobility.

Bangladesh has one of the oldest family planning programmes in southern Asia. Started as a voluntary effort in the 1950s, the programme has evolved through different stages. It gained special momentum during

---

Basic demographic facts

Population (in millions)   111
Population growth rate (per cent per year)   2.2
Total fertility rate (births per woman)   4.2
Contraceptive prevalence rate   45

Source: S. N. Mitra et al. (1994) *Demographic and Health Survey 1993–1994*, National Institute of Population Research and Training (NIPORT) (Dhaka: Mitra and Associates; and Calverton MD: Macro International Inc.).

---

the 1980s and 1990s when the government declared population was the nation's largest problem. The total fertility rate declined from 7.0 births per woman in 1975 to 4.2 births per woman in 1991, due to intensive family planning programmes undertaken by the government. One key characteristic of the Bangladesh family planning programme is its extensive outreach services. Some 35,000 village-level workers, supported by both government and non-governmental organizations (NGOs) visit couples in their homes to provide contraceptive information and supplies. In this way, the programme overcomes the cultural constraints that limit women's mobility outside of their homes in many communities. The 1993–94 *Demographic and Health Survey* (DHS) found that 42 per cent of modern method users relied on field workers' visits to their homes.[4]

The Bangladesh programme is considered a family planning 'success story' because of the relatively high contraceptive prevalence rate (45 per cent) and low fertility rates that have been achieved. The box above gives a summary of the country's current demographic facts.

The Bangladesh government has set a target to reach the replacement fertility level (the fertility rate at which the population will no longer continue to grow) by the year 2005. A study conducted by the Bangladesh Planning Commission identified three issues which must be addressed to reach that goal. These elements are to increase contraceptive prevalence to 70 per cent; recruit younger family planning acceptors; and provide an appropriate method mix for them.

To achieve this, the government has set up a comprehensive health and population programme, called the Fourth Population Programme and Health Project (FPHP) during the fourth five-year plan. The project is to be funded over a period of five years (1992–96) by a consortium of donor agencies under the coordination of the World Bank.[5] The four principal components of the project are:

- strengthening family planning and maternal and child health services delivery

- improving efficiency in health services delivery
- strengthening support activities for the delivery of family planning and health services
- enhancing women's and children's nutrition.

There is a major shift of focus in the government health programme towards women, children and the poor. Strong emphasis is placed on improving the quality of care, rather than merely expanding physical facilities. To enhance quality of care, the FPHP has adopted a multi-faceted approach to the sector which includes training, provision of adequate supplies, improvements in management and supervision and appropriate incentives. Finally, there are increasing efforts to promote community participation and communication in the health services field.

The targets to be achieved are listed in the box below.[6]

The use of incentives and disincentives continues to be part of the Bangladeshi population policy in the fourth five-year plan. Acceptors of permanent methods or those who have practised family planning for more than five years are to be given preferential treatment at government facilities which control the allotment of housing, loans and the like. Concretely, this means that families with no more than two children will receive an income tax benefit. Families with more children will receive no consideration regarding the allotment of government housing and land. After the second child, families will be charged fees for subsequent deliveries at government hospitals. Financial assistance may be introduced in the case of a child's death when a couple is a permanent method acceptor. Appointments, overseas posting, foreign training and government and non-government services may be given preferentially to people with smaller families.

Fourth Population Programme and Health Project targets

The targets include (among other items) the reduction of:

- population growth rate from 2.11 to 1.82
- total fertility rate from 4.3 to 3.4 (per woman)
- maternal mortality rate from 570 to 450 per 100,000 live births
- infant mortality rate from 110 to 80 per 1,000 live births

the increase of:

- contraceptive prevalence rate from 39 to 50 per cent
- total number of family planning acceptors from 8.2 million to 12.3 million.

Source: FPHP.

Except to save a woman's life, abortion is illegal in Bangladesh under the Penal Code of 1860. Nevertheless, first trimester termination of a possible pregnancy is widely practised under the name 'menstrual regulation' (MR). This practice has its legal basis in an interpretation by the Bangladesh Institute of Law and International Affairs which says that the procedure is 'an interim method to establish non-pregnancy'.[7] The government plans to make amendments in the law involving birth and death registrations. Medical termination of pregnancy within the first sixteen weeks would be allowed by authorized medical practitioners and paramedics on a number of grounds such as protecting the mother's health, if birth defects are suspected, because of certain socio-economic conditions or in cases of pregnancy resulting from rape or incest.

The current government of Bangladesh recognizes that the provision of health care is not the sole responsibility of the government. Cooperation and collaboration among the public, private and NGO sectors is seen as essential for sustainable improvement in the health-care delivery system. NGOs in Bangladesh already play a significant role both in family planning and health care. Since the NGOs have greater resources focusing on smaller geographical areas, they are able to provide markedly better quality of care than government facilities. NGOs are thus encouraged to support and complement the government's population control programme. Currently, they are mostly involved in community-based distribution of contraceptives.

Reviewing the present and past population policies, the following points become apparent:

- Women are the focus of the national and NGO programmes. Men are systematically excluded from family planning programmes.
- Though much has changed in the societal attitude towards family planning and the small-family norm, Bangladesh society remains very conservative. Family planning is still regarded as a private matter and couples do not want their practices to be known.
- Knowledge about family planning is universal in Bangladesh; however, it is not clear how effective this knowledge is. That is, it is not known whether or not clients have enough knowledge about the details of many methods to make informed choices.
- Bangladesh's family planning programmes are method-oriented instead of client-oriented. Although declared a 'cafeteria-style' approach, clients do not always have choice. In most cases, it is the provider who chooses on the client's behalf. Also, there is no provision for counselling and supplying contraceptives to single adolescents who need them. This results in unsafe abortions and unwanted pregnancies.
- In Bangladesh, religion serves to dissuade couples from using family planning. Efforts were made to involve religious leaders in solving this

problem. At the Bangladesh Academy for Rural Development (BARD), several research studies were done on what the Qur'an says in favour of family planning. Its findings were used subsequently by the programme. Also, the government has introduced several schemes to involve the Imams, Islamic religious leaders, in family planning. Its success in doing so is not well documented. However, it is felt that there still remains more to be done on this issue.

Study design

The Bangladesh case study looks at the strengths and weaknesses of the current family planning programme by focusing on the quality of care provided to clients as well as describing the availability, functioning and quality of health and planning activities in the Dhaka division of Bangladesh. The emphasis is on service delivery in basic health services (so-called first-line service delivery points) and the provision of contraceptives by community-based distributors. It was intended to contribute to the debate on how to improve the country's family planning programmes as a whole. The study was done under the auspices of the Bangladesh Women's Health Coalition (BWHC), an organization that offers women reproductive health care at reasonable cost. BWHC's guiding principle is that informed choice is as essential to a reproductive health programme as are medical safety and access to contraceptives.[8]

The sample of family planning service providers (comprised of the most experienced and oldest family planning service centres) was proportionally selected from NGO and government clinics. The selected organizations were the Family Planning Association of Bangladesh (FPAB), Family Planning Services and Training Centre (FPSTC), Concerned Women for Family Planning (CWFP), Bangladesh Women's Health Coalition (BWHC) and government family planning service delivery points in the urban areas Dhaka and Narayanganj and also the rural districts Tangail and Narshingdi.

In each area, data were collected through interviews with service providers, observations of provider–client interactions, exit interviews with clients and in-depth interviews of some non-clients. Both qualitative and quantitative methods were used (see Table 8.1).

It is important to note that findings from this survey are not representative for all of Bangladesh. The sample was taken from selected rural and urban areas from the Dhaka area division. Bangladesh has another five divisions. Due to the limited budget available for the appraisal, the researchers limited the sample size regarding the number of health centres and community distributors included and the number of observations made.

The visited health centres generally provide family planning services

Table 8.1 Sample covered by the study

Samples	Number
Family planning agencies	5
Private clinic /providers	4
Drugstores or pharmacies/providers	4
Service delivery points/providers (NGO + gov't)	(15 + 4) 19
Community-based distributors (NGO + gov't)	(11 + 4) 15
Exit clients interviewed at the service delivery points	45
Provider–client interactions observed at the service delivery points	38
Exit clients interviewed at community-based distributors	60
Provider–client interactions observed at the community-based distributors	75
Provider–client interactions observed at private clinics	8
Provider–client interactions observed at commercial outlets	12
Non-clients interviewed	38
Focus group discussions with adolescents (21 male + 14 female)	6

Source: Field data; S. Kabir and H. Chaklader.

from Saturday through Thursday. (Friday is a holiday in Bangladesh.) All family planning services are available on these days.

The providers

The researchers observed that the proportion of female doctors was greater in NGO clinics than in the government ones. Most of the family planning workers had been working in family planning for a long time, approximately ten years. They had generally received training on family planning in their original curriculum and had received refresher training since then.

An important characteristic of the Bangladesh family planning programme is the large number of community-based distributors of contraception who have been trained. These distributors are called 'family welfare assistants' (FWAs) in Bangladesh. Each FWA is responsible for approximately 600 eligible couples, i.e. married couples of reproductive age.[9]

All the interviewed community-based distributors were female and the majority were between the ages of thirty and forty. Among them, approximately half had attended secondary school. They were paid workers, receiving US$50–75 per month. Some received additional benefits either in kind or cash, depending on their ability to reach targets. For example, those distributors reaching their targets might receive two to four cents for each case of IUD insertion, or an appreciation certificate, crockery or gift towels. Those covered by the study had worked in their present capacity for an average period of nine years. When asked whether their gender affected their work, only one distributor responded that it did. In total, 80 per cent of the community-based distributors included in the study had received refresher courses. The lack of refresher courses and the short duration of the training are some of the reasons why half of the community-based distributors said that they thought their training was inadequate. Six out of ten had attended a refresher course within the last year. Most had received training from the Family Planning Association of Bangladesh and Concerned Women for Family Planning.

Study findings

Free and informed choice of methods   The study found that women and men in the research area can choose from a wide range of contraceptive methods at health centres (see Table 8.2). It should be noted that progestin-only pills and diaphragms are not available. In addition, only two cases of Norplant® insertion carried out by the Family Planning Association of Bangladesh were observed during this study. They were part of a pilot project.

All methods are usually available at health centres, with the exception of spermicides. The choice provided by community-based distributors is less extensive; the main methods being the contraceptive pill and condoms. The distributors usually have only one brand of pill available while the

Table 8.2 Percentage of NGO and government service delivery points with specified methods available

	NGO health centres	Government health centres	NGO community-based distributors	Government community-based distributors
Contraceptive pills	93	100	100	100
Condoms	93	100	100	100
Spermicides	14	0	27	0
Injectables (Depo-Provera®)	93	100	55	50
Copper T	79	100	0	25
Menstrual regulation	36	100	0	0
	(n=15)	(n=4)	(n=11)	(n=4)

Source: Field data; S. Kabir and H. Chaklader.

health centres usually have two or three. The data show that some community-based distributors do provide injectables, and this follows the government's policy as part of a pilot project. This is not the case in the other countries taking part in this study. Problems with their resupply were reported in a study on factors affecting discontinuation of injectable methods in Bangladesh.[10]

The price of contraceptives Contraceptive costs at government and NGO service delivery points are very low due to extensive subsidies. Drugstores and private clinics sell these items for their actual market price. Generally, pills are dispensed in twenty-eight-day cycle strips. The cost of the combined oral pill is in the range US$0.17–0.50 for one cycle, depending on the brand. The cheaper brands are available at government and NGO service delivery points. To have an IUD inserted, the client pays only US$0.19 at a service delivery point while a private clinic will charge between US$1.19 and US$2.38. A packet of four condoms generally costs US$0.02–0.10 in all of the studied areas. Injectables cost US$0.02–0.10 at the service delivery points. At drugstores, they sell for US$0.59. Menstrual regulation is performed at service delivery points for a price varying between US$2.38 and US$35.70. Vasectomy and tubectomy are mostly provided by government and NGO service delivery points free of charge.

Restrictions There are official restrictions regarding age, marital status and spousal consent when certain contraceptive methods are chosen at service delivery points. Oral contraceptive pills are not given to women above the age of thirty-five or those who are unmarried. In the same way, condoms are not dispensed to unmarried women. Women who have no children or only one child or who have pelvic inflammatory disease cannot receive an IUD. Injectables are unavailable for women who are unmarried, older than forty-five or who have only one child. Menstrual regulation is not available for unmarried women, except in life-threatening cases where it is performed after obtaining consent from the woman's parents or older siblings. Sterilization, both male and female, has the highest level of restriction. Tubal ligation is restricted if the woman is considered too young or too old, or if she has fewer than two living children, when the younger child is under five and/or if spousal consent is lacking. Vasectomy is denied to men with fewer than two living children, when the younger child is less than six years old and/or if spousal consent is lacking. The number of children is applied as a restriction for male and female sterilization and for long-acting methods (IUDs and injectables) which can have a detrimental effect on fertility. It is interesting to note that comparatively more restrictions are applied for female sterilization.

The question remains whether or not these restrictions or guidelines are based upon health risks or other reasons. From the researchers' findings it seems that there are many instances where restrictions are based and enforced upon social, cultural, religious and patriarchal factors that go beyond any health risk involved. Because Bangladesh is a conservative, Muslim society, no services are provided to unmarried people of either sex. However, these individuals often get around official restrictions by going to commercial outlets which keep no personal records and require no interview. Spousal consent is rarely required here.

The provision of balanced and objective information   To assess the quality of information provided to clients, information materials used during consultations were reviewed by the researchers. These included brochures, pamphlets, pictorials, flip charts and contraceptive samples. Most of the service delivery points (89 per cent) had written materials available for clients. All materials were written in the national language, Bengali, and included illustrations. However, these were not routinely given to them. NGOs were found to use their own materials as well as those provided by the government. Most of the providers were satisfied with the materials provided for consultations. They generally displayed all of the available materials in their examination rooms. Clients could pick up the materials while they waited. According to the providers, people did not have any difficulty understanding them. However, the question remains whether or not these materials provide balanced information. The researchers observed that the risks and side effects are not always given adequate attention in the information materials.

The commercial outlets lacked most of the necessary materials. The data from observations show that information materials were not used during consultations and flip chart instruction sheets and contraceptive samples were rarely used in these outlets.

Observations of provider–client interactions further revealed that more than 80 per cent of the providers greeted clients in a warm and friendly way. Clients seemed to feel at ease when coming to the health centre. Most providers used the local dialect when speaking with clients. While assessing the provider–client interaction, it was found that all the providers encouraged people to decide for themselves which method would best meet their needs and gave the clients information on various methods (see Table 8.3). During consultations, providers most often mentioned pills, the copper IUD, injectables and condoms. The client was usually told how the method she was using worked, how it should be used, its contraindications and side effects and how any side effects could be managed. The information provided on how the method worked was quite superficial. While describing side effects, providers tried not to raise anxiety or fear in the client. There was less discussion on different contraceptives' effectiveness in preventing pregnancy. Sometimes the providers were in a hurry and allowed no time for questions. Less than

Table 8.3 Observations on the quality of client–provider consultations (%)

	Service delivery points	Community-based distributors
Encouraged clients to decide themselves about which was best method	100	100
Encouraged clients to switch methods if having problem	94	0
Gave clients a respectful and friendly greeting	79	89
	(n=38)	(n=75)

Source: Field data; S. Kabir and H. Chaklader.

half of the providers asked whether or not the client had any questions. Overall, the consultations were mainly provider-oriented. Clients were advised to switch methods if they experienced a problem.

The salespeople in drugstores generally greeted people in a friendly way. They didn't encourage people to choose among various methods. They provided pills and injectables mainly on request.

Table 8.4 shows clients' reasons for visiting the service delivery points. These vary from resupply and check-ups to wanting to discontinue a method. The majority of clients within this study came for resupply. In service delivery points, providers asked six out of ten clients about their

Table 8.4 Observations at service delivery points and commercial outlets on provider–client consultations (%)

	Service delivery points	Commercial outlets
Purpose of visit by client:		
resupply	40	81
consult about a problem	21	16
to switch methods	21	4
to obtain a method	18	9
Provider inquired about:		
reproductive plans	63	47
breastfeeding	29	11
problem with current method	58	60
managing side effects	86	35
willingness to switch methods	51	20
	(n=38)	(n=75)

Source: Field data; S. Kabir and H. Chaklader.

reproductive plans and if they had problems with their current method. Nearly all clients were told how to manage side effects. The community-based distributors inquired about reproductive plans in five out of ten cases. They asked about breastfeeding in only one out of ten and asked about problems with current methods in six out of ten cases. They explained how to manage side effects only to three or four out of every ten clients. Providers at service delivery points and the community-based distributors mostly referred clients who wanted a method that was un-available. Sales clerks in drugstores did not ask about reproductive plans. They did ask about problems with the methods used with every other client and told six out of ten how to manage side effects.

Quite a substantial percentage of providers stated that they would recommend what the client wanted, depending on what was most appropriate. Condoms, IUDs and injectables were most frequently recommended at health centres while combined pills and condoms were the two most popular methods among pharmacists and private clinic staffs. Other methods, including spermicides, Norplant® and natural family planning were recommended much less frequently. Female sterilization was the most recommended method for those wishing to have no more children. About 64 per cent of the providers also recommended male sterilization.

Clients' perspective on the quality of counselling and information pro-vided In all, forty-five clients were interviewed when leaving the service delivery points and another sixty clients were interviewed at the community-based distributors. They were all married. The majority of them were between twenty and twenty-five years of age, illiterate and had a family income of more than US$50 per month.

The contraceptives currently used by these exit clients are shown in Table 8.5. The majority of the clients at community-based distributors

Table 8.5 Contraceptives currently used by exit clients interviewed at the service delivery points/community-based distributors (%)

Methods	Clients of service delivery points	Clients of community-based distributors
Pill	26	40
Condom	11	2
IUD	13	27
Injectables	47	30
Norplant®	3	2
	(n=45)	(n=60)

Source: Field data; S. Kabir and H. Chaklader.

Table 8.6 Type of information on contraceptive methods received by exit clients (%)

Information	Service delivery points	Community-based distributors
Explained clearly how the methods work	69	73
Showed how to use the method	71	72
Described possible side effects	69	80
Told what to do about side effects	31	25
Told where to get method	72	83
Asked if they had questions	11	2
	(n=45)	(n=60)

Source: Field data; S. Kabir and H. Chaklader.

used pills while the majority of service delivery point clients used inject-ables.

Table 8.6 shows clients' responses on the quality of services received at these service delivery points and community-based distributors. Approximately 70 per cent of the clients were told how their method worked and how to use it. More clients at community-based distributors were told about side effects than those at service delivery points. Surprisingly, only 11 per cent of the clients at service delivery points and 2 per cent at community-based distributors were asked if they had any questions.

Table 8.7 shows an assessment of the overall quality of services provided at the studied areas using the selected indicators. A majority of the clients reported that they were received warmly and found the information given to them easy to understand. Most of them obtained the method they desired. They were informed about the date of the next visit. They

Table 8.7 Quality of services received at service delivery points and community-based distributors as perceived by exit clients (%)

Indicators	Service delivery points	Community-based distributors
Clinic staff was friendly	96	85
Easy to understand	100	97
Desired method received	93	92
Told when to return	89	80
Would encourage friends to visit it	98	82
Overall satisfaction	93	97
	(n=45)	(n=60)

Source: Field data; S. Kabir and H. Chaklader.

said that they would encourage their friends to visit the same facility. They also reported that they were satisfied with the services provided.

Avoidance of incentives and disincentives   Given the past controversy of incentives offered in the form of food relief to contraceptive acceptors, this part of the study was very important in Bangladesh. The survey findings reveal that acceptors of sterilization are given incentives at service delivery points. These usually include a sari for a woman and a lungi for a man, plus US$3 to cover transportation costs and an improved diet. Those women undergoing tubal ligation also receive some rice, wheat and sugar at a subsidized price for a certain period of time. Almost half of the family planning workers and community-based distributors interviewed reported that incentives are given in the form of cash and gifts to prospective clients. Incentives are thought to be one of the most effective tools in achieving the country's demographic goals. Current incentives include a benefit of 4 to 6 cents given to IUD acceptors and an incentive of about 14 cents given to Norplant® clients when they come for their follow-up visit. These clients also become eligible to receive loans and vocational training by relevant service providers.

At the same time, some sanctions are imposed on non-users of family planning services. For example, both governmental units and NGOs impose sanctions on non-users including the denial of credit and vocational training among other actions. Because family planning providers receive a monthly salary, their payment is not dependent on the number of acceptors. However, researchers found that a small benefit is given to providers for each IUD insertion.

Reporting on the incentives provided in Bangladesh, the researchers Cleland and Parker Mauldin suggested that cash payments to sterilization clients perform a valuable function in removing cost barriers that would otherwise deter the very poor from making use of this method of birth control.[11] The provision of incentives 'exceeds its official purpose of compensation for costs associated with the procedure and acts as an inducement, particularly for men and the very poor'. The authors describe a regular October peak in the number of sterilizations performed co-inciding with the lean inter-harvest period, when employment is low and money is in short supply. Still, the authors suggest, the element of inducement works only if there is an underlying strong desire to limit family size. According to them, the payments made to government field workers do not influence their priorities. Even for a highly successful worker, income from this source would amount to only 10 per cent of the regular salary.

A health-care infrastructure that enables safe use   Following the guidelines developed in the study, the Bangladesh team observed the adequacy of

Table 8.8 Service delivery points having minimal facilities and materials for family planning services (n = 18)

Facilities and materials	Percentage
Separate room for examinations	72
Separate area for examinations	28
Clean examination area	73
Water available	78
Blood-pressure cuff available	94
Vaginal speculum available	72
Examination table	100
Needles/syringes sterile	94
Other equipment clean	83
Inventory kept	100
Adequate storage	100
Records kept	100
Written guidelines and manuals available	67

Source: Field data; S. Kabir and H. Chaklader.

the health-care infrastructure in the health centres. The study found that 72 per cent of the service delivery points had separate examination rooms. The rest had separate areas for examination. All of the service delivery points observed used sterile equipment. Table 8.8 shows the proportion of community-based distributors who have these facilities. The conditions in service delivery points were found to be quite good with clean floors and a nice atmosphere. Most of the service delivery points had blood-pressure cuffs and all them had examination tables. The majority of service delivery points also had vaginal speculums available. Disposable needles and syringes were used. Contraceptives were kept in adequate storage facilities. Client records were also kept in systematic order. Most of the providers kept the clients' histories/records in a book, but, in some instances, they were contained in files. The researchers found the private clinics to be in better condition in terms of facilities and material.

All community-based distributors had a record book. They generally did not have equipment to measure blood pressure. Approximately four out of every ten had the community-based distributor procedure manual and approximately six out of ten had a flip chart with information about methods for clients. Less than 50 per cent had information materials on the pill for clients (see Table 8.9).

Adequacy of check-up during consultations Service delivery point providers carried out better check-ups than community-based distributors. Table 8.10 shows the percentage of providers in service delivery points

Table 8.9 Community-based distributors having facilities and materials (n = 15)

Items	Percentage
Community-based distributor record book	100
Blood-pressure cuff	6
Stethoscope	0
Community-based distributor procedure manual	38
Flip chart/book	56
Contraceptive sample kit	38
Referral slips	7
Condom instruction sheet	50
Diaphragm	0
Pill instruction sheet	31
Pamphlet on sterilization	13
Other	–

Source: Field Data, S. Kabir and H. Chaklader.

Table 8.10 Service delivery points and community-based distributors performing check-ups during consultation with new clients (%)

Check-up	Service delivery points	Community-based distributors
History taken	61	37
Contraindication checklist used	44	19
Blood pressure checked (hormonal method)	44	2
Pregnancy excluded	50	0
If blood pressure was high, action taken	3	0
	(n=38)	(n=75)

Source: Field data; S. Kabir and H. Chaklader.

and community-based distributors who performed selected check-ups during consultations with new clients. During these interactions, a reproductive history was taken in only 60 per cent of the cases at the service delivery points and 38 per cent of the community-based distributors. Pregnancy was excluded in only 50 per cent of delivery point clients, but not in any of the clients visiting the community distributors. Between one-fifth to half of the providers checked clients' blood pressure though practically no action was taken if it was found to be high.

Advice when breastfeeding Injectables, IUDs and condoms were most often suggested for breastfeeding women. When a client was breastfeeding, approximately one-third of community-based distributors said they would advise pills (not always specifying which type). Service delivery point providers usually did not advise using pills in this situation.

Management of side effects When providers were asked to specify how they would manage clients experiencing severe abdominal pain while using an IUD, they gave a number of responses including advising clients to switch methods, removing the IUD, telling them to take drugs or consult with a doctor, to rest and/or restrict hard work and that they would carry out a physical examination.

Various responses were also received from providers asked how they would manage a pill user experiencing severe headaches. It appeared that many providers did not know how to interpret the headache and only tried to reassure their clients that they should continue.

Community-based distributors of contraceptives have learned basic skills on how to deliver family planning services at the community level with back-up support from qualified personnel based at the nearest service delivery point. Most (53 per cent) of them referred their clients to the nearest service delivery point for proper management of the client's side effects.

Integration of services The most common services provided at the service delivery points studied were maternal and child health services. The majority also provide services for other curative problems as well. However, sexually transmitted disease (STD) care and prevention was rarely a component of the services.

Views of contraceptive users and non-users on the provided quality of care To obtain qualitative data that would supplement the quantitative survey, an in-depth interview was carried out with a group of married women and their husbands. All couples wanted to delay their next pregnancy. The group was comprised of twenty-three women and fifteen men. The majority of the interviewed women were between the ages of fifteen and twenty, while most of the men were between thirty and forty years of age. A majority of the women had schooling ranging from five to ten years and had been married between the ages of sixteen and twenty. Their monthly family income was mostly below US$75.

Members of the group were asked which contraceptive methods they had heard of, where they had heard about them and how they had heard about them (i.e. the method of communication). Most men and women were familiar with pills and condoms. More women knew about IUDs and injectables than men. Knowledge about female sterilization was greater among women while more than half of the men knew about permanent contraceptive methods. The most commonly cited source of contraceptive knowledge for women was NGO field workers. For men, government health complexes are the main sources of information. When learning about contraception, informational material which was well understood by them had been used in less than half of the instances.

A majority of the respondents viewed government service delivery points as having qualified staff and a full range of contraceptives. However, quite a number of them asserted that the staff was sometimes harsh with them, asking too many questions and insisting on spousal consent before giving them contraception. They also complained of long waiting times and a shortage of staff.

When asked about ways to improve family planning services, a large number of suggestions were put forward, including: extending the number of methods available and increasing the number of staff and the presence of female doctors.

Focus group discussion with adolescents A total of six (two urban area and four rural area) focus group discussions were conducted with thirty-five unmarried adolescents (twenty-one male and fourteen female) in the community working area. Only 16 per cent of the participants were illiterate, most came from middle-class families. The themes discussed were:

- knowledge about service delivery points in the area
- services available at these delivery points
- the need for family planning
- contraceptive knowledge
- suggestions for improvement.

Respondents from the urban area were most familiar with the services of NGOs and private clinics, and only a few could say something about government facilities. Those from the rural areas stressed the NGO facilities. This may be due to the fact that NGO activities are focused in rural areas.

When asked about the need for family planning, participants replied that it was necessary to keep the family small and control fertility. The respondents from urban areas were knowledgeable about pills and con-doms, but this information was mostly superficial. Rural respondents knew more about the functioning and use of different contraceptives than the urban respondents. When asked how to improve service delivery at these centres, they put forward several suggestions.

- Facilities at the centres should be expanded so that waiting time is reduced and more individual attention can be given.
- Comprehensive services should be provided so that available options are increased.
- Evening clinics for women should be held, and service hours should be expanded. Some services should be provided on holidays.

Conclusions

Bangladesh has formulated a population control programme which has a strong emphasis on demographic goals. The government is committed to providing the population with a free and informed choice of fertility-regulating methods. As this study has shown, availability of methods is good in the Dhaka division. On average, providers at service delivery points have been working in family planning for ten years. They have received basic training in family planning services and sometimes refresher courses. However, this training is not up to the desired standard for providing quality services. Providers' attitudes towards fertility-regulating methods affect choice. In many cases, information on managing side effects is insufficient. The review of providers' health-care practices shows that advice given to clients and their reactions to women experiencing side effects vary and often are not medically justified. This indicates a need for better provider training and regular refresher courses on these issues for all providers.

Although Bangladesh has the widest possible range of methods available at service delivery points, services are provided only to married women of reproductive age. This severely limits the availability of services to others who may need them, such as teenagers, single women, older women and men. In addition, providers' personal preferences for certain contraceptives and abortion affect choice.

Restrictions are imposed on contraceptive availability such as marital status, age of the youngest child and the number of children. These restrictions are often not medically justified.

Family planning services are provided by a wide range of agencies comprised of government and NGO service delivery points, community-based distributors, private clinics and commercial outlets such as drugstores. There are no substantial differences between the NGO and government services in the availability of methods. The interaction between NGO providers and government providers differs as NGO workers develop a closer rapport with their clients and seem more committed to their work. Generally, NGO workers provide more extensive and understandable information to clients so that they can make an informed choice. Community-based distributors tend to offer less choice than the health centres. They were found to supply only one type of pill and only half of them were found to have injectables in stock. However, community distributors do increase accessibility of family planning services. At times, clients at NGO service delivery points had choices among more than one brand of pill. This was not the case at the government service delivery points studied. Some NGOs provide infertility and STD/HIV services which are not provided at government service delivery points.

The paid community-based distributors who supply contraceptives through both governmental and NGO programmes provide a vital link between the community and the formal service delivery points. All of these community distributors are female, and most are middle-aged. They are trained by clinical staff at the nearest service delivery point but receive inadequate supervision. Community-based distributors generally stock pills and condoms. They motivate and counsel clients about contraception but are supported by poorly developed referral services. Sufficient information on risks, side effects, suitability and long-term consequences are not always discussed clearly with service clients. Community distributors especially put little effort into informing clients on how to manage side effects. Information materials are readily available in service delivery points and with community-based distributors, but they are rarely used in provider–client consultations.

In conclusion, it can be said that the current family planning programme is mainly method-oriented. To convert it to a real 'cafeteria-style' approach, more efforts should be made to provide objective, complete and correct information about contraceptive options before the clients are asked to make a choice. To improve the situation, efforts should be made to train providers adequately and sufficiently with frequent retraining and intensive supervision. There is also a need to ensure a constant supply of a wide range of methods and facilities at all service delivery points and to community-based distributors. Efforts should also be made to bring men and older members of the family into family planning as they are the ultimate decision-makers. Programme administrators could consider implementing users' fees in order to recover costs and make the programme financially sustainable. The researchers found a gap remained between providers' and clients' views on family planning services regarding the dissemination of 'effective' knowledge for making 'informed' choice, follow-up services and managing clients' complications. Lastly, assistance is needed to develop the quality of client counselling and care in the private clinics and commercial outlets. From the study's findings, it is clearly evident that quality of care issues are more meticulously addressed at present by NGOs compared to government or private clinics and commercial outlets.

In light of these conclusions, the following recommendations are made.

Recommendations

Provide more basis for informed choice To justify the programme being called a 'cafeteria-style approach', more attention should be paid to client counselling and provider–client interactions. Clients' right to receive objective, complete and correct information on contraceptive options before choosing one must be recognized. They should receive information about contraindications for use, possible side effects, the risk factors involved

and long-term consequences. Client counselling sessions must allow sufficient time to answer client concerns.

Examine the use of incentives and training The use of appropriate
incentives to motivate family planning providers needs to be examined.
Providers need to receive adequate and frequent training to carry out
their work efficiently. They should also have training on developing interpersonal skills to listen effectively to clients' needs and concerns.

Involve men in family planning In a traditional society like that of
Bangladesh, it is the man of the household who makes the decisions
regarding family planning. At the same time, women remain the focal
point of the national and most NGO programmes. Such programmes
systematically exclude men. To reverse this situation, family planning
services should be made accessible to men. They should be encouraged
to play a more active and responsible role in them.

Improve contraceptive supply Although the density of workers in
Bangladesh is one of the highest in the world, mechanisms to supply
contraceptives at the village level still need much improvement. Various
types of community health workers in villages could work as storage
holders and could form an effective link between the villages and the
government's supply system. Other actors in civil society, such as older
women and men, committed women, elected officials and midwives, should
be drawn into the programme and given training in family planning. These
people could then provide quality information to people in their villages
and also provide some contraceptives. When clients request contraceptives
that such actors cannot supply, the clients can be referred on to appropriate
health-care workers or service delivery points.

Restructure fees for services Currently, the government provides most
family planning services free of charge. However, this may be difficult to
continue in the future, particularly where development aid has started to
decline. Policy-makers must start thinking about charging user fees to
recover costs and make the programmes financially sustainable.

Encourage greater cooperation The strengths of the NGO programmes,
i.e. provider–client interaction, commitment and motivation, management
support and systems, should be shared with the government. This will
assist in improving the quality of care in the government family welfare
system.

About the authors

Sandra M. Kabir is the founder president and special adviser to the Bangladesh
Women's Health Coalition and overseas development manager of Population

Concern in London. *Hasina Chaklader*, MSc, BEd, is the deputy director of research at the Bangladesh Women's Health Coalition.

Notes

1. B. Hartmann (1987) *Reproductive Rights and Wrongs: The Global Politics of Population Control and Contraceptive Choice* (New York: Harper and Row).

2. United Nations Development Program (1993), 'Decentralization for Local Action', *Report on Human Development in Bangladesh*, p. 1.

3. S. N. Mitra et al. (1994) *Demographic and Health Survey 1993–1994*, National Institute of Population Research and Training (NIPORT) (Dhaka: Mitra and Associates; and Calverton, MD: Macro International Inc.).

4. J. Cleland et al. (1994) 'The Determinants of Reproductive Changes in Bangladesh', in *A Challenging Environment* (Washington, DC: World Bank), p. 2.

5. World Bank (1991) 'Bangladesh Managing Public Resources for Higher Group', *Publication 9379 BD*, p. 2.

6. These are 1990 figures. The demographic data presented in the box on page 113 are more recent estimates and differ slightly from the baselines set out in the targets.

7. M. S. Ali et al. (1978) *Report on Legal Aspects of Population Planning*, 31 (Dhaka: Bangladesh Institute of Law and International Affairs); and J. A. Ross et al. (1996) 'Country Report on Gender, Sexuality, Reproductive Health', paper presented at the Asia and Pacific Regional Network on Gender, Sexuality and Reproductive Health and Fora on the Teaching of Health Social Science Conference, Cebu City, the Philippines.

8. B. J. Kay et al. (1991) *Quality/Calidad/Qualité – The Bangladesh Women's Health Coalition* (New York: The Population Council).

9. J. L. Ross et al. (1996) 'Country Report … '.

10. S. Kabir et al. (1989) 'Factors Affecting Discontinuation of Injectable Methods in Bangladesh', *Journal of Family Welfare*, 35(4): 28–37.

11. J. Cleland and W. Parker Mauldin (1990) *The Promotion of Family Planning by Financial Payments: The Case of Bangladesh*, Working paper No. 13 (New York: Research Division, Population Council).

CHAPTER 9

Efficiency at What Price?
Two Districts of Chiengmai Province, Thailand

Napaporn Havanon

Thailand is one of the few developing countries which has experienced a rapid decline in fertility over the last two decades. Since the end of the Second World War, improved medical technology and public health have brought about a rapid decline in the death rate while birth rates remain high. In 1996, the country had an estimated population of 60 million people. This represents more than a sevenfold increase since 1911 when the population was estimated to be 8 million.

In 1965, four major government hospitals in Bangkok opened family planning clinics. In 1968, the Thai government, concerned about the rapid population growth, decided to add population policies to its national development plans. Here, the emphasis was placed on expanding family planning services to people living in rural areas who were not yet accustomed to the concept of family planning. Nurses and auxiliary midwives were trained to distribute birth control pills at more than 3,500 health stations in rural areas. As a consequence, by the end of 1971, birth control pills were available throughout the rural areas.

Since the mid-1970s, there has been a substantial decline in fertility in both rural and urban areas of the country. Between 1969 and 1979, marital fertility fell by approximately 40 per cent while contraceptive prevalence among married women of reproductive age increased from approximately 15 per cent to approximately 50 per cent. The total fertility rate has declined from 6.3–6.6 births per woman in the early 1960s to 5.8 in 1970, 4.5–4.9 in 1975, and 2.1 in 1990. It has been estimated that the population in the year 2025 will be 80 million.

The population policy officially adopted by the government in 1970 states that the Royal Thai Government would support voluntary family planning in order to reduce the population growth rate from more than 3 per cent to 2.5 per cent. The government intended to use family planning as a means to control population growth which in turn would facilitate the country's socio-economic development. Abortion is illegal though it is carried out, often under unsafe conditions.

Today, controlling population growth and increasing contraceptive prevalence rates are major goals of the current five-year national plan. Expanding services to those not presently served and improving the quality of family planning services are included in the plan as a means to achieve the population target and not as goals in themselves.

At present, Thailand has undergone its forth five-year plan (1992–96). Within the plan, the population growth rate has been set at 1.2 per cent at the end of the plan period. The contraceptive prevalence rate has been set at 77 per cent, which is extremely high. To achieve this goal, the plan has been set to expand family services to outreach populations including hill tribes, out-of-school youth in rural areas, urban poor and construction workers.[1]

In addition to the efforts of the Ministry of Public Health, the private sector has also contributed to this family planning initiative. However, the estimation of private organizations' contribution to overall contraceptive prevalence appears to be very low. Taking into account all contraceptive methods used by married women in 1984, it was estimated that only 5 per cent of all contraceptive users nationally used the largest private organization as their source of contraceptive supplies or services.[2] Other non-governmental outlets providing family planning services include private clinics, hospitals and drugstores. Of these, drugstores are the main source of contraceptives, particularly for people in urban areas and adolescents. However, compared to government outlets, the private sector has played a minimal role in providing family planning services. This study therefore focuses on government services.

It should be noted that although the country's family planning programmes have been very successful when measured by sharp declines in total fertility rates and rapid increases in contraceptive prevalence rates, other reproductive health problems still remain. The widespread occurrence of unwanted pregnancy and unsafe abortion as well as increasing rates of HIV infection reflect the programmes' shortcomings. As will be shown later, family planning programmes in Thailand have, by and large, ignored the broad issues of sexuality and gender relations. The services, therefore, have been responsive only to those people whose behaviour conforms to traditional norms, particularly married women. The programmes emphasize contraception as an end (i.e. lower fertility and population growth rates) rather than a means for women to achieve good reproductive health. Clients of family planning clinics receive only limited information about their sexual health. Services related to unwanted pregnancies have been negligible in the programmes. Sexual education in broad terms has never been provided to either married women or to outreach groups, particularly teenagers and single women. While Thailand's population programmes

Table 9.1 Types and number of service delivery points and commercial outlets and the number of client–provider interactions observed in the survey

Type	Number	Interviews with providers	Observation of client–provider interviews	Exit interviews
Rural health clinics	10	10	56[1]	60
District hospitals	2	2	17[1]	20
Private clinics	4	4	–	–
Drugstores in district areas	6	6	18[2]	–
Total	22	22	91	80

Notes: [1] Using the observation method.   [2] Using the mystery client method, i.e. the researcher poses as a client and purchases contraception.

Source: Field data; N. Havanon.

have been called a success by some, there has been a call for a profound change in the programme from women's health advocates. The results of this study provide support to the call for setting a new agenda on population policy and family planning programmes.

Study design

Chiengmai, a province in the northern region of Thailand, was purposely selected for this study. This province is composed of nineteen districts. Two districts were examined for this study, one located near the provincial urban area and one located in a remote area. Within each district, five sub-district health centres in rural areas and one district hospital in an urban area were selected. A total of ten health centres and two district hospitals were selected as research sites. Data collection included observations of provider–client interactions, and in-depth interviews with providers and clients were carried out. In addition, the research team conducted in-depth interviews with groups of people who did not currently seek services at the health centres. These included male and female teenagers and unmarried men and women in both rural and urban areas. Table 9.1 gives an overview of the type and number of interviews and observations conducted.

Study findings

A free and informed choice of methods   As in Thailand's other rural areas, health centres in the areas studied are the primary service delivery points. There are approximately two midwives stationed at each health centre. They provide family planning services for about 500–600 women of

Table 9.2 Availability of specific methods provided at service delivery points and commercial outlets

Method	Rural health clinics	District hospitals	Private clinics	Drugstores
One or more types of combined pill	10	2	4	6
Progestin-only pill	0	0	3	6
One or more types of injectables	10	2	4	3
Implants	0	0	0	0
Norplant®	0	0	0	0
Condom	10	2	4	6
Diaphragm	0	0	0	0
One or more types of spermicide	0	0	0	0
One or more types of IUD	1	2	0	0
One or more types of female sterilization	0	2	0	0
	(n=1)	(n=2)	(n=4)	(n=6)

Source: Field data; N. Havanon.

reproductive age. The district hospital has at least one doctor responsible for family planning services. However, those who actually provide family planning services are mainly nurses. The district hospitals offer family planning services to approximately 1,700 women of reproductive age. Virtually all clients are currently married women. No teenagers, single women or men and divorced or widowed women came to the visited service delivery points during the time of the survey. Informal interviews with providers at the delivery points revealed that it is normal for the service delivery points to have only currently married women requesting family planning services. The average client age was between thirty-two and thirty-four. All had at least one child.

A survey conducted in 1987 showed that knowledge of at least some method of contraceptive was virtually universal among married Thai women of reproductive age. Knowledge of oral contraceptives, IUDs, injectables, and female and male sterilization was close to universal, with well over 90 per cent of the survey's respondents knowing of them. In contrast, barrier methods such as the diaphragm, foam and jelly, were much less widely known, mentioned by only 17 per cent.[3]

The availability of methods provided at the rural health centre is very limited. In general, only oral pills, injectables (Noristerat® is the most popular) and condoms are provided. Microgynon® is the most popular pill available (found at all ten outlets). Usually only one type of oral pill is available. At the district hospitals, more methods were available including oral pills, injectables, condoms, IUDs (Copper T 380A® and Multiband®), female sterilization and vasectomy. Drugstores provide only oral pills and injectables. However, illegal postcoital pills and menstruation-inducing pills which are not available at government outlets are generally available at most drugstores. The menstruation-inducing pills which contain ethisterone, ethinylestradiol, and cyanocobalamin are recommended by sales clerks at drugstores for pregnant women who want to have menstrual regulation. Generally, contraception obtained at drugstores is available without a prescription (see Table 9.2).

Restrictions Officially, there are no restrictions on contraceptive choice based upon a client's age or sex. However, adolescents and single women and men seldom visit these outlets to obtain advice about family planning or contraceptive methods. In Thai society, restrictions for women regarding premarital sex have made it difficult for teenagers and single women to come to health centres or hospitals for family planning services. They feel too shy or embarrassed to walk in and ask for services. Generally, they prefer to receive methods available at drugstores where no interviews are done and no personal records are kept.

Cost of methods Contraceptives cost very little at government outlets, including rural health centres and district hospitals, as the government subsidizes the costs of all methods. For example, the cost of oral pills is about US$0.40 for three strips. One injectable also costs about US$0.40. To have an IUD inserted, clients pay only about US$0.80. Condoms are generally given free of charge. In contrast, the cost of oral pills at drugstores ranges between US$0.60 and US$7. A condom costs about US$0.60. Costs of menstrual-regulation pills range from US$0.60 to US$1–2. Since the cost of contraceptive methods at government outlets is quite low, cost does not seem to have a great impact on people's choice. However, the limited availability of method choices at rural health centres seems likely to have some impact on client choice.

Adolescents and methods In-depth interviews with both male and female teenagers revealed that these groups had very limited knowledge of family planning. Most of them viewed family planning as an issue for married people. Generally, they knew some types of contraception such as oral pills, injectables, condoms and sterilization and some details about them. For example, some of them knew that oral pills had to be taken every day, that injectables had to be given once every three months and that sterilization was for those who did not want any more children. However, almost no one mentioned how these methods worked or any side effects or possible restrictions related to their use. They all knew that people could obtain oral pills and injectables from health centres and hospitals or at drugstores. The young people interviewed saw condoms as a method for men to use when visiting commercial sex-workers. No female teenager mentioned that she had ever used any type of contraception. Only male teenagers indicated that they used condoms with commercial sex-workers or had bought postcoital pills for their non-commercial sex partners.

Sexual education for teenagers is very limited. There is no regular course on this subject given in schools. Those who were interviewed mentioned that the school arranged to have health workers give lectures on AIDS once or twice a year. The information given on these occasions was mainly related to the danger and the transmission of the HIV virus. Using condoms was mentioned during the lectures as the way to protect against transmission of the disease, rather than to prevent pregnancy. Both male and female teenagers said that they had learned about oral pills and injectables from observing their mothers or other married women using these methods. Information on selected contraception including oral pills and condoms was also obtained from advertisements in magazines, newspapers, television spots and the radio. Such information, however, was limited only to brands, types and availability. Information obtained from friends of the same sex was more detailed but still inadequate. Owing to the fact that postcoital pills are not officially allowed to be sold in drugstores, the media gave very limited information on this method. Not all young people interviewed knew about this method. Male teenagers were more likely than female adolescents to know about this method. However, their knowledge was limited and to some extent incorrect. For example, some of those interviewed believed that one postcoital pill was only sufficient for one act of intercourse. If intercourse had occurred twice, they thought the woman needed to take two tablets. No one knew the maximum number of pills that should be taken within one month. Neither did anyone know about possible side effects if the pills were used as regular contraception.

Male teenagers mentioned that postcoital pills were generally bought in a secret and quick manner. They explained that they would wait until the drugstore was not busy and then approach a sales clerk to buy the pills. Normally, the sales clerks packed two tablets into a small plastic bag. This would cost between 10 and 20 baht (US$0.50–0.80). No explanation or written material was given with them at the drugstore.

Adolescents' main source of supplies for contraception was drugstores. The teenagers interviewed shared the opinion that services at government health centres were for married people. This is partly because messages delivered by health centres (posters, booklets and verbal communication) were targeted at married people and also because teenagers felt uneasy about going to health centres for family planning services. At health centres, they said, clients had to register and have interviews. They complained about the lack of privacy there. They said they found the services at drugstores quicker and more responsive to their needs.

Interviews with female teenagers revealed that they seldom discussed contraception with their girlfriends. They felt that it was not appropriate for women to bring up such issues in normal conversations. Some expressed the feeling that 'good' women should not pay attention to those issues. Talking about contraception might imply that they wanted to have sexual relationships with men. Only with very close friends would they talk about it. Unlike their female counterparts, young men felt more free to discuss contraception with male friends. The topics discussed were none the less limited to the practical issues of obtaining postcoital pills, how the pills should be taken and their effectiveness in preventing pregnancy. Restrictions with the method and its possible side effects on women's health were completely ignored in their conversations and concerns.

On the whole, both male and female teenagers in the study had very limited opportunity to learn about sexuality in general and family planning in particular. Social norms, which place restrictions on women's involvement in premarital sex, shape the way in which young women are socialized about sexuality. Providing information on sexual behaviour and family planning to young women, it is believed, may encourage young women to violate such norms. Young men, on the other hand, are taught to have sexual relationships with commercial sex-workers instead of their girlfriends. Messages given to young men centre on how to protect oneself from contracting sexually transmitted diseases from commercial workers. No emphasis is placed on their role in caring and taking responsibility for their sexual relationships with girlfriends. As a result, both young men and women are likely to be naive and ignorant when pregnancy, sexually transmitted disease contraction or other health-related problems occur. These problems come at a high cost. Undergoing an unsafe abortion, being forced to leave school or being threatened or abandoned by family and relatives are not uncommon penalties for young, pregnant women. Young men, on the other hand, may face the risk of contracting sexually transmitted diseases from women they consider 'safe'. Many assume that their girlfriend has not had sexual experiences with other men and, therefore, there is no need to use condoms. At present, there has been no practical effort from related organizations to tackle these problems.

The provision of objective and balanced information   Most service delivery points had written material available for clients. However, few providers gave that information directly to them. They often displayed all available materials in the waiting area. Clients could pick up information if they wished. All materials were written in Thai with illustrations of contraceptive methods. The information given provided a basic introduction to

Table 9.3 Percentage of (exit) clients who received specific types of information in rural health clinics and district hospitals

Type of information	Rural health clinic	District hospital
Informed clients how the methods work	42	50
Explained how to use the methods	52	55
Informed clients about side effects	45	40
Discussed management of side effects	42	50
Informed clients where the methods were available	47	50
Asked clients if they had any questions about the methods	38	45
Number of exit interviews	60	20

Source: Client exit interviews; N. Havanon.

the method and focused on its effectiveness. No information about side effects or how to manage side effects was provided.

The study found that a substantial number of clients visiting government outlets were not well informed about method choices. The information they received also tended to be limited and the interactions between clients and providers were generally described as one-way communication. About one-half of the clients said that the health providers did not explain how the contraceptive method worked when they first obtained it. In addition, only one-third of the interviewed clients were told about side effects.

Table 9.3 shows that the quality of the provider–client interactions is not substantially better in the district hospitals than in the rural health facilities. However, interviews indicated that providers encouraged people to decide for themselves and always suggested switching to a more appropriate method if the client had a problem with the method currently used.

Quality of counselling   The observations in the rural health clinics and district hospitals (see Table 9.4) revealed that the clients are only rarely asked about reproductive goals. Women are also hardly ever asked if they are breastfeeding.

The recommendations that providers at health centres gave for delaying and spacing children were mainly limited to the available methods, including oral contraceptive pills and injectables. Only 10 per cent of the providers at the health centres studied said that they would recommend an IUD, Norplant®, or condoms for birth-spacing. Providers at district hospitals tend to recommend condoms in addition to pills and injectables. Other methods such as the diaphragm, spermicides and natural family planning

Table 9.4 Quality of provider–client interactions for clients who came for resupply (%)

	Rural health clinic	District hospital
Inquired about reproductive goals	16	24
Inquired about breastfeeding	4	8
Inquired about methods currently used	29	41
Number of observations	56	17

Source: Field data; N. Havanon.

are neglected by providers. Natural family planning in this context refers to the 'rhythm method' which is perceived by health personnel to be ineffective.

Advice to breastfeeding women   The advice given to breastfeeding women was judged to be inadequate. Providers at both rural health clinics and district hospitals had very limited concerns about the link between breast-feeding and appropriate family planning services. They were unlikely to ask whether or not a client was breastfeeding. In addition, the providers were reluctant to answer the survey questions regarding advice given to breastfeeding women. Most providers could not give accurate advice to breastfeeding women. Some of them were aware that oral pills should not be recommended. However, they seemed to lack knowledge of when breastfeeding women could become fertile again.

Providers' preferences   Female sterilization was the most common method recommended for those wanting no more children. About one-half of all providers also said that they would recommend male sterilization. Inject-ables were recommended by one-half of all providers. The providers at district hospitals also recommended methods such as Norplant®, IUDs, oral pills and condoms. None of the providers at the rural health centres said that they would recommend Norplant® to those who wanted no more children. Some rural health centre providers said that they would never recommend the diaphragm, spermicide, Norplant® or natural family plan-ning. Providers at the district hospitals mentioned only natural family planning as a method they would never recommend.

A health-care infrastructure that enables safe use   Approximately two-thirds of the health centres had separate examination rooms. The rest had separate examination areas. The centres' conditions were quite good with clean floors and a pleasant atmosphere. All health centres were found to have blood-pressure cuffs and examination tables available. Almost all

Table 9.5 Number of service delivery points offering selected reproductive health services

	Rural health clinic	District hospital
STD care was also given	0	2
HIV/AIDS care was given	0	2
Infertility care was given	0	2
Maternal and child health care were given	10	2
Total number of SDPs	10	2

Source: Interviews with providers; N. Havanon.

service delivery points had a vaginal speculum available. Needles and syringes were usually disposable. Contraception methods were kept in adequate storage. Client records were kept but not in a systematic order. Most providers kept client records in books. No filing system was observed.

Only district hospitals were found to offer health-care services related to sexually transmitted diseases (STDs). The spread of AIDS in Thailand was beginning to become a cause for alarm at the beginning of the 1990s. The first case of AIDS was identified in Thailand in 1984. Within a short period of time (since 1988), the prevalence of HIV among Bangkok's intravenous drug users increased to 30–40 per cent.[4] In 1989, increasing numbers of HIV infections were observed among female commercial sex-workers and, later, in the general population. It was estimated, based on the HIV Sentinel Surveillance data, that there were between 200,000 and 400,000 HIV-infected people in Thailand at the end of 1991. It has been projected that if the current trends continue, by the year 2000 about 2–4 million people will become HIV-infected and there will be about 350,000–500,000 AIDS cases. AIDS will be the leading cause of death, accounting for 30 per cent of all deaths.[5]

Providers at rural health centres indicated that clients requesting these services would be referred to district hospitals (see Table 9.5). At the same time, the rural health centres did offer preventive services by providing information about STDs and AIDS, and the ways to prevent these diseases, to people in villages and in schools. Maternal and child health-care services were provided at both rural health centres and district hospitals, but no infertility care was given.

Conclusions

The success of the population policy in Thailand is by and large based on the ability of the government to reduce the population growth rate to a level that would facilitate socio-economic development. Very limited concern has been given to the quality of health services provided for women, particularly regarding reproductive health. So far, Thailand's family planning services have been directed at groups specifically to limit population growth, namely married women of reproductive age. Teenagers, single women, men and those above reproductive age have not yet received much attention from the programme.

The methods offered are also limited. The country's family planning services promote the use of oral contraceptives, injectables and condoms. District hospitals also offer IUDs and sterilization. Other barrier methods are rarely available. Young men often turn to drugstores to obtain emergency contraception.

The types of services provided by the Thai national family programme are limited to those serving married women wanting to control births and to increase the number of contraceptive users. However, the increase in contraceptive prevalence does not necessarily imply that those who want to prevent pregnancy are able to do so. The problem of unwanted pregnancy has been evident in Thailand for many decades,[6] as also reflected in the abundant availability of alleged abortifacient pills in drugstores. This problem reflects the deficiencies of health and family planning services. The study points to the special attention required for adolescents who do not feel comfortable visiting the primary health-care centres. More 'anonymous' reproductive health-care outlets are needed for this population group. At present, drugstores fulfil their needs.

While, at present, adolescents' main source for contraception is drugstores, these outlets do not provide information on the methods sold. Sexual education and family planning information in schools are very limited. To prevent unwanted pregnancies, the provision of family planning services must be comprehensive. This includes sex education, especially for adolescents, and quality services which offer accurate and complete information about contraceptive methods available in the country.

Even for those clients coming to receive family planning services, information is limited. While information materials are available in the Thai language, this research study has shown that they are rarely used during client–provider consultations. Complete, objective information on contraceptive methods is lacking. Most of these interactions are one-way conversations with the provider leading the conversation. Often the method of choice is provided without explanations on how it works and possible side effects.

The widespread occurrence of unwanted pregnancy, unsafe abortions and an alarming increase in HIV infection rates reflect the programme's limitations in addressing all of these issues. The provision of family planning services and sexual education are not comprehensive and sensitive to the needs of all men and women.

These conclusions lead to the following recommendations.

Recommendations

Expand services to other groups of users Family planning services should be sensitive to the needs of all women and men including married and single women, women of reproductive age and those around the age of menopause.

Provide a broad focus for adolescents Sexual education and counselling services for young people should be integrated with existing family planning programmes. For outreach groups, especially adolescents who may engage in sexual relationships but who are not aware of their risk behaviour, services must be given outside family planning clinics. Mobile teams should be set up to visit them regularly at schools or places of work. Self-diagnosis of STD symptoms should be provided in addition to contraception information. Those having symptoms should be encouraged to come to health centres or hospitals for treatment. Services for outreach groups should be provided under the reproductive health programme rather than the family planning one.

Integrate family planning into reproductive health care As fertility decline in Thailand has been pervasive for more than two decades, the national family planning programme should be reoriented to a new strategy encompassing all aspects of reproductive health which enables men and women to undertake sexual activity safely. To improve women's reproductive health, universal access to good quality contraceptive services is mandatory. Facilities should offer a wide range of services including accurate information, appropriate counselling and a choice of contraceptive methods, STD/HIV care and infertility prevention and services.

Provide services for STDs and HIV/AIDS With the rapid spread of the HIV virus in Thailand, family planning programmes should take the step to include client services for the prevention and treatment of sexually transmitted diseases including HIV. Clients visiting health centres or the hospital for family planning services should receive information on the symptoms of HIV infection and should be encouraged to have STD screening and diagnosis. Those having STD infections must get high-quality treatment and counselling. They should be informed about their risk of contracting other STDs including HIV from their sexual partner(s). Counselling on negotiation to convince their partner(s) to use condoms is essential. Male sexual partners should be encouraged to visit family planning clinics for counselling. Information on their risk of contracting the HIV virus should be given as well as advice on safe sex practices.

About the author

Napaporn Havanon, PhD, is deputy dean of the Graduate School at Srinakharinwirot University in Bangkok.

Notes

1. K. Wongboonsin (1995) *Population Policy and Programmes in Thailand 1929–Present*. Institute for Population Studies, Chulalongkorn University, Bangkok.

2. J. Knodel et al. (1987) *Thailand Reproductive Revolution* (Madison: University of Wisconsin Press).

3. N. Chayovan et al. (1988) *Thailand Demographic and Health Survey 1987*. Institute for Population Studies, Chulalongkorn University, Bangkok.

4. Thai Division of Epidemiology (1992) 'National HIV Sentinel Surveillance Report'. Unpublished manuscript, Bangkok.

5. Thai Working Group (1991) 'Estimation and Projection of HIV/AIDS in Thailand'. Unpublished manuscript, Bangkok.

6. S. Koetsawang(1993) 'Illegally Induced Abortion in Thailand'. Paper presented at IPPF SEAO Regional Programme Advisory Panel Meeting on Abortion, 29–30 October, Bali, Indonesia.

Additional references

Chao, D. and Allen, K. B. (1984) 'A Cost–Benefit Analysis of Thailand Family Planning Program', *International Family Planning Perspectives* 10(3): 75–81.

Khoo, S. E. (1979) 'Measuring the Family Planning Program's Impact on Fertility Rates: A Comparison of Computer Models', *Studies in Family Planning* 10: 137–45.

Prasartkul, P. et al. (1983) 'The Population Project: Organization and Input', in *Impact, Effectiveness and Efficiency of AFPH Programs on Family Planning Status in 20 Provinces* (Bangkok: Institute for Population and Social Research, Mahidol University).

CHAPTER 10

Taking Adolescents Seriously: Four Areas of Finland

Arja Liinamo, Maija Ritamo, Annukka Heimonen,
Teija Launis, Riikka Pötsönen, and Raili Välimaa

The decrease in the national birth rate which began early in this century continued in Finland until the 1960s. The only exception to this trend occurred during the years immediately following the Second World War. The total fertility rate for women in Finland fell until the early 1970s. Since that time, there have been only slight changes. Finland today belongs to the group of countries with low overall fertility. The average number of children per woman is less than two. Although there has been little change in the overall fertility rate during the past few decades, a noticeable change can be observed in the fertility rates of certain age groups. At the end of the 1970s, the fertility rate fell within the fifteen to nineteen, twenty to twenty-four and thirty to thirty-four age groups. However, a slight rise was seen in the thirty-five to thirty-nine-year-old age group. This change in the fertility rates signals the fact that women are having children later in life. The median age for first birth rose from twenty-seven in 1970 to 28.8 in 1990.

Between the years 1971 and 1986 there was a shift in contraceptive use away from natural methods towards more reliable ones. In 1989, one in five women used an IUD and 16 per cent used hormonal pills. Condom use dropped from 27 to 18 per cent during this time. Interestingly, adolescents choose more reliable contraceptive methods than adults. Contraceptive use also begins at an increasingly younger age in Finland. In 1981, a study found 7 per cent of sixteen-year-olds and 22 per cent of eighteen-year-olds were using contraceptive pills. A follow-up study done in 1993 found that these numbers had increased to 18 and 37 per cent respectively.[1]

Finnish health-care services are good by international comparison. Health care has traditionally been regarded as primarily a state responsibility. The national health authorities together with professional experts and voluntary associations have made studies, given guidelines and arranged training about contraception and sexual behaviour for municipal health personnel as well as for teachers. The local authorities must provide primary health-care services. Alone or in collaboration with other munici-palities, they maintain health centres which provide health, family planning, preventive health services, maternal and child health and school health-care services. Most primary health-care services are given free of charge as are some contraceptives (IUDs and pills) for first-time users. Women constitute the majority of health-care system users. In Finland, more than half of all women (57 per cent) obtain contraception from public health services, the others receive it from private doctors. Most young women under age twenty-five use public health services.[2] Family planning activities have been carried out within primary health care since the early 1970s and even before that as part of midwifery services in municipalities.

Today, maternity clinics operate within the area health centres. During a normal pregnancy, a women is examined ten times by a public health nurse and three times by a doctor. Use of the maternity clinics has been enhanced by the fact that in order to qualify for her maternity benefit, a mother must have had a health examination before the end of the fourth month of pregnancy. This benefit is given in the form of baby clothing and care accessories. More than 80 per cent of the women take this benefit in goods, the rest in a cash equivalent. Since 1971, the items included in the benefit package include condoms with instructions on how to use them and how to order more.

In Finland, increasing numbers of fathers take part in childbirth preparation training which is a part of health centres' maternity care. School health-care services and sexual education are offered to both boys and girls. As part of family planning policy, the Ministry of Social Affairs and Health sends sexual education material by post to all sixteen-year-olds and their parents. This leaflet includes information about dating, human relationships, sexuality and family planning. A sample condom is also included. The message given is that responsibility for contraception and family planning rests with both partners.

NGO family planning services

In addition, since 1941, the Family Federation of Finland (FFF) has operated as a non-governmental (NGO) population and family policy organization with twenty-two welfare and health-care organization members. It provides examinations and treatment for infertile couples, contraceptive services, family and genetic counselling and carries out public relations and publishing. It conducts two family planning clinics and a separate clinic for young people which give advice on sex, dating and contraception. It also publishes teaching materials for schools. The FFF also markets condoms, mostly those made by a firm which it owns.

Private health-care services are also available alongside the public health-care system. There are private medical centres and doctors in every town. Compensation may be claimed from the sickness insurance scheme for the fees requested by private doctors regarding examinations, treatment and prescribed medicine.

Abortion

Until 1950, abortion was a punishable crime in Finland.[3] When the nation's first law allowing abortion was passed in 1950, it stated that abortions could be performed based upon medical, eugenic and social/ethical reasons. The law was meant to reduce the number of illegal abortions taking place at the time. However, for the two decades that it was in force, the national, illegal, abortion rate did not decrease significantly. As a result, in 1970 a new law was passed that made social conditions grounds for an abortion, instead of just being additional factors as they had been under the older law. Social reasons for allowing an abortion are interpreted very broadly in Finland. This means the procedure can be done if the delivery or care of a child would place a significant strain on the mother, taking into account her living conditions and any other circumstances relating to her or her family. Illness of the mother or foetus, the mother's age (under seventeen or over forty) and the number of children already in the family (four or more) also qualify as social reasons. In Finland, more than 85 per cent of the abortions performed have been done on the grounds of social conditions. Abortions carried out on social grounds must be done before the first twelve weeks of pregnancy have passed. They can be carried out later on medical grounds.

Abortions are done in hospitals granted permission to perform them by the National Board of Medicolegal Affairs. Most of them are done in a poly-clinic setting. If the pregnancy is less than twelve weeks old, a woman is given permission to obtain an abortion after receiving written permission from two doctors. In special cases, the National Board of Medicolegal Affairs can permit an abortion up to the twenty-fourth week of pregnancy. In 1993, most abortions were performed on women between the ages of twenty and twenty-four. More than half of the abortions were performed on women who already had a child.

After a pregnancy is terminated, the woman must receive counselling on contraception. Finland is the only country in Europe with a decreasing number of abortions for those under nineteen years old. Its total number of abortions has continuously decreased since 1973.

Study design

In Finland, four areas were studied, two in the southern part of the country (the town Vantaa and the rural area Riihimäki) and two in the centre of the country (Jyväskylä and the rural area Mid-Finland). All of the health units studied were governmental family planning units. These units are usually located near or at least within easy reach of public transportation. The distances vary between 200m and 16km, the average distance being 5km from a client's home to the nearest family planning unit.

The providers

In total, thirty-three staff members from family planning units were interviewed for the study. Eighteen of them were public health nurses, six were public health nurses who were also midwives. Three were midwives and six were medical doctors. Of these staff members, 75 per cent said that family planning was a part of their basic vocational training. However, seven staff members replied that their training did not include family planning. All of the nurses and midwives and five of the medical doctors were women. Only one medical doctor interviewed was male. Fifteen of the providers worked as school nurses. Four were located in Vantaa, four in Riihimäki, five in Jyväksylä and two in Mid-Finland. Some of the school nurses also worked in other sectors of primary health care such as family planning and child health.

Study findings

Profile of clients When asked about their usual clie.::s, the staff members said that family planning units were visited by women between the ages of thirteen and fifty-two who came with questions related to contraception. Usually, young women wanted contraceptive pills and older women wanted an IUD. On extremely rare occasions, the services were used by men. According to the providers, wealthier people often used private-sector services instead. Clients seldom came to the units to discuss infertility problems (see Table 10.1).

Providers' opinions about services for adolescents When asked what factors they consider when a client is a young girl or a boy, most providers said that they would consider the client's situation as a whole, not just questions relating to contraception. They said they would talk with the client about relationships and dating, hygiene, smoking, drinking and their present need of contraception. To make the information clear to them, providers said their approach was more specific and concrete than with adults. According to the providers, discretion, confidentiality and safety are the most important factors in this situation. The adolescents are told that they can always contact the staff if they have questions.

About half of the providers thought that young people do not ask questions about sexuality on their own initiative. However, during

Table 10.1 Client backgrounds (n = 54)

	Percentage	Number
Age		
14–20	28	15
21–30	42	23
31–40	30	16
Total	100	54
Marital status		
Married	30	16
Cohabiting	28	15
Single	37	20
Divorced	5	3
Total	100	54
Education		
Intermediate school	60	32
Senior school	22	12
Currently studying	18	10
Total	100	54
Monthly family income		
<US$1,111[1]	24	11
US$1,111–<US$2,222	33	15
US$2,222–<US$4,444	41	19
>US$4,444	2	1
Total	100	46[2]

Notes: [1] US$1 equals 4.5 Finnish marks. [2] The number given for family income is different as some clients refused to provide this information.

Source: Client interviews; A. Liinamo et al.

observations, some adolescents asked surprisingly numerous and un-inhibited questions, for instance, about orgasm, pain during intercourse and contraception. The providers said that adolescents should know how the method they are using works, how effective it is, how it should be used and its possible side effects. Young people are also reminded of the importance of remembering to take the pill regularly. They are also told that pills will not protect them from sexually transmitted diseases.

A free and informed choice of methods In Finland, a variety of contraceptive methods are easily available. If a method is out of stock at the unit a client visits, she is usually referred to another unit. It is extremely rare that a client has to wait to receive the method she wants, for example, due to a delay in the arrival of new supplies.

Pills Clients receiving oral contraceptives for the first time receive their first strips of pills free of charge from the family planning unit. However, clinics differed in how they carried this out in practice. In Vantaa, clients under the age of eighteen received pills for nine months while clients above eighteen received only a three-month supply. In Mid-Finland, all clients receiving pills for the first time received a free, nine-month supply. Clients requesting resupply received their pills on prescription from the chemist and had to pay for them themselves. In Vantaa, the pharmaceutical committee of the public health centre had selected the brands of free pills on the basis of industry offers.

Generally, doctors recommend the type of pill they consider most suitable for the client. However, there was some flexibility about this in practice. One public health-care nurse said that it was possible to get the first pills from a nurse if the client was in a hurry to have them. Another nurse said that waiting for a doctor's appointment caused unnecessary delay in starting contraception and that a nurse should be able to give the first pills after which a doctor's appointment would follow as soon as possible. In her opinion, a delay could cause unwanted pregnancy.

Condoms Condoms are available at chemists and other shops and kiosks without a prescription. Condoms can also be bought from vending machines. However, they are not distributed in family planning units, schools or student health-care units. The units have some condom samples that are given out as the need arises or for educational purposes. For example, if the client has a sexually transmitted disease or if the client has several short-term relationships. Sometimes a school nurse may give out single condoms to boys and girls. Some school nurses said they gave out condoms to students in the eighth and ninth grades (fourteen- and fifteen-year-olds) for educational purposes during their physical examinations. At one school, however, this was not possible as the principal denied permission to distribute condoms. At some schools, both boys and girls came to the school nurse for condoms. One school nurse stressed that she handed them out for educational reasons only, not for use. In Mid-Finland, condoms were not distributed at all. In Vantaa, condoms were distributed to eighteen-year-olds when they were called up for military service.

Diaphragms and spermicides Diaphragms were not available when this study was conducted. Usually units did not even have an example of a diaphragm on hand. A few staff members said that some clients had recently asked about the diaphragm. (Diaphragms have been available from pharmacies since the summer of 1996.) Spermicides (foams, pessaries) are not available at the units but can be bought at the chemist's without a prescription.

IUDs IUDs are available in family planning units and clients usually receive the first IUD free of charge. This is not so for the hormonal IUD

(Levonova®) which is more expensive than the other type of IUD. Levonova® is a contraceptive method in which contraceptive efficacy (hormonal pills) and ease of use (IUD) have been combined. This IUD releases 20 micrograms of the hormone levonorgestrel daily. It can be used for five years. Other IUDs can be bought at the chemist's without a prescription. In the area of Jyväskylä, clients have to pay for their first IUD. Usually a doctor inserts the IUD in one of the family planning units. Afterwards, the client is asked to buy a similar IUD at the chemist's and return it to the family planning unit to replenish the supply. The researchers were told that the demand for hormonal IUDs had increased among women nearing menopause.

Implants Implants (Norplant®) are not found in family planning units. This method must be bought from the chemist with a prescription. A doctor can insert it at the health centre. One doctor in Riihimäki said that new implants were no longer being inserted and only those who had received implants previously were given new ones. A public health nurse in Mid-Finland said that only a few implants had been given. The reason for this did not become clear during the interviews.

Sterilization Sterilizations are performed only at hospitals. To obtain one, a doctor at the family planning unit writes an admission note for the client. The client pays a twenty-four-hour hospital charge but he or she does not have to pay extra costs for the operation. Some health-care workers mentioned that a client has to wait a long time (up to eighteen months) to have the sterilization done. Providers also mentioned that when different alternatives were discussed, vasectomy was recommended because of the ease and speed of the operation.

Emergency contraception Postcoital pills are not available at the units. Clients requesting them are usually referred to the doctor on duty who can write a prescription for these pills. Postcoital pills are also available at health centres. In one unit in Vantaa, a nurse said she could write prescriptions for them if it was necessary. Another nurse would then phone the doctor who would write an order for postcoital pills and contact the chemist. In this way, the client can get the pills directly from the chemist without delay.

Client counselling and recommended contraceptive methods   Health-care workers said they encourage people to decide for themselves which contraceptive method would best meet their needs, and to do so they give clients information about different methods. According to the providers, women know a lot about the different alternatives. During a consultation, the provider discusses the client's situation and the need and duration of contraception with her. The provider then recommends methods that are suitable and advisable but in the end it is the client who decides. Health

Table 10.2 Methods which providers had recommended to clients during the last three months (n = 32)

Method	Percentage of those interviewed who recommmended it	Number of those interviewed who recommended it
Pill	100	32
Condom	81	26
Non-hormonal IUD	44	14
IUD with hormones	22	7
Norplant®	9	3
Female sterilization	9	3
Spermicide	6	2
Male sterilization	6	2

Note: Other methods such as the female condom, diaphragm and preventive tampon (a tampon with spermicides) were not recommended by providers during the last three months.

Source: Provider interviews; A. Liinamo et al.

workers recommend the use of condoms, especially to adolescents. When changing partners, clients are also advised to use a condom in addition to their other contraceptive method, if they are using one. If a client has problems with the method she is using, the method is not automatically changed. The client's condition is monitored and often she is referred to the doctor. The client is advised to switch methods if the problem cannot be solved.

Table 10.2 shows the family planning methods those interviewed had recommended to their clients during the past three months. The most commonly recommended methods were pills, condoms and the IUD. Spermicides were usually recommended to be used with a condom.

Most often, providers said they would recommend pills or condoms for those wanting to delay their next pregnancy. For those who wanted to have no more children, providers would often recommend the IUD or sterilization. Half of those interviewed said that they would never recommend natural family planning. A few providers had a negative attitude towards implants.

When asked whether providers discussed other alternatives with a client considering abortion, those interviewed said they seldom saw such clients as they would probably go straight to the health centre or would be referred there. If a client considering abortion came to the family planning unit, the provider discussed different options with her, including abortion, giving birth, adoption and the system of social support. One-third of the health-care workers explicitly said that they bring up the possibility of adoption. In their discussion with the client, the providers stated they consider the needs of the client and her possible support network and, ultimately, they respect the client's decision. They said they avoid taking a stand in the decision-making. Young people are especially encouraged to discuss the situation with their parents. Even if providers do not approve of abortion, they said they bring up the subject and try to remain neutral.

The providers interviewed said that the quality of existing services should be secured in spite of the decreasing resources for preventive health services. They thought the availability of such services should be even better. Some providers said family planning services should not be integrated into public health care but rather kept separate in order to have truly professional and specialized staff. They felt that the more sides that become involved in family planning, the more diverse the practices were going to be.

Providers said more condoms should be available for distribution and the free distribution of pills should be ensured. Some providers wanted to concentrate more on social relations so that their work was not so method-centred. The providers also wanted to have more information on new books and publications in the field of family planning. They asked for feedback on this project's research findings regarding them.

Restrictions applied by service delivery points   There are no restrictions to providing contraceptive methods in Finland aside from those with a medical rationale. Practices are based on good medical practice and national recommendations. For example, the preconditions for obtaining a sterilization are prescribed by law.[4] However, the interviews indicated that the attitudes, opinions and experiences of the health-care workers affected their recommendations of methods. One provider said that she recommended hormonal methods only if there was clearly a need for family planning, that is, if the relationship was lasting. Some providers took a critical view of implants and IUDs with hormones. Some health-care workers mentioned that implants were suitable for women unable to take their pills regularly either due to negligence or some other reason.

Results of the observations   In addition to interviews, the researchers observed sixty-three client–provider interactions in the family planning units. Generally, during them the client's entrance received no special attention from the provider. The providers greeted clients quickly and mechanically, most providers shook hands with the client and smiled. The observers did not get a clear picture of the visit's purpose at the beginning of the consultation. The provider did not ask why the client was there as the appointment had been made by telephone and the visit's purpose was then discussed. Providers also had the client's records containing background information.

Table 10.3 Reasons for observed provider–client consultations (n = 54)

Reason	Percentage	Number
Family planning follow-up	58	31
Desire to change method	13	7
First visit	9	5
Problem with method	2	1
Desire to stop using method	2	1
Other reason	16	9
Total	100	54

Source: Client exit interviews; A. Liinamo et al.

A typical family planning client was a woman wanting contraception. Young women who had not given birth yet used or ended up using pills; more mature women who had already given birth mainly used the IUD. Table 10.3 shows the most common reasons for the visits according to client exit interviews.

The most common reason for the visit was follow-up, for example, prescription renewal or having a Pap smear. The second most common reason was the client's desire to change the method. Approximately every tenth visit was a first visit to the unit. Other reasons for visits included, among others, a check-up after delivery, menstrual pain or pain during intercourse.

In most observed cases, providers did not ask about the client's reproductive goals (see Table 10.4). This may be due to the fact that most of these clients came for follow-up visits. This question did come up in first visits when a woman wanted to start using a contraceptive method. One of every five clients was presented with the direct question, 'Is there a

Table 10.4 Quality of provider–client interactions (n = 63)

	Percentage	Number
Inquired about client's reproductive goals	19	12
Inquired about client's problems with method	65	41
Problems with method reported by client (among the 41 clients who had been asked about problems)	66	27
Client decided to switch methods	22	14

Source: Provider–client observations, A. Liinamo et al.

need for a long-term contraceptive?' or 'You don't want children, then?' Five clients were asked about breastfeeding. The provider could see from the client's record if the woman was breastfeeding and the date of the child's birth. Most of the clients did not have breastfeeding children. If the client was breastfeeding, she was told she could not use hormonal methods. She was mostly told to use a condom and have an IUD inserted six months after delivery.

Two-thirds of the clients were asked if they had experienced problems with their current method. Of these clients, two-thirds had in fact encountered problems. In most cases, the providers discussed how to manage the problems. As a consequence, approximately one-fifth of the clients decided to switch methods. Reasons for switching to another method included smoking, a need for longer-term contraception, a problem with the current method and the contraceptive's reliability.

Family planning methods mentioned most often during the consultations were the pill, the copper IUD, the hormonal IUD and the condom. The client was usually told how the method she was using worked, how it should be used, its contraindications and side effects and how side effects could be managed. The information about how the method worked was quite superficial. The provider did not check whether or not the client understood the contraceptive effect of the method. The provider did describe possible side effects to the client but tried not to cause anxiety or fear in her. The providers stressed the importance of remembering to take the pill regularly. There was less discussion about the reliability of contraceptive methods. Health habits, such as smoking, diet, physical exercise and alcohol, did come up in the discussions. Clients were often reminded to examine their breasts but were rarely shown how to do this. Mainly young clients were told about using condoms together with the pill. This was rarely mentioned in discussions with older clients.

The atmosphere during consultations was usually pleasant and providers were friendly. Clients almost always had a chance to ask questions. However, sometimes the providers were in a hurry and had no time for questions. Less than half of the providers asked whether the client had any questions. Information about follow-up visits was provided when the client was about to leave. Follow-up was planned depending on the client's situation. Clients were encouraged to contact the unit if there was a problem.

Adequacy of the physical check-up during the consultation   During the consultations, the client's medical history was taken and possible contraindications were covered during the initial interview held by the nurse or doctor. These things are not asked during every visit as the information is recorded on patient information cards or in a database that is easily available.

Blood-pressure readings were taken especially from clients using pills. If the pressure was higher than normal for clients of that age, the pills were not automatically changed but the pressure was monitored. If the client had high blood pressure, an agreement was made with her that she would come and have her blood pressure taken regularly. Often high blood pressure was linked to excitement or stress in the client's life situation. In one case, high blood pressure was said to have been caused by nervousness stemming from the observer's presence in the examining room. Two clients were given a pill prescription for a shorter than normal period (three to six months). However, sometimes monitoring arrangements were not made.

Clients were never directly asked about the possibility of pregnancy. Perhaps this was due to the fact that most clients were using a reliable contraceptive method at that time. The providers did, however, inquire when the client had had her last period and thus they were able to exclude pregnancy. Two clients had a pregnancy test immediately after their consultation.

Time spent with clients The duration of the consultation with a public health nurse varied from between ten to fifty minutes, the average being about twenty-two minutes in length. Consultations with a doctor lasted from four to twenty-three minutes, with the average length being twelve minutes. Follow-up visits were short when the client did not have any problems. First-visit clients and those experiencing problems with their method stayed longer. The provider's own personality seemed to have an influence on the length of the consultation. Some providers talked more and gave more explanations, some did not talk that much and concentrated on the procedures. Nurses had reserved more time for each consultation than doctors. This may be the reason why the observer was able to sense more of a rush during some of the doctors' consultations.

One point that caught the observer's attention was how provider-oriented the consultations were. The provider steered the conversation and was the active party in it. It appeared that the provider proceeded mechanically. Client participation depended on the client's own activity and her ability to ask questions.

In the initial interview, the provider did not ask what the client already knew about family planning. In other words, it was not meant to test the client's existing knowledge of family planning. The providers often assumed that the client knew more about contraception than she actually did. For example, a nurse said to a fourteen-year-old girl, 'I guess you know the contraceptive effect of this method?' The question contained a pre-conception of the answer and the client was not necessarily even expected to answer. Questions were often suggestive, such as, 'And you have no problems with your period?'; 'Everything's OK?'; 'You probably aren't interested in an IUD?'; 'You are healthy, aren't you?'; 'You haven't had any hormones, have you?', and 'I guess you are a bit afraid of inserting the IUD?'

The examinations and operations were described to the client clearly and knowledgeably before the examination and during it. The provider noticed the possible pain caused by the examination and empathized by saying, 'You may feel this, does this hurt?' or, 'Relax, now breathe and you will be all right'. The provider talked a lot during the consultation, but there was little reciprocal conversation. The provider tried to bring up as many points as possible. There was little discussion about the client's life situation. Client's children were discussed but men or her relationships were hardly mentioned. With young clients, however, the providers asked about their studies and possible personal relationships.

Sometimes clients brought up important and even delicate matters but often the provider passed over them quickly and did not take them up. This included subjects such as depression or sexual reluctance. When discussing a client's habit of smoking or drinking, the provider did not try to moralize but attempted to give her positive feedback, such as, 'It's great that you have given up smoking.'

The provider and the client were usually on fairly equal terms though, as mentioned, the provider tended to be in control of the consultation. The interaction between a provider and a young client often showed signs of a different attitude. Often providers talked to a young client as if she was a child. Although clients said they felt the staff was easy to understand there were some difficult terms such as spermicide, speculum and dilator which some clients did not understand. In most cases, the doctors and nurses used humorous, everyday language during the consultations. The humour often enlivened the consultation and made it less formal.

Client exit interviews Fifty-four per cent (29) of the fifty-four interviewed clients were currently using hormonal pills as their family planning method, 24 per cent (13) were using the condom and 16 per cent (9) were using the IUD. Three clients were using no method at all. At the time clients received their current method, 16 per cent of them (9) really wanted to use another method, for example, implants or sterilization.

Surprisingly, many clients said that they did not receive instructions or that the information they did receive was superficial. Clients receiving their first contraceptive method got the most information about the pill. They were told how the pill should be used, what kind of side effects it can have and how it works. Its reliability, contraindications and the management of its possible side effects received less attention. Some other methods – natural family planning, spermicides, the diaphragm and the preventive tampon (a tampon containing spermicides) – were mentioned but were not really recommended.

Poor knowledge Not one of the women interviewed during the exit interviews knew the contraceptive effect of the method she was currently using or had just accepted. Four clients gave incorrect information about the contraceptive effect. For example, a woman using the pill said: 'The ovum comes off during the week you don't take the pill, that's when you get pregnant.' One-third (17) of those interviewed said that they did not know the method's contraceptive effect. Two of them were not even interested in knowing it. One said, 'The main thing is that it is contraceptive.' Forty-one per cent (22) of the clients mentioned something about hormones; for example, 'The hormone has an effect on the womb', or something about using the method: 'You need to take pills regularly and you won't get pregnant.' They were, nevertheless, unable to explain how the method actually worked. One-fifth of those interviewed were able to mention at least one thing about how to use the method.

Majority is satisfied Ninety-one per cent (49) of the clients felt that they had received the family planning services that they wanted and nine per cent (5) said that they had partially received the service they wanted. Two of those who had partially received the service they wanted disagreed with the provider about the best method for them. Two said that they did not get what they wanted as they would have liked to have had an examination during the consultation. Only one client complained that the information was insufficient. Fifty-nine per cent (32) of those interviewed were very satisfied and 41 per cent (22) were satisifed with their visit to the unit. Those who were satisfied would become very satisfied if they received more information and more specified instructions concerning contraception and sexually transmitted diseases since, as one said, 'You don't always know what to ask.' They expressed a wish to handle everything during just one visit so that they did not have to come back repeatedly. They wished that they did not have to wait so long for a consultation and that they could visit the unit in the evening. They also wished for more conversation and listening from the provider as they felt the client should be taken seriously and not be underestimated.

Family planning clients usually get an appointment at the unit within a week. In the waiting room, they have to wait up to ten minutes. Almost all of those interviewed (93 per cent) considered the opening hours convenient. Four clients wished that they could visit the unit in the evening. All of the interviewed clients felt that the staff was friendly and easy to understand during the consultation. Almost all of the clients (94 per cent) would encourage their friends to come to the same unit if they wanted family planning services.

Clients had some ideas about developing family planning services. Some wanted more consultations by telephone and during evenings. They also wanted to have a better system for making appointments because in some units appointments are made by phone only during limited hours reserved each week. Clients said that the unit should be close by, 93 per cent (50) of those interviewed said that the services were easily attainable. They felt the services should be specialized and that young people should have a unit of their own. It was considered important that the services were free of charge.

When asked about the influence of price on the contraceptive method chosen, every fifth client said that the price did affect their choice. On two occasions, the observer wondered whether or not the free delivery of pills made the client choose them.

Male partners and male providers Not one of the clients observed had visited a family planning clinic with her partner. A few said that they had visited a maternity clinic with their husband. When asked whether the clients had discussed contraception and the most suitable method for them with their partners, 65 per cent (35) said that they did discuss this with their partners. Four of them, however, said that they made the decision themselves. Twenty-four per cent (13) of the clients interviewed said they did not discuss contraception with their partner and made the decision themselves. One-fifth of those interviewed did not have a steady relationship or did not need contraception at the time of the interview.

One client's opinion about sharing responsibility was: 'The men should buy condoms and women take care of the IUD and the pill.' One client said: 'I felt funny coming alone because I thought that couples come here together as it was taught at school.' Approximately half of those having a steady relationship said that their partners knew as much about the method they were using as they did. Three said that their partners knew even more about it. More than half felt that their partners did not know as much about it as they did.

One-third of those interviewed said that the doctor's gender did not make a difference to them. Two clients stressed the professionalism of the doctor as a more important point and two said that personality was a more important factor than gender. About half of the clients (26) said that they would rather see a woman, because, for example, she understood better, she knew things from her personal experience and therefore the procedures were more comfortable. Some felt the situation was so intimate that it was easier and more natural to talk to a woman. Some women also had better experiences with female doctors. One client said: 'On regular matters I don't mind a male doctor, but when I'm there for contraception I only blush and think that he doesn't understand anything.' Another said: 'I'm more nervous and shy when I see a male doctor' and that, 'It would be less natural to consult an old man.'

The provision of balanced and objective information The informational material used during consultations included, among other things, examples of contraceptives. Clients also received written information material. Sometimes the provider went through brochures with the client, but usually understanding the information was left to the client.

About half of the providers were satisfied with the informational material distributed to family planning clients. Brochures were handed out as the need arose, not automatically. Many of the brochures were published by pharmaceutical companies and therefore the information might not be objective. Some providers expressed their dissatisfaction at not being in a position to decide what kind of material was obtained and some said that the brochures were old-fashioned and should be replaced by newer versions. Often the provider went through the informational material with the client during the consultation but a more careful reading was meant to be done at home. According to the providers, people did not have any difficulty understanding the material.

The providers said they needed more information to answer questions relating to contraception. It was felt that the informational material for family planning clients should be improved and that it should be available in more languages since the number of foreign clients was constantly increasing.

Most of the clients (82 per cent) had received written informational material. In most cases, they had received brochures about pills or IUDs that were published by pharmaceutical companies. In Finland, all of the material is in Finnish. However, in addition, at some units clients can also receive information in English or Swedish. One-third of the clients receiving written information had gone through it with the provider. All who had time to read through the material said that they had understood it.

Regarding their own information sources, only half of the providers said that books and guides on contraceptive methods were available in the unit. However, pharmaceutical companies' brochures were more common and there was not much other literature available. Usually the nurses and doctors stated they did not have time to read literature during their working days. A few providers stressed that they needed to study in their own time to stay up to date.

The providers' opinions about family planning methods for breastfeeding women were very similar. Almost all of those who answered this question believed that the condom was the best method to use during breastfeeding and said that it would be OK to insert an IUD six months after delivery. Three providers said they would also recommend using spermicides together with a condom. One provider said he would also recommend progestin-only pills. No providers mentioned the lactational amenorrhoea method (LAM).

Adolescents and family planning information Focus group discussions were conducted with ten groups at five secondary schools: two schools in Jyväskylä and one school in every other research area (Vantaa, Riihimäki, and Mid-Finland). There were two groups in each school. In total, thirty-four girls and twenty-seven boys aged fourteen and fifteen discussed dating, sexuality and contraception in the ten groups. The size of the groups varied from four to nine members. Two groups consisted of both boys and girls, the rest of the groups were single sex.

The adolescents' knowledge of family planning services varied some-what in different groups and by sex. Boys knew less about the different units than girls. If their girlfriend needed pills or if they needed to discuss abortion, they were not sure where to get information and help. According to adolescents, birth control is, nevertheless, one of the most central questions in the sexual instruction they have received. It is probably girls' earlier maturation that has made them become more personally acquainted with the services available. The discussions also made it clear that girls feel more responsible for contraception.

The quality of family planning services led to a discussion in only a few groups. Boys didn't seem to have any experience of using the services. Girls' opinions and experience of the quality of the services were very different depending on the treatment they had been shown. Some girls were satisfied with the services, some had very critical comments about the providers and their work which were based on personal experience. Adolescents valued the first contact in the unit very highly. Being respected and listened to, experiencing friendliness, objectivity and communication skills were regarded as extremely important.

Sources of information Adolescents said that they talked a lot about matters concerning sexuality and dating with their friends but less about contraception. Although adolescents are oriented towards their friends and peers, they seemed to need the viewpoint of an adult or an expert as well. The information adolescents got from their parents varied signi-ficantly. Some considered discussions with their parents at home as normal, some said that they did not talk about such things with their parents at all. Often adolescents wished that they could discuss such issues more openly with their parents. On the other hand, some adolescents said that their parents tried too hard to bring up sexual education. The media were mentioned as significant sources of information for adolescents.

Girls mentioned the need for more information on certain, specific themes. Most common of all were sexually transmitted diseases but adoles-cents wanted to hear more information about abortion and personal relationships as well. The predominance of contraception in sexual educa-tion made adolescents think about the possibility of unwanted pregnancy and its consequences, abortion in particular. Nevertheless, adolescents did not know very much about abortion, such as, with whom you should talk about it, how to have the procedure and its cost. Adolescents did not bring up ethical dilemmas related to abortion. Adolescents' knowledge of sexually transmitted disease was superficial. Everyone mentioned AIDS, but chlamydia, which harms many more young people although its consequences are not as extreme, was not that familiar.

The researchers also asked the adolescents about the amount of education concerning personal relationships provided at school and whether they felt a need for it. Boys did not take a clear stand on this kind of education in all discussions but often said that this side of the matter was not that important. Some also said that one could not teach about personal relationships as each one was different. Girls wished for more focus on social skills as they found it difficult, for example, to refuse sex. One group of girls also criticized the prejudice found in the material being distributed. They felt that the responsibility for getting pregnant, for example, fell upon the girl's shoulders. In their opinion, joint responsibility and the boy's participation have not received sufficient attention.

Adolescents who had previous experience with family planning services were satisfied with the services they had received. However, most young clients found it difficult to say whether they were satisfied because they had so little experience with family planning services. One young client was pleased that providers took her blood pressure. Some adolescents had heard from their friends or had experience themselves that the staff were friendly. One young client said that she would like to have more concrete information. Another client said that in principle the services were good but that the staff should listen to the client more, they should not press their own views and put words into the client's mouth.

The significance of communication and getting information came up clearly during exit interviews with young clients too. The starting point was that, 'You have the courage to come to the unit.' The young clients considered it important that the staff were friendly, gave detailed information about things and were ready to converse. A discussion about various options, a confidential atmosphere and an acceptance of the adolescent were seen as essential during the consultation. Young clients also wanted to get to know the provider. One said, 'It should always be the same person.' They felt the providers should not be hurried and it should be stressed that contraception and going to a family planning unit were natural. Young clients wanted to be taken seriously. One young client hoped that they did not 'look down on young people'. Another client said that providers should not ask about things they do not have to know, for example, something about the client's partner or if the client had short-term relationships.

Young clients emphasized that they would like to have more information about services and where to find out more about them. They wanted more services just for young people: as one said, 'Places where you could just go to get information and you didn't necessarily have to talk.' They also wished that they could visit the family planning unit as a school group. Young clients stressed that they should not receive a lecture on morals. On the contrary, they felt that the provider should stand by the client.

Adolescents' opinions on various contraceptive methods   When asked in focus groups to list different kinds of contraceptive methods, the adolescents mentioned the condom immediately. The pill, the IUD, spermicidal foam, the diaphragm, implants and sterilization were next mentioned. Natural family planning came up in some groups but the adolescents knew that it was very unreliable. They knew about postcoital pills but did not regard them as a contraceptive method. Both boys and girls knew the most common methods but girls were able to list more of them immediately. Some boys did not have a clear picture of an IUD, sterilization or spermicidal foam, for instance.

When listing the advantages of using condoms, adolescents mentioned that it provided protection against sexually transmitted disease and prevented pregnancy. They said the disadvantage was that it could break during intercourse. Moreover, girls said that boys did not want to use a condom, preferring instead that the girl use the pill. On the basis of group discussions, girls seemed to accept fairly easily boys' negative and doubtful attitudes toward condoms. Adolescents considered condoms to be easily available. They knew that one could buy them at shops, petrol stations, the chemist's and from vending machines. Usually adolescents did not feel embarrassed about the idea of getting condoms. However, they did mention that the reactions of other customers or staff sometimes made the situation awkward.

In the participating adolescents' opinion, the pill is the most reliable contraceptive method, provided that it was taken regularly. However, they also brought up its possible side effects: weight gain, mood swings and possible effects on the liver. One group of girls also discussed the correlation between smoking and the pill and the risks that might follow if pills were used for a very long time. Adolescents said that pills should be used only in a long-term relationship. When discussing the availability of the pill, girls knew how to get it, but boys were mostly unsure. According to adolescents, they could be obtained from a school nurse or a doctor at a health centre.

In other words, adolescents were able to name different contraceptive methods. However, the knowledge they had of them was quite superficial, especially among boys. Girls knew considerably more about different methods, which might be due to the fact that they already had personal experience. Both boys and girls knew a lot about the advantages and disadvantages of the condom and pills. Their knowledge of other methods was quite poor.

Use of incentives and disincentives No incentives or disincentives are tied to the use of family planning services in Finland.

Management of side effects When a woman using an IUD comes to the family planning unit complaining of severe abdominal pain, health-care workers usually take into account that the pain may be connected to her contraceptive method. A nurse interviews the client and conducts the basic examination, among other things checking whether the IUD is still in place. Two health-care workers emphasized the importance of a pregnancy test, two nurses said that they would remove the IUD if that was necessary. The nurses would also refer to doctors. Doctors conduct a more thorough examination and eliminate the possibility of inflammation.

When a woman using the pill comes to the unit because she is suffering from headaches, a nurse or a doctor asks her questions and tries to find out whether the headache and the pill are related. They discuss other possible reasons for the headache and take her blood pressure. Pills are not automatically changed. If the headaches are prolonged or severe, the health workers advise changing pills or stopping pill use.

Conclusions

Family planning services and methods in Finland are inexpensive and sometimes free. The counselling that clients receive remains technical and focused on the provider. There is an assumption that those seeking contraception already know a great deal about the various methods and the ways they work. However, client interviews done for this project revealed that knowledge of contraceptives and their effect was actually quite poor.

The contraceptive pill and IUD are the two most commonly provided methods. It is noteworthy that the diaphragm was not even available in the country during the study. In addition, while condoms are sold at drugstores and chemists, they are seldom available at family planning centres. There needs to be more discussion with clients about other possible options including barrier methods and more natural family planning methods. There is also a great need to develop more objective information and materials for use in family planning counselling. At present, most of the available material has been published by pharmaceutical companies.

The researchers found that most of the interactions they observed between clients and providers were done in a friendly and kind atmosphere. After the visit, most clients were very satisfied (59 per cent) or satisfied (41 per cent) with their consultation. However, communication was technical in nature and focused on the provider. Most clients remained passive, mainly answering questions and listening. This study found that clients were not encouraged to ask questions or express their own values, attitudes, fears, doubts and/or problems with providers. Providers usually carried out the consultation following an interview form used in their clinic. The questions they asked were routine and the manner in which they were asked was often suggestive.

Through the interviews and observations, the researchers found that providers seemed to assume that adult clients especially already knew a great deal about contraceptives and how they worked. In Finland, the media provide a great deal of information on family planning and sexual education which could contribute to providers' beliefs about clients' knowledge. During observations, providers gave superficial information to clients without asking what they already knew or wanted to know. At the same time, client interviews showed that the information they had received about the contraceptive effect of their method was quite poor. Not one of the clients knew it accurately. Observations also found that discussing sexuality or related subjects, e.g. sexual reluctance, is not easy for some professionals and, therefore, some providers ignore client attempts to broach these subjects. Also, providers seemed to assume that young clients needed information on prevention of STDs/HIV, but that older clients did not.

Many of those coming to clinics for family planning advice are unmarried adolescents. This study included focus group discussions with adolescents in order further to explore their experiences, knowledge and family planning needs. The findings indicated that providers need to have the motivation and skills to meet the needs of this special group.

Young people knew the types of contraceptives but their knowledge on them was quite superficial, especially among boys. Condoms and oral pills were the best-known methods. Their knowledge of sexually transmitted diseases was also quite low; AIDS was well known but chlamydia was not familiar to them.

Adolescents' most common information sources concerning family planning were friends, school, parents, magazines, books and television. Focus group participants emphasized the need for better information about available services, separate units for young people, cooperation between schools and family planning units and the need for good information and educational materials.

Men's role in family planning is often lacking. At the same time, an increasing number of fathers in Finland are taking part in prenatal training. About 60 per cent are present during their child's birth. Family planning units do not reach men. According to providers, only a few boys visit the units although when adolescents are taught about family planning in school, girls and boys are encouraged to visit them together. Such messages may make male participation greater in the future. The accepted principle that contraception is a shared responsibility must become more recognized and carried into practice if men are to become more involved.

Recommendations

More focus on client counselling and interaction   Even though providers are experts in their field and know a lot about family planning, they should pay more attention to what and how they tell their clients about family planning. The purpose of each visit should be discussed by the provider and client. The provider should verify what the client already knows. It is important that providers allow the client to talk during the consultation. This can be encouraged through open-ended questions. Clients should be given time to absorb new information. Providers need to be comfortable with family planning topics so that they are able to discuss even the most sensitive and intimate matters. The provider should recognize a client's nervousness and try to relieve it by being friendly and breaking the ice with humour.

Improve services for young people   Providers and adolescents offered many suggestions about developing family planning services for young people. Adolescents felt that they should have a separate unit. It should not be too difficult to come to the unit and use the services. The services should remain free of charge. Clients should be able to come to the consultation without an appointment and practices should be flexible. The cooperation between family planning units and schools should be improved. For example, students could make more frequent educational excursions from schools to family planning units. More attention should be paid to information about services and information material for young people.

Offer providers special training for adolescent clients   The information gathered from the focus groups discussions suggests that providers need to have the motivation and special skills to offer the best possible services to adolescents. This calls for training in listening and advising skills targeted at this group.

Provide objective and balanced information   There is a great need for health units to have more objective informational material regarding all contraceptive options. At present, they rely heavily on information produced by the pharmaceutical industry.

Increase method choice   Finnish providers usually recommend contraceptive pills or IUDs to clients seeking a family planning method. Clients need to be made more aware of other family planning options including barrier methods and more natural methods. These methods can be better options for some women and should be presented during counselling sessions. The provision of some methods for free (pill/IUD) while clients must pay for others creates a bias in choice.

Integrate services? Some providers felt that family-planning services should not be integrated into public health care units but maintained separately in order to have truly professional and specialized staff. Currently, family planning services focus on contraception. Issues such as sexuality and STD/AIDS prevention receive less emphasis. At present, no clear guidelines exist for the management of issues such as infertility (an increasing problem in the country) within primary health care. The family planning services could be improved by paying more attention to these issues. Also, the needs of special groups, for example, immigrants and disabled people, should be better taken into consideration when developing services.

Call for shared responsibility Men's role in family planning needs to be strengthened and encouraged. Although men have played a large role in creating family planning policy, services at the primary health-care level are carried out by women, for women. There needs to be increased emphasis on men and women's joint responsibility for family planning. This principle is recognized but needs support in practice if men and boys are to become more involved.

About the authors

Arja Liinamo, MS, is a researcher at the University of Jyväskylä's Department of Health Sciences. *Maija Ritamo* (Master's degree in social sciences) was the project leader of this study in Finland. She works for the National Research and Development Centre for Welfare and Health in Helsinki. *Annukka Heimonen* and *Teija Launis* are pursuing degrees in health education at the University of Jyväskylä's Department of Health Sciences. *Riikka Pötsönen*, MS, and *Raili Välimaa*, MS, are researchers at the University of Jyväskylä's Department of Health Sciences.

Notes

1. E. Kosunen (1996) *Adolescent Reproductive Health in Finland: Oral Contraception, Pregnancies and Abortions from the 1980s to the 1990s*, Vol. 486 (Tampere: University of Tampere).

2. S. Sihvo et al. (1995) *Raskaudenehkäisy ja terveyspalvelujen kaytto. Tuloksia vaestopohjaisesta tutkimuksesta 1994 (Contraception and Use of Health Services: Results of a Population-based Study 1994)*, STAKES series: 27/1995.

3. This information on abortion in Finland is summarized from Ministry of Foreign Affairs (1994) *International Conference on Population and Development 1994: Finland's National Report on Population* (Ministry of Foreign Affairs).

4. Sterilization may be carried out at the request of the client under the following conditions: (i) if the person is alone or with a partner, if the client

already has three minor children in her/his care, if a woman has already given birth to three children; (ii) if the person has reached the age of thirty; (iii) if a pregnancy would endanger the life of the woman; (iv) if a woman's chances of preventing pregnancy by any other means are exceptionally poor; (v) if there is reason to believe that the offspring of the client would have or would develop a grave illness or physical defect; (vi) when, because of illness of the person involved or another comparable reason, the capacity of the client to care for a child is severely limited.

CHAPTER 11

Reproductive Rights, Really? Five Private Reproductive Health Clinics and Selected General Practitioners' Practices in the Netherlands

Evelyn Schaafsma and Anita Hardon

Family planning services in the Netherlands have gained a worldwide reputation for good quality and efficiency, as indicated by a high acceptance of modern contraceptive methods (approximately 70 per cent of reproductive-age women)[1] and a very low abortion rate (approximately six abortions per 1,000 women per year).[2] The idea that reproductive rights are adhered to in the Dutch context is generally taken for granted. But is the situation really so positive?

Characteristic of the Netherlands is the fact that contraceptive services are not primarily available in specialized family planning clinics, but rather offered mostly by general practitioners (GPs) who provide basic health services to the population. Contraceptives are also available in hospitals where gynaecologists provide postpartum contraception such as IUDs, sterilization and other methods to women who are referred by their GP. The GP practices account for 90 per cent of the contraceptive services provided in the Netherlands; private sexual and reproductive health clinics run by an organization called the Rutgers Foundation account for only 10 per cent of the services provided. This chapter suggests that the quality of care provided by these two channels of care differs.

Dutch policy on population and contraception

The aim of contraceptive services in the Netherlands is to prevent unwanted pregnancy. Much attention is paid to population groups considered to be at risk: migrants and adolescents. The relatively high abortion rate among these groups is the main issue of concern. The country has no explicit population policy. In 1983, the government's aim was to achieve a stable population of approximately 14 million, the number of inhabitants at the time. In 1988, the policy was slightly rephrased to create more conditions for men and women to combine parenthood with work (for a so-called 'child-friendly' society), based on recommendations made regarding a policy for emancipation.[3]

The government's policy is to respect each couple's right to decide freely and responsibly on the number of children they wish to have. Responsible decision-making implies that couples have to be well informed about sexuality and that they use reliable contraceptives, generally defined as hormonal methods, the IUD or sterilization. The government policy is sometimes characterized as pro-natalistic because families with children receive a subsidy to support the extra costs involved in their upbringing. However, this benefit covers only part of the actual costs of raising children. Thus it can hardly be seen as an incentive for having children.

In 1981, after years of political struggle, abortion was legalized in the Netherlands. The abortion law was a compromise between conservative and more liberal political parties. The compromise was drawn up under great pressure by the national women's movement which called for women to be 'the boss in their own belly'. Under the abortion law, abortion is permitted in emergency situations, that is, when a woman cannot cope with the pregnancy for either medical, mental or social reasons. Physicians must determine if the pregnant woman's situation is such that one can speak of an emergency. The law requires a woman requesting an abortion and the physician to whom the woman has turned to consider the options for five days before concluding whether or not to perform the abortion. Abortions are conducted at registered clinics, most of which are members of an organization called the Stimezo Foundation, or in hospitals. So-called menstrual regulation, which is done within sixteen days after missed menstruation, does not fall under the abortion law and can therefore be done without restrictions in registered clinics. This liberal policy has not, however, led to an increase in the number of abortions performed, as critics strongly predicted. On the contrary, the abortion rate in the Netherlands is the lowest in the world.

What is remarkable about the Dutch situation is that there are no governmental family planning clinics. The general practitioner practices where contraceptives are prescribed and the pharmacies and drugstores where contraceptives are provided are all privately owned. The Rutgers sexual and reproductive health clinics and the Stimezo abortion clinics are owned by private foundations that operate on a non-profit basis with financial support from the Dutch government, although recently the continuation of these subsidies has come under scrutiny.

In the Netherlands, health care is financed through a mixed system of voluntary insurance offered by competing, private insurance companies and a central governmental fund which provides basic insurance for those who meet income requirements. Health-care clients are reimbursed directly for the services that they receive. Until recently, contraceptives were financed by the government in its basic insurance fund (called the AWBZ, Algemene Wet Bijzondere Ziektekosten) but, as of 1996, only abortion remains covered by this fund. Contraceptives are now included in both obligatory, basic insurance plans and voluntary insurance packages offered by private companies. However, this may change in the future. For instance, in 1995 the Minister of Health announced a proposal to sell oral contraceptives over the counter. This was met by strong opposition by the Parliament, service providers and women's organizations. Eventually, the minister withdrew her proposal. The private sexual and reproductive health clinics do not have a contract with the insurance companies and therefore clients must pay for services themselves. Costs for barrier methods are generally not reimbursed by insurance companies.

Service delivery in practice

According to the National Association of General Practitioners, there are 4,800 general practitioner practices in the country of which approximately 650 run an incorporated pharmacy as well.[4] Most clinics are staffed by one or two doctors. The Rutgers and other related clinics are much less accessible. They are located in only nine cities and serve the surrounding regions.

In the Netherlands, the general practitioner deals with all kinds of problems and questions regarding illness and health. Therefore, family planning services are only a small part of the family doctor's tasks. More than half of the family doctors interviewed for this study said that they carry out ten or fewer family planning consultations each month, with a maximum of forty consultations a month. In contrast, the Rutgers clinics are specialized in sexual health and providing family planning services is a major task. According to interviewed staff, the clinics carry out 120–400 family planning consultations per month.

Both general practitioners and the Rutgers clinics provide services from Monday to Friday. Services from family doctors are mostly available during the day, starting at 8 or 9 a.m. and continuing until 5 or 5.30 p.m. During the day, clients can phone for an appointment or to request a resupply of oral contraceptives. Most family doctors are available every day for consultations, but an appointment is required. All Rutgers clinics' services are available at least during one part of each day, and usually all day. It is advisable to make an appointment, but it is not compulsory. The clinics are also open for consultation and other services one or two evenings each week. Pill users are advised to come for check-ups once a year.

In general practitioner clinics, all consultations are given by trained physicians. Telephone requests for a resupply prescription for the contraceptive pill are handled by assistants, but a doctor must sign all prescriptions. In the Rutgers clinics, doctors and nurses are available for consultations. A nurse can always ask for a doctor if necessary.

Most of the country's GPs are male, only 18 per cent of currently registered GPs are female. However, the percentage of female doctors is increasing rapidly. The ratio of male/female family doctors for doctors under the age of forty is 72:28 and the ratio of doctors currently in training is 55:45.[5] This study found that in four out of ten GP practices, women could choose to visit a female doctor.

An advantage of the Rutgers clinics is that most of their doctors are female. Depending upon the clinic's size, there are also as many as three female nurses practising there. However, it is not known if the opportunity to see a female doctor to discuss family planning issues is a major reason for clients to visit Rutgers clinics.

Study design

The study was conducted in different regions of the Netherlands. Small villages with a minimum of family planning services were included as well as large urban areas, where all possible services are available. All large Dutch cities offer a choice of services and referral possibilities. The options include male and female general practitioners, a Rutgers clinic, one or more general hospitals and gynaecologists, one or more specialized abortion clinics such as Stimezo (which includes first-line counselling and sterilization), other specialized hospitals and clinics offering in vitro fertilization (IVF), sterilization, pharmacies, chemists/drugstores and vending machines for condoms. The capital, Amsterdam, even has a specialized condom shop called the *condomerie* which supplies all kinds of condoms. In small villages, the family doctor's practice usually has its own pharmacy. Villages usually also have chemists selling over-the-counter medicines, condoms and spermicides.

The forty-three general practitioners included in this research were interviewed at their practices. It was not possible to receive permission from the scientific committee of the National Association of General Practitioners to observe consultations with clients in these practices, hence this part of the study could not be done.[6] Five of the nine Rutgers clinics were visited and provider interviews were held. These clinics differed in size and region. In four clinics, a physician and a nurse were interviewed. In one clinic, only a physician was interviewed. A total of thirty-six client–provider interactions were observed at these clinics and those clients were all personally interviewed afterwards. Clients visiting the Rutgers clinics were by no means representative of the Dutch population. For example, only two clients had children. The average age was quite young: twenty-four years old. In addition, most of those interviewed at the clinics were highly educated. All of the clients interviewed were native Dutch and spoke the Dutch language. Except for one male client and one couple, all of the interviewed clients were female.

Focus group discussions were done with a group of women above the age of forty, and with young women between the ages of seventeen and nineteen who lived in a northern, non-urban area. Discussed topics included information and education on family planning, experience with contraceptives and family planning services; AIDS and contraception; and the role of the male partner.

Study findings

Free and informed choice of methods   When visiting a general practitioner for contraception, clients usually receive a prescription for hormonal pills which they must pick up at a pharmacy. As some doctors in small villages run their own pharmacy, they are also involved in the actual distribution of contraceptives. If no prescription is necessary, such as in the case of condoms or spermicides, the client visits a chemist shop and buys the method over the counter.

The pharmacy system works well. If clients have a prescription, they generally have no problem obtaining the desired contraceptive. If the method happens to be out of stock, resupply is ensured in one or two days. In this sense, availability of methods is very hard to define in the Netherlands. Condoms are available at all chemists and at vending machines located on streets. A special display has been developed for chemists where condoms can easily be seen and obtained in a self-service way. These displays are used a lot and are almost never out of stock. According to a recent study by the Dutch Consumers' Union (Consumentenbond), almost all of the condoms sold in the country conform to European standards but, in practice, they vary greatly in the quality of accompanying client information and price per condom. The ingredients contained in the condoms' accompanying cream or jelly are seldom mentioned. This suggests the need for further investigation due to frequent complaints of irritation by users.[7]

GPs usually stock a small amount of pills (for special cases), injectables and morning-after (postcoital) pills. Morning-after pills are hormonal preparations that can be used between twenty-four and seventy-two hours after unprotected intercourse. Sometimes these can simply be picked up from the GP's assistant or, with a prescription, they can be obtained at the nearest pharmacy. IUDs are present in 40 per cent of GP practices. In these practices, the doctors insert the IUDs themselves. Sometimes a client has to pick up a new IUD at the pharmacy to replace the practice's supply. Very few family doctors have diaphragms available in their practice, nor do they have diaphragm-fitting rings to measure the needed size. They usually do not advise them and do not know how to fit them should a woman request one. Consequently, clients asking for diaphragms are usually referred to Rutgers clinics.

The methods available at Rutgers clinics include oral contraceptives, IUDs, injectables, morning-after pills and diaphragms. These methods are generally in stock at the clinics. Due to the reimbursement scheme, however, women are often given a prescription by the clinic doctor and referred to a pharmacy to obtain oral contraceptives. Methods that do not need a prescription and are not reimbursed by insurance companies, such as condoms and spermicides, can be bought at the clinic. For sterilization and abortion, referral to a general hospital or specialized clinic is needed. The research done for this book found that all clinics had the contraceptive pill, condoms, diaphragms, spermicides and IUDs available. The progestin-only pill was available in four out of five clinics and injectables were present in three of the five clinics during the researcher's visit.

In interviews, service providers were asked which methods they had prescribed to their clients during the past three months (see Table 11.1).

The data in Table 11.1 show that all GPs and Rutgers clinic providers prescribed the pill during the past three months. The majority of GPs also had advised clients on IUDs. Contraceptive methods which were prescribed or advised by a minority of GPs included spermicides, the diaphragm, morning-after pills and abortion, whereas all Rutgers providers mentioned the diaphragm, morning-after pills and abortion. Advice on condoms seemed to be given equally by both types of providers. With

Table 11.1 Percentage of providers who prescribed or advised clients on specific methods during the last three months (n = 52)

Method	General practitioners	Doctors in Rutgers clinics
Pill	100	100
IUD	81	66
Male sterilization	70	44
Condom	60	55
Injectables	58	66
Female sterilization	56	66
Morning-after pills	35	88
Diaphragm	23	100
Abortion	21	77
Progestin-only pills	14	11
Spermicides	2	44
Natural methods	2	11
Number of respondents	43	9

Source: General practitioner interviews; E. Schaafsma.

respect to sterilization, it is important to note that these doctors referred for male sterilization more often than for female sterilization, which is a consistent pattern in the Netherlands. In their prescription patterns, Dutch GPs seem to favour the combined contraceptive pill, paying less attention to alternative forms of contraception such as condoms and diaphragms.

Costs of methods Currently all costs for family planning methods obtained from or advised by the general practitioner are covered by nearly all health insurance companies for all clients. However, there are some slight differences. For example, the diaphragm is not always reimbursed by health insurance companies. Condoms and spermicides are never reimbursed. Their prices do not differ substantially if one looks at different delivery points. Condom prices differ more by type of condom than by type of selling point. Regular condoms cost about US$1 each in pharmacies, chemists, supermarkets, condom vending machines or Rutgers clinics. Therefore, regarding cost, it does not matter where one buys condoms. The women's condom is much more expensive than the male version. One such condom, Femidom®, costs about US$2, making it twice the price of a male condom. This might influence the choice for a female condom adversely. A tube of spermicide, which should be used with a diaphragm and can be used with condoms, costs around US$7. Diaphragms, when ordered through pharmacies, cost approximately US$10.

At the Rutgers clinics in 1996, each consultation is done for a non-reimbursable fee which must be paid immediately. At the clinics, the pill and injectables cost approximately US$20 and services for insertion of an IUD or diaphragm (including the cost of the method and the consultation fee) is around US$40. Referrals from a Rutgers clinic are also not reimbursed. Therefore, in the case of a sterilization, Rutgers clinic clients are referred to their family doctor who, in turn, refers them to a hospital. An abortion at a Stimezo clinic is free as it is covered by the basic governmental insurance (AWBZ).

Young girls can obtain the pill free of charge at Rutgers clinics thanks to pharmaceutical industry sponsorship. For this reason, they do not have to buy the pills first at a pharmacy and wait for reimbursement as older women have to do. Also, clients under the age of eighteen pay a lower consultation fee. For these reasons, adolescents might be more inclined to go to a Rutgers clinic once a year to obtain the pill. The Rutger clinic in Amsterdam also has special consultation hours for migrants that are free of charge due to city subsidies.

Overall, barrier methods are the most expensive contraceptive methods in the Netherlands. This is due to the fact that condoms are not reimbursed at all; additional spermicides to be used with diaphragms are not reimbursed; and because family doctors almost always refer clients requesting diaphragms to Rutgers clinics. Those consultations are not reimbursed.

These costs may lead to a negative choice for both diaphragms and male and female condoms. Paradoxically, if clients are referred to a gynaecologist who then fits them for a diaphragm, the costs are reimbursed. Of course, this is rarely done in practice.

Because clients have to pay and travel more for services at Rutgers clinics, this influences a real free choice of services. Some participants of the focus group discussions stated, however, that they liked the idea of leaving their village to receive family planning counselling. They felt that it was more anonymous. They said they felt as if they were being watched in their village when buying condoms from a shop or at a vending machine. They also did not want to discuss family planning with their own doctor.

Costs incurred during a first visit might also be a barrier. However, if clients then find out that they are treated very well at the clinic, they may accept the extra costs. Interviews with Rutgers clinic clients revealed that the majority of them would recommend the clinic to friends because of great service. However, they also said they would advise friends to go to their family doctor because of the costs.

Restrictions Providers were asked about any non-medical considerations used when advising against specific family planning methods. All interviewed providers in the Netherlands declared that they never apply non-medical restrictions to contraceptives. Some family doctors said they would not recommend a specific method, or in a few cases disapproved the use, but they said they would never forbid anyone. If doctors opposed using a specific method, it was always based upon medical risks. If a client is persistent, she or he can have a prescription or referral. This is also true for the Rutgers clinics. Here, no restrictions were found for non-married couples, adolescents or those without spousal consent. Still, despite the declaration that non-medical restrictions are not used, age restrictions were mentioned for the pill (too young or too old) by 18 per cent of the GPs and one Rutgers provider. Two of the forty-three interviewed GPs saw low intelligence as a restriction for pill use. This was not mentioned by Rutgers providers. Most providers said they would not advise the pill to people who are forgetful or who lead an irregular life.

Forty-four per cent of the family doctors interviewed said that age was a restriction for sterilization, although the majority were eager to point out that age should not be the only argument used to discourage sterilization. They said they felt that having no children was relevant and that psychological and emotional stability were necessary. They said the choice had to be made by the client her/himself and not by the partner. A combination of individual factors influence family doctors' decision to give positive or negative advice on sterilization. For some family doctors, the age restriction for men is more strict than that for women. Their explanation for this is that figures show that men regret sterilization more often than women.

Regarding the IUD, age restrictions were mentioned by very few family doctors. The concern they had was risk of sexually transmitted infections and the related risk of pelvic inflammatory disease. Doctors saw not yet having children while having a wish to have them in the future as a relative restriction for IUDs and/or injectables. They were apparently not yet aware of the latest professional guidelines set out by the Dutch Association of General Practitioners (NHG) which state that age and having had children should not be considered when prescribing IUDs.[8] The NHG believes that the increased risk for pelvic inflammatory disease is related to inserting IUDs when women have an STD. Hence, their main advice is to take precautions to ensure hygienic insertion. For example, if women have vaginal infections, these should be diagnosed properly and treated if necessary before the IUD is inserted.

Recommendations given for specific conditions The providers were asked to specify which methods they would advise in specific circumstances. All of the providers interviewed who advised specific methods recommended oral contraceptives to space or delay having children. Some family doctors added that this method was their first choice. The majority of GPs also offered other options such as IUDs or condoms. Most of the family doctors thought these methods were second choices. However, their advice depended on the situation. For the IUD, advice was based upon the client's age, whether or not they had children, the period of delay and the client's sexual behaviour (promiscuity). In cases of promiscuity, some family doctors always advised condoms or the 'Double Dutch' method (pill plus condom). The same alternatives were mentioned by Rutgers providers. These providers more often expressed the idea that specific recommendations depended upon the client's wishes. Hence, some providers did not mention any specific method.

If a client wishes to have no more children, sterilization is the method mentioned most often by providers. It is interesting to note that male sterilization is recommended slightly more often by family doctors. Seven GPs said they prefer male sterilization for medical reasons. Rutgers providers did not mention any difference between male or female sterilization. Many providers distinguish between a permanent and reversible method. Some family doctors said they do not promote sterilization because they have seen too many regrets. The client's age and the partner influence recommendations regarding sterilization. If clients are too young, other reversible methods such as combined pills, condoms or the IUD are recommended. Rutgers providers commented less on circumstances, but again stressed that the wish of the client is the most important aspect to consider.

When asked which methods they would never recommend, the majority of providers stated that they would not recommend natural family planning methods such as periodic abstinence and withdrawal. Spermicides were never recommended for use alone. Differences between family doctors and Rutgers providers do not seem to be that great except for their advice regarding diaphragms. Slightly more than one-third of the interviewed GPs would never recommend this method. Some thought it was unreliable. Others said they did not have enough experience with it. Progestin-only pills were not recommended by about 20 per cent of the GPs because of unreliability. Rutgers providers did not bring up this point.

Clients' motivation to use contraception Family doctors and Rutgers clinic providers were asked whether or not they encourage clients to use contraception. Fifty-eight per cent of the family doctors interviewed said that they do. Target groups included (mostly female) adolescents, postpartum mothers, those who have just used the morning-after pill or have had an abortion, women with large families, migrants, clients who have conditions where pregnancy is contraindicated, and clients being advised on sexually transmitted disease prevention. Most family doctors said it depended on the situation. The GPs who said they did not motivate their clients to use family planning gave reasons such as: 'People have their own responsibility' or 'Clients do not want us to be paternalistic'.

Providers at all the visited Rutgers clinics said that they encouraged clients to use contraception. Adolescent girls and boys receive special attention. For example, if a client enters the clinic for a sexually transmitted disease, they are often motivated to use contraception as well. All of the clients who came to the clinic for the morning-after pill or an abortion were also encouraged to use contraception. The Rutgers clinic providers are more regularly confronted with young people who do not use any contraceptive and who visit the clinic for morning-after pills. Therefore, they are perhaps more eager to motivate clients than family doctors.

Balanced and objective information Information on fertility, sexuality, STDs, HIV/AIDS and safe-sex strategies begins during primary school in the Netherlands and continues into secondary school. For the past few years, family planning has not only been given as part of biology lessons on reproduction, but it is also included as part of more socially oriented classes on relationships and society. Family planning education first became part of the school curriculum in the 1970s. As a result, a large segment of women of reproductive age and their male counterparts should know how to prevent pregnancy in a safe manner. However, the focus group discussions held with young people showed that the quality of family planning and sexual education depends a lot on the teacher. Because family planning used to be taught with biology as a part of human reproduction, it was possible to avoid discussing family planning in a social context.

Both younger and older focus group participants said that the general practitioner was not regarded as a source of information on family planning. Most women said they know what they want from their GP beforehand and ask for a specific prescription or a needed referral. Women above the age of forty who took part in the focus group discussions said that they did not know anything about reproduction, sex or family planning when they were younger. Anything they did know, they had learned from friends. For this reason, they felt it was very important to tell children about sex and family planning. The focus groups suggested that both younger and older women see the mother as the most important source of information, followed by friends. Although they said the media were not an important information source, many items on sex and family planning appear on television, in newspapers and in women's magazines. These messages might subconsciously influence discussions between friends and between a mother and child. For example, in the early 1980s, the media highlighted negative aspects of the contraceptive pill based upon new scientific findings. This information convinced many women to stop using the pill. Family planning information given to young people today is often linked to AIDS prevention.

Information provided by family doctors   GPs give information on family planning methods in either verbal or written form. In nearly all of their practices it was possible to find brochures or pamphlets on methods in the waiting room. In a recent study, women were asked about their pill use and the role of the family doctor.[9] More than half of the interviewed women said they did not need any additional information from their GP. From this study, it appears that family doctors give less and less information on family planning because women already know things about it. The small minority of interviewed women who did want more information on different methods did not receive the information they wanted.

Table 11.2 shows to what extent information materials were available in GP practices and at the Rutgers clinics.

Eighty-four per cent of the GPs interviewed said written materials in Dutch were present at their practice. Approximately one-third of the clinics had information in languages other than Dutch. These were prepared especially for migrants. Languages mentioned were Turkish and Arabic (for Moroccan immigrants), but items in French and English were sometimes available as well. In contrast, all Rutgers clinics had information materials available in Dutch and other languages. Some GPs said they rarely used written materials and, indeed, such materials were not present in their waiting room. Twenty-one per cent of family doctors used different kinds of pictures during consultations, in addition to written material, 26 per cent made their own drawings to clarify matters and 12 per cent referred to books that clients could borrow or buy.

Table 11.2 Percentage of general practitioners and Rutgers clinics with general information available (n = 52)

	GP	Rutgers
Dutch materials available	84	100
Materials available in other languages	33	100
Other materials		
examples	21	100
pictures	26	100
books advised/available on loan	12	100
Number of service delivery points	43	9

Source: Provider interviews; E. Schaafsma.

Most available brochures or patient information leaflets focus on one method or one brand. Only one brochure was mentioned that gives information on all family planning methods. This brochure is sponsored by Schering, a pharmaceutical manufacturer which sells different contraceptive pill brands. This brochure was used by many of the interviewed GPs.

In contrast, the Rutgers clinics make available written materials developed by their own education department. Leaflets are available on the pill, IUD, sterilization, the diaphragm, morning-after pill, female condom and male condom. These leaflets can be obtained in the waiting room, but are also used during consultations. Other informational material used includes examples of all methods, dolls and pictures of the human body.

It was found that informational materials were used in approximately half of the consultations observed at Rutgers clinics. In 37 per cent of the cases, the information was already known, so no explanation was needed. In 11 per cent of the cases, examples of methods were used and in two cases (6 per cent) other visual material was used. Informational material was used if it was found to be necessary and effective. Only seven of the observed consultations involved new users of contraception. In those cases, many kinds of materials were used including examples, pictures and leaflets. In exit interviews, all of the clients who read the leaflets said the written information was comprehensible and written in their own language.

During observations at Rutgers clinics, the researchers focused attention on the specific types of information provided to clients. Afterwards, during exit interviews, clients were asked about the information they had received (see Tables 11.3 and 11.4).

The observations gave the impression that the quality of information given at Rutgers clinics is generally good. Providers take time for clients and many items are discussed, even if clients visit only for a check-up or

Table 11.3 Number of clients who received specific information by type of method adopted (n = 34)

Information given	Pill (15 resupply/ 4 new users)	IUD (3 new users)	Morning-after pill (12 new users)
Discussed how it works	5	2	3
Discussed use	10	0	11
Discussed contraindications	4	3	2
Discussed side effects	9	3	12
Discussed how to manage side effects	1	1	5

Source: Clinic observations; E. Schaafsma.

resupply. Nineteen cases of pill use were observed including four new users and fifteen cases of resupply. How to use the pill was discussed ten times and side effects came up nine times. All new users were told about its use and side effects. Contraindications were not mentioned to new users.

New users of the morning-after pill received a lot of information before it was provided. Effectiveness, use and side effects were always or nearly always explained. Management of side effects was discussed only in half of the cases. In some clinics, however, the packet containing the

Table 11.4 The type of information given at Rutgers clinics as reported in exit interviews (numbers of clients) (n = 32)

	Yes, today	Yes, previous visit	Partly	No	Information not needed
Explained how it works	21	4	2	1	4
Showed how to use	18	3	1	1	9
Described any side effects	22	3	0	4	3
Discussed management of side effects	16	3	1	8	4
Discussed where available	25	4	0	0	3
Asked if there were any questions	24	2	0	5	1

Source: Rutger clinic exit interviews; E. Schaafsma.

morning-after pills also includes an anti-emeticum to alleviate vomiting resulting from taking the pills.

The three observed consultations of IUD users all involved new users, although two clients already had prior information. How the IUD works and its effectiveness were discussed twice. Contraindications and side effects were mentioned in all observed interactions. Management of side effects was discussed once, but some providers told clients to come back if they experienced any problems (including side effects).

The exit interview data confirm that generally information is adequately provided during consultations at Rutgers clinics (see Table 11.4). An important finding is that twenty-four of the thirty-two clients (75 per cent) reported that the provider had asked if they had any questions. The data, however, suggest that side effects are not always discussed during consultations.

Incentives and disincentives   In the Netherlands, there is neither a system of benefits for family planning users or providers nor any sanctions against non-users. Physicians' salaries do not depend on whether or not clients are users. The pharmaceutical industry's influence, however, might be an incentive for doctors to prescribe more hormonal contraceptives. Industry representatives promote pill brands to doctors. Thirty-seven per cent of the family doctors interviewed said that they meet with drug company representatives. At least one provider at each Rutgers clinic sees such representatives. These drug representatives mainly promote the contraceptive pill. GPs could also be influenced by drug advertisements sent by mail or printed in medical journals or by information presented at medical conferences organized by drug companies.

A health-care infrastructure that enables safe use   In addition to assessing the quality of the information provided at Rutgers clinics, the researchers also assessed the adequacy of the examination given during consultations with new users. Two patient–provider interactions were observed where an IUD was inserted. This was done in a hygienic manner (clean sheets, gloves, washed hands, clean room and materials, etc.). It was not observed if the speculum used had been sterilized. All other materials used were disposable. All of the Rutgers clinics visited had clean examination rooms with blood-pressure cuffs. The pleasant atmosphere of the consultation rooms seemed to enable free and relaxed interaction between the client and provider. In GP practices, the researchers found clean examination rooms and separate consultation rooms. It was not observed if the speculums used were sterilized in accordance with the standard protocol on hygiene. Disposable gloves and blood-pressure cuffs were observed. The Dutch protocol on IUDs stresses that IUDs should be inserted in a hygienic manner and describes this process in detail.

During interviews, Dutch providers were also asked what kind of

Table 11.5 Advice to clients if breastfeeding (%)

Advice if breastfeeding	GP	Rutgers
Contraception unnecessary	0	0
Use combined pills	60	55
Use progestin-only pills	9	22
Use condoms	51	88
Use diaphragm	12	44
Use spermicides	0	0
Use IUD	28	66
Use injectables	0	0
Start contraception after breastfeeding stops	0	0
Do not know	0	0
Depends on age of child	0	0
Number of providers	43	9

Source: Provider interviews; E. Schaafsma.

contraception they would recommend when a women was breastfeeding. The results are given in Table 11.5.

The majority of interviewed Dutch providers mentioned the combined pill as a possible contraceptive to use while breastfeeding, although some providers were reserved in prescribing it. Their comments included: 'It is not a first choice, but it is wanted by women'; 'Information should be given on declining breastfeeding'; 'Only light pills used'; 'Prescribing only after six to eight weeks'. These comments suggest providers are aware of the fact that combined pills influence the quantity and quality of breast-feeding, but that this fact does not make them reject combined pill use when a woman is breastfeeding. The lactational amenorrhoea method (LAM) is never mentioned and progestin-only pills are infrequently advised. This may be explained by the fact that Dutch providers see progestin-only pills as an unreliable method in general. One family doctor said that advising use of these pills while breastfeeding was old-fashioned. The IUD was mentioned by less than one-third of the family doctors. They did not see it as a first choice, also because it can be placed only six to eight weeks after delivery. The advice given by Rutgers providers differs on a few points. Condom use was mentioned more often than pill use or the IUD. Rutgers providers offered more possible solutions. Therefore, the percentage of providers advising an IUD, progestin-only pills and the diaphragm was higher. The attitudes towards combined pill use did not differ substantially. It is remarkable that the health practitioners did not express any awareness of the contraceptive protection offered by complete breastfeeding by women who are not yet menstruating again and whose infant has not yet reached six months of age.

Table 11.6 Advice to women with abdominal pain during IUD use (%)

	GP	Rutgers
Physical examination	70	66
History taken	23	55
Referral to a gynaecologist	7	22
Check for pelvic inflammatory disease	67	33
Remove IUD	60	44
Pregnancy test or test for sexually transmitted diseases	7	11
Switch method	7	0
Number of providers	43	9

Source: Provider interviews; E. Schaafsma.

The providers were further asked what they would do if a client presented herself with abdominal pain while using an IUD; or with severe headaches while using the contraceptive pill. Their advice can be found in Tables 11.6 and 11.7.

The majority of interviewed providers saw abdominal pain as a potentially serious situation. Therefore, most doctors said they have to check carefully for pelvic inflammatory disease and would have to determine treatment afterwards. Some also pointed out the possible treatments. It is striking that 60 per cent said that the IUD probably has to be removed, as this is not the first-choice treatment according to the Dutch guidelines on IUDs. These first advise medication, and if there is no response then removal.[10] Rutgers providers mentioned removal of the IUD more often than medication.

With respect to a client's complaint of severe headache during pill use,

Table 11.7 Advice to women with severe headaches during pill use (%)

	GP	Rutgers
Advise to continue for some time, check again later	44	11
Stop the pill	0	0
Take history of menses	7	44
Search for other causes	23	11
Switch method	17	33
Switch brand	81	100
Other	9	0
Number of providers	43	9

Source: Provider interviews; E. Schaafsma.

the majority of GPs interviewed said to switch pill brands. Nearly half of the GPs interviewed first advised continuing for some time and then having another check-up after two to three months. If the headaches persisted, the majority of GPs would then switch brands. Some advised stopping pill use for a while and then switching brands. During all of the interviews, switching brands was mentioned by more than 80 per cent of the family doctors and all of the Rutgers clinic providers. Four out of nine Rutgers providers take a menses history to find out whether or not the headache occurs during the pill pause period. In doing so, they check when the headache occurs, during menses (a) or during the pill use period (b). The solution for problem (a) is removing the pill pause. The solution for problem (b) is often another brand or sometimes another family planning method. Guidelines for oral contraceptives were developed in 1989 and were the first of their kind. However, they do not include suggestions on how to handle cases of severe headache.

Conclusions

Reviewing the results of the GP interviews, it can be concluded that, in general, Dutch GPs do respect free and informed choice. No strict, non-medical restrictions are applied in the Netherlands and GPs seem to respect clients' wishes. Today in the Netherlands, doctors generally accept the idea that clients should decide for themselves. Unfortunately, as no data could be collected from actual client–GP interactions, it is not known how GPs apply this view in practice.

Most GP prescriptions are for the contraceptive pill which is used by two-thirds of the women using contraception in the Netherlands. One reason for this high rate of pill use could be the fact that doctors prefer to prescribe the pill more than other methods because they consider other methods too unreliable (barrier methods) or less appropriate for other reasons. Women, on the other hand, indicated in the focus group discussions that they know which method they want when they go to see their GP. Usually they want the pill. Free and informed choice is explicitly mentioned in the Dutch professional guidelines on oral contraceptives. Here, it is said that the GP should focus on information and counselling. If a woman asks for the pill, the GP has to ask if she has already considered other methods and if she has any questions.[11] An important service provided by Dutch GPs and the Rutgers clinics is emergency contraception in cases of unprotected intercourse.[12]

Interviews with providers and observations and exit interviews carried out at Rutgers clinics show that providers give their clients a genuine choice of methods and provide adequate information. In general, it was observed that a lot of information was given on several methods. Free choice in the Rutgers clinics is, however, affected by costs. Consultations with doctors at Rutgers clinics and the methods provided there are not reimbursed by insurance companies.

Costs also affect free choice in GP clinics, where only medical contraceptives are reimbursed. That is, barrier methods are generally not paid for by insurance companies. Barrier methods are thus the most expensive contraceptive methods for clients in the Netherlands.

In GP practices, brochures and pamphlets on family planning methods are available. However, the brochures are often not objective (produced by industry) or are rarely used. The pamphlets produced and used by Rutgers clinics are very usable and provide balanced, objective information.

In the Netherlands, Rutgers clinics and GP practices are well equipped to ensure safe fertility regulation. They are staffed by medical doctors who are trained in family planning during their university education. During GP interviews however, doctors stated that they do not attend refresher courses. Rutgers providers do take refresher courses.

Both GPs and Rutgers clinics offer an appropriate constellation of health services. Because the GP is the key person for primary health care in the Netherlands, sexually transmitted disease care, HIV/AIDS care, infertility treatment, maternal and child health care and unwanted pregnancy counselling can be obtained through them. The care is not specialized, but adequate referral can be given. Rutgers clinics offer specialized care on sexually transmitted diseases, HIV/AIDS, unwanted pregnancies and sexuality counselling. The latter offers the opportunity to treat family planning in a broader perspective, instead of from a purely technical/ medical approach.

It can be concluded that, in general, reproductive rights are adhered to in the Netherlands. The quality of care can be qualified as good. However, looking closely at the results, a few observations can be made. The GP as a family planning provider is very accessible. All Dutch citizens have a GP who is located near their home. Because of their broad tasks, however, GPs cannot be expected to specialize in family planning. Also, for some adolescents the fact that the GP is the family doctor may become a barrier to consulting him/her on family planning. Adolescents frequent the Rutgers clinics. Clinics like those run by the Rutgers Foundation offer specialized care, if necessary. Their providers are specialized in family planning and offer an appropriate constellation of other related reproductive health services. Services at the Rutgers clinics, however, are more expensive because they are not completely reimbursed and their services are available only in nine cities.

The data included in this chapter demonstrate that the Rutgers clinics provide good quality of care for clients compared to the general practitioners interviewed. This can be seen in such elements as the wider range of methods offered to clients and the availability of better information materials. At the same time, Rutgers clinics remain relatively inaccessible due to the distance many clients must travel to visit them.

Recommendations

Provide objective information General practitioners should be encouraged to use more objective information materials during consultations. This should include the new leaflets on contraception produced by the Dutch Association of General Practitioners. Such materials diminish reliance on industry-produced information that highlight certain methods.

Increase choice The contraceptive pill is the most commonly used and prescribed contraceptive in the Netherlands. In the future, research could be done to give insight on when the pill might be a less positive possibility. For example, this could be the case if women become more concerned about side effects caused by the pill. More attention could be given to the IUD, since the new standard developed by the Dutch Association of General Practitioners on IUDs has diminished the number of contra-indications regarding its use. This study has revealed that GPs apply restrictions to IUDs because of perceived risks for pelvic inflammatory disease and related infertility problems. New professional guidelines emphasize that the method can be used in women who have no children or who are at risk of STDs, as long as they do not have an STD when the IUD is inserted.

Promote barrier methods Based on the data presented here, GPs are especially unlikely to advise women to use the diaphragm, even though the diaphragm is often prescribed at Rutgers clinics. One could conclude that family doctors need to become more informed about the benefits of female barrier methods and should discuss them more often as an option for women seeking contraception. Discussions on such barrier methods should include the female condom.

At the same time, a debate has to be initiated on the promotion of male condoms as contraceptives as condoms can enhance male responsibility.

End reimbursement differences Consultations provided at Rutgers clinics should be reimbursed by insurance companies. That this is currently not the case is an important impediment to people's (especially adolescents', young adults' and migrants') right to a free and informed choice of methods. The price disincentive currently working against barrier methods should also be removed and these methods should be reimbursed.

Inform breastfeeding women about their contraceptive options The findings suggest that GPs should be provided with more information on the methods of choice for breastfeeding women, including the lactational amenorrhoea method (LAM). Women need to know that use of combined pills while breastfeeding affects the quantity and quality of their breastmilk.

Encourage more cooperation General practitioners and Rutgers clinics need to make better agreements about the provision of family planning care on a regional basis. Family doctors should refer clients more systematically to the Rutgers clinics for services that they themselves do not offer. GPs should also be trained in gender-sensitive approaches that have been developed during the past twenty years in the area of women's health-care services.

About the authors

Evelyn Schaafsma, Pharm D, is a pharmacist and director of the Science Shop for Medicines at the University of Groningen in the Netherlands. *Anita Hardon*, PhD, is head of the Medical Anthropology Unit at the University of Amsterdam.

Notes

The authors would like to thank Elske Straatsma, Marijke Anna Vermaas, Ellen Mommers and Jannemieke Bokma for their field work assistance. In addition, Nicolien Wieringa and Elly Engelkes have given very valuable suggestions for the text. Anne Drews is also thanked for her work in writing the initial Dutch policy review which was presented during the first phase of the research project.

1. M. L. E. Delft (1991) *Social Atlas of Women*, Part 1 (Rijswijk: Social and Cutural Plan Bureau).

2. J. Rademakers (1992) *Abortus in Nederland 1991–1992. Jaarverslag van de landelijke abortusregistratie (Abortion in the Netherlands 1991–1992. Annual report of the national registration of abortion)* (Utrecht: Stimezo).

3. G. Beets and P. Verloove-Vanhorick (eds) (1992) *Een Slimme Meid Regelt Haar Zwangerschap Op Tijd (A Smart Girl Plans Her Pregnancy Ahead of Time)* (Amsterdam: Swets and Zeitlinger), pp. 18–19.

4. National Association of General Practitioners (LHV) (1994) *De Huisarts in Getallen (The General Practitioner in Figures)* (Utrecht: LHV).

5. Ibid.

6. A request made to the Institute for General Practice at the University of Groningen to have medical students carry out the observations as part of their training in family health was also denied because of the large demands already placed upon the students.

7. Anon (1996) 'Veel slechte condooms te koop' ('Many poor condoms for sale'), *Consumentengids* 6: 348–51.

8. NHG (1991) 'NHG Standaard: Het Spiraaltje' ('NHG Standard: The IUD') *Huisartsen en Wetenschap (General Practitioners and Science)* 34: 89–94.

9. P. Vennix (1990) *De Pil en Haar Alternatieven (The Pill and Its Alternatives)* (Delft: Eburon).

10. NHG (1991) 'NHG Standard: The IUD'.

11. Ibid.

12. It has been suggested that the use of morning-after pills in cases of

unprotected intercourse is probably a factor that contributes only slightly to the
low incidence of unwanted pregnancy in the Netherlands and related low abortion
rates. See E. Ketting (1994) 'Is the Dutch Abortion Rate Really That Low?', *Planned
Parenthood in Europe* 23(3): 29–32.

Additional references

Kremer, J. and Haspels, A. A. (1991), *Geboortenregeling Bij de Mens* (*Birth Control*), 8th
    revised edn (Lochem: De Tijdstroom).
NHG (1989) 'NHG Standaard: Het Spiraaltje' ('NHG Standard: The IUD') *Huis-
    artsen en Wetenschap* (*General Practitioners and Science*) 32: 62–5.
— Protocol Commission (1993), 'Desinfectie en sterilisatie' ('Disinfection and
    Sterilization') NHG Protocol Brochure No. P25 (Utrecht: NHG).
— (1996) 'Voorbehoedmiddelen' ('Contraceptives') (leaflets).

PART THREE
Conclusion

CHAPTER 12

Reproductive Rights in Practice: A Comparative Assessment of Quality of Care

Anita Hardon

Reproductive rights are this book's point of departure. In more concrete terms, these rights include the right of women and men to be informed and have access to their choice of safe, effective, affordable and acceptable methods of fertility regulation.[1] Quality of care, in this light, is not a means to achieve high contraceptive acceptance rates and low fertility, but rather a way to diminish the unmet need for contraception. Women's health activists have tended to relate low quality of care and the violation of reproductive rights in family planning services to the demographic aims of governments in their population programmes. The assumption has been that when a government provides family planning with the explicit aim of reducing population growth, women are not provided with a free and informed choice. Instead, they believe women are coerced into using longer-acting methods or permanent ones which effectively lower fertility rates. The question remains: Is this in fact the case?

Chapter 2's policy review has demonstrated that most of the governments of the countries included in this collaborative appraisal have mixed aims for their family planning programmes. Bangladesh is the country with the most evident demographic goals. The fourth five-year development plan of the government of Bangladesh set out to reduce the country's total fertility rate from 4.3 to 3.3 births per woman and the population growth rate from 2.11 to 1.82 per cent per year by 1995. The current Kenyan population policy can also be characterized as primarily demographic in nature. It includes goals such as reducing the population growth rate, encouraging Kenyans to have small families, lowering fertility rates and motivating men to adopt and practise family planning. Mexico, Nigeria and Thailand all have policies that combine health and fertility reduction goals in their population programmes. For example, by the year 2000, Nigeria's National Population Policy aims to reduce the proportion of women who bear more than four children by 80 per cent, reduce the present rate of population growth from 3.3 to 2.0 per cent, and reduce infant mortality to 30 in 1,000. Bolivia, Finland and the Netherlands are three countries in which family planning policies lack demographic objectives.

Chapter 2 pointed out gender bias in policies that implicitly or explicitly still target married women in an attempt to reduce fertility levels, generally failing to involve men actively in fertility regulation.[2]

Incentives and disincentives

Family planning programmes can use a variety of incentives and disincentives to bring individual behaviour into conformity with a government's demographic objectives.[3] Sanctions and incentives are interrelated. An incentive to one contraceptive user often implies a sanction for a non-user. Incentives in this appraisal are defined as rewards in kind or cash to people who have accepted a contraceptive method or to the provider who recruits the acceptor. Such rewards can be provided at the service delivery point or indirectly by granting the acceptor access to better housing, food subsidies, free health care, employment, a higher income or other benefits which are inaccessible to those who have not accepted contraception. Sanctions include penalties for people who refuse to use contraception, i.e. barring access to housing, loss of work permits, denial of food subsidies, or limiting the number of children per family granted access to free health care.

Sometimes the same incentives are available to all clients accepting a contraceptive method. In other situations, users of particular contraceptive methods – for example, women undergoing sterilization – receive incentives while users of other contraceptive methods such as the pill do not. When this is the case, the incentives are used to promote certain methods more than others.

In theory, some incentives can broaden individuals' choice and/or help facilitate it. An example of an acceptable reward to users is the reimbursement of expenses made to use the method, such as those related to transportation. An important acceptable reward to providers is the provision of free health services to community-based distributors who, in many countries, receive very little or no compensation for their work. The incentives and disincentives highlighted in this study are those that diminish choice and penalize those who choose not to use contraceptives, and those that reward service providers in relation to the number of contraceptive acceptors that they recruit.

Provider incentives and disincentives related to the number of contraceptive acceptors that they mobilize are not in keeping with principles of reproductive rights. This is due to the fact that such rewards or punishments aim at meeting targets instead of meeting clients' needs.

Using these definitions of incentives and disincentives, this collaborative study found that such a system of rewards and punishments occurs only in one of the countries studied: Bangladesh. Thus, incentives and disincentives were not found to affect quality of care and adherence to reproductive rights in the studied areas except, possibly, in that country. The review of Bangladesh's policy brought out the fact that acceptors of permanent methods or those who have practised family planning for more than five years are to be given preferential treatment at government facilities which control the allotment of housing, loans and the like. In the country's service delivery points visited, it was determined that incentives were given to sterilization clients. Women received a sari while men were given a lungi, both men and women received US$3 compensation to cover transportation and food costs. Providers in Bangladesh also received a small benefit for each IUD inserted. By using these incentives, it is clear that the programme encourages the use of permanent and longer-acting methods.

National family planning systems

In all of the countries where the quality of care appraisals were conducted, public and non-governmental family planning services co-existed. The policy review described in Chapter 2 points to differences in the types of agencies that provide family planning services in the countries studied and their relative importance. In Thailand and Finland, family planning services are primarily provided by the government in primary health-care centres. In the Netherlands, the services are almost always provided by private family physicians. In Bangladesh, Kenya, Mexico and Nigeria, the services are offered by a variety of agencies, including government, non-governmental organizations (NGOs) and private for-profit clinics. In Mexico and Bolivia, insurance companies are important providers of contraception. These institutions cater to people who are employed and pay insurance fees to them. The government in these settings caters to people who don't have regular, paid employment and those who cannot afford to visit a private clinic. In Nigeria and Kenya, Catholic and Protestant NGOs play an important role in the provision of health care. The services provided by these agencies vary. The countries also differ in the extent to which they provide community-based, family planning services. Data included in this book have shown that Bangladesh's family planning programme is successful primarily because of its 'doorstep delivery' of methods. Community-based distributors also operate in Kenya, Nigeria, Mexico and Bolivia, but in a much less intensive manner. Thailand, Finland and the Netherlands do not use a system of community-based distribution.

Quality of care assessments generally focus on the range of methods provided within particular services. This book assesses quality of care in the various services available to women and men through government,

NGOs, insurance agencies, private clinics, pharmacies and community-based distributors. The range of methods provided by these various agencies differ. In Kenya, for example, the clinics run by Catholic health services provide only natural family planning methods while the government's service delivery points offer a relatively wide range of methods. In the Netherlands, private physicians usually do not fit diaphragms, but the NGO clinics do. The advantages of having a choice of contraceptive services is rarely included in statements on reproductive rights. Still, it must be noted that in situations where one agency is not capable of meeting everyone's needs, the availability of other services offers a wider mix of methods.

Integrating reproductive health services

In light of the ICPD declarations on reproductive health, it is important to know to what extent the centres studied integrate family planning services within comprehensive, reproductive health care. Assessing the *integration* of services fell outside of this study's scope. However, each country's researchers did check if reproductive health services, other than family planning, were offered at the centres. In general, it was determined that this was the case in the service delivery points. The most common aspects included were maternal and child health care and the prevention and care of STDs/HIV.

Studying the degree to which reproductive health services are integrated requires more in-depth study of the ways in which services are provided. One would need to know, for example, if women coming to immunize their children are also given a chance to receive a resupply of their contraceptive method and vice versa. In the same way, if women have an IUD inserted are they screened adequately for STDs? In addition, are infertility problems also treated? The Nigerian researchers commented: 'While family planning is provided at the same location as maternal and child health (MCH), this does not imply integration.' They found that only the clinics of the Planned Parenthood Federation of Nigeria actually integrated services, providing in addition to family planning, advice and counselling to infertile and sub-fertile couples and other reproductive health services.

One particular type of first-level service that needs more study related to this topic is community-based distributors. This group is responsible for only a fraction of the family planning services offered in the areas studied. Such distributors are disadvantaged as they do not provide services other than family planning and in fact give only a limited choice of methods. Also, in practice it is difficult for community-based distributors to maintain confidentiality and clients' privacy. In clinics, this is more easily done. In the future, implementation of reproductive health-care programmes calls for a reassessment of the role of community-based distributors.

Given the extent to which the first-level clinics were found to offer multiple reproductive health services, one can conclude that a basis for integrated reproductive health care is already present at that level of primary health care. The extent to which the various components are meaningfully integrated; the reproductive health elements that are lacking; and clients' preferences and needs regarding change must still be evaluated. The focus group discussions held in Finland revealed that clients preferred specialized family planning services. There is also evidence from the studies that integrated reproductive health services do not enhance access to family planning for adolescents as cultural barriers keep them from visiting the services.

Perhaps the best implementation of reproductive health care is to allow clients to choose between comprehensive, integrated reproductive health care and more specialized family planning services and other health-care services. In the various settings where this book's research was done, differences were found in the level of existing integration. Often government clinics offered a variety of primary health-care services and NGO clinics. Those affiliated with the International Planned Parenthood Federation (IPPF) especially were more specialized in family planning and reproductive health.

Having now described the organization of health services in the countries and the level of integration of family planning in more general reproductive health care, it is time to compare the actual quality of care provided to men and women in local-level service delivery points as reported in the country studies. This will be done by examining a number of key elements, starting with the choice offered to clients in the services, i.e. the range of methods provided to men and women. Attention will then be given to the information that accompanies the methods. These two elements are the most important ones to evaluate in order to assess the extent to which reproductive rights are adhered to in practice.

Choice of contraceptive methods

A choice of methods refers to both the number of methods offered to clients on a reliable basis and the spectrum of method options.[4] Offering methods on a reliable basis implies that the methods are rarely out of stock. Ideally, a client should be able to obtain the method of choice during any given visit to a service delivery point and have access to emergency contraception if the method fails.

Defining a satisfactory choice is not easily done. Minimal requirements regarding method choice at service delivery points are that the services provide:

- contraceptive options for men and for women
- birth-spacing methods and permanent methods
- hormonal methods and non-hormonal methods
- provider-dependent contraception and user-controlled methods
- contraceptive options for breastfeeding women
- emergency contraception and safe abortion services.

The choice of modern contraceptive methods designed for men is technologically limited today. Family planning services can currently offer only condoms and sterilization. The public is repeatedly confronted with media reports on new hormonal methods for men, such as the hormonal injection developed by the World Health Organization (WHO). In practice, none of the studied family planning clinics offered an expanded choice for men. Methods such as the one under development by WHO are still in an experimental stage. It is likely to take years, if not decades, before such a method is ready for routine use in family planning programmes. Even if this happens, it is highly questionable if such methods will prove acceptable to men.

The present range of options designed for use by women is much wider. Hormonal methods are available, as well as barrier methods, IUDS and different forms of female sterilization. Some of these methods, i.e. IUDs, hormonal injections, implants and sterilization, require providers to administer; others such as hormonal pills and barrier methods are under the user's control. Satisfactory choice for women implies that they can choose between these various forms of contraception.[5] In addition, from a women's health perspective it is essential that emergency contraception is available for use after unprotected intercourse and that safe abortion services are accessible in case of method failure, unwanted pregnancy or a pregnancy that threatens the life of the pregnant woman.

Breastfeeding women seeking contraception need access to safe alternatives to the combined contraceptive pill as studies have shown that its use when lactating decreases the quality and quantity of breastmilk. Ideally, apart from IUDs, sterilization and barrier methods, lactating women should be offered the choice of progestin-only pills and informed about the lactational amenorrhoea method (LAM). LAM is the scientific name for a method that women have been practising for centuries, i.e. breastfeeding as a natural protection against pregnancy. After extensive review of scientific data, international experts have put forward guidelines indicating that breastfeeding is an effective form of contraception as long as the mother has not started to menstruate again, the infant is not yet receiving significant amounts of food other than breastmilk, and the baby has not yet reached six months of age.[6]

The data presented in Table 12.1 overleaf show that a wide range of birth-spacing methods were available to clients in the research areas in

Bangladesh, Finland and the Netherlands. In Bolivia, Kenya, Mexico and Thailand the range is considered average with three methods generally available. In Nigeria, the range is limited. Of the developing countries studied, the research area in Bangladesh has the widest range of methods available in first-level, service delivery points. On average, nine out of ten service delivery points offer four different methods: pills, injectables, condoms and IUDs. In addition, seven out of ten delivery points provide menstrual regulation services. This relatively good availability could be due to the fact that the research area is Dhaka division. More remote areas in Bangladesh are likely to have poorer contraceptive availability. Recall though that Bangladesh is also the country with the most demo-graphically driven population policy of the countries involved. It has received a great deal of donor support, which also may explain the accessibility of contraceptives. In Thailand, the unavailablity of IUDs in the majority of primary health-care centres is apparent. At the first level of government health care, women in the research area in northern Thailand can basically choose between hormonal injectables or hormonal pills. If they want IUDs, they must be referred to the district hospital. In the two European countries studied, an interesting difference appears. In Finland, family planning and student health-care units are specialized in family planning and provide a wide range of methods. In the Netherlands, family planning is handled by general physicians who often do not have the methods available in their practices. Instead, they refer clients to drugstores, the hospital or NGO health centres to obtain the methods.

The diaphragm is conspicuously missing in all of the research settings in the eight countries. The lack of access to barrier methods for women is remarkable given the fact that women often discontinue using hormonal methods because of health concerns such as headaches, weight changes, dizziness and nausea. In the absence of barrier methods, women wanting to avoid hormonal methods only have the IUD as an alternative. However, the IUD requires screening for sexually transmitted diseases to ensure safe insertion. It is thus a more complex method to provide. Barrier methods, which lack systemic effects and can be self-administered, clearly are an attractive solution for women with such concerns. In fact, the absence of diaphragms in the spectrum of available methods is one of the main weaknesses observed in the country studies.

Another less apparent weakness is the fact that programmes in develop-ing countries tend to have only one or two types of combined pills available. For women to use the contraceptive pill in a satisfactory manner, it is essential that they can select a brand from different combinations and dosages of oestrogen and progestins. In Finland, the Netherlands and Kenya, women can choose between brands. In the other countries, choice is limited.[7] Providing women with choice regarding brands of combined contraceptives is also important in the light of new evidence of increased

Table 12.1 Provision of a range of birth-spacing methods

	Nigeria	Kenya	Bolivia	Mexico	Bangladesh	Thailand	Finland	Netherlands
Overall assessment	Limited range	Wide range	Average range	Average range	Wide range	Average range	Wide range	Wide range
Main methods available[1]	Combined pills; condoms	Combined pills; condoms; IUDs; progestin-only pills	Combined pills; condoms; IUDs	Combined pills; condoms; IUDs	Combined pills; injectables; menstrual regulation; IUDs	Combined pills; injectables; condoms	Combined pills; condoms; IUDs; progestin-only pills	Combined pills; morning-after pills; condoms; IUDs; injectables; progestin-only pills
Diaphragm	Rare	Rare	Not available	Not available	Not available	Not available	Not available	Rare
Legal abortion services	No	No	No	No	As menstrual regulation	No	Yes	Yes
Non-medical restrictions on use of the pill[2]	Severe: marital status, spousal consent	Severe: age mainly age	Limited: mainly age	Limited: age,	Limited: marital status, spousal consent	None	None	None
Perceived quality of counselling	Good	Good	Good	Good	Good	Good	Good	Good

Notes. [1] In more than 60 per cent of surveyed service delivery points.   [2] 'Severe': 50 per cent or more service delivery points apply restrictions; 'limited': less than 50 per cent of service delivery points apply restrictions.   *Source*: Field research data; A. Hardon.

deep venous thromboembolism risks (blood clots in veins) related to use of so-called third-generation, progestin pills (pills containing gestodene or desogestrel). Women should be offered a choice between pill brands and told about the relative advantages and disadvantages of the various types of combined pills.

It is remarkable that although this research was done in diverse settings, the types of contraceptives available in the services are similar. Combined pills, IUDs, condoms and sterilization are available to women nearly everywhere. It is clear that family planning programmes have achieved amazing coverage of these contraceptive technologies in the research areas of the eight countries.

There are, however, a few technologies that are rather particular to certain countries. In Finland, an IUD containing the hormone levonorgestrel was available in all of the family planning clinics visited. This IUD can have particular advantages for women who suffer from excessive bleeding during menstruation. In the same way, once-a-month injectables are commonly found on the Mexican market. The advantage of these contraceptives is that they cause fewer menstrual disturbances than the injectables given every three months. Although they were found to be available in only a few of the studied service delivery points (5 per cent) in Mexico, they were more commonly found among community-based distributors (23 per cent).

When contraception fails, women need access to safe abortion services. In Nigeria, Kenya, Thailand, Bangladesh, Bolivia and Mexico, access to abortion is legally restricted. Only in the Netherlands and Finland is abortion available on broad socio-medical grounds. The field data show that despite Bangladesh's restrictive law on abortion, menstrual regulation services are available in the government's family planning programme up to ten weeks after the last menstruation. When performing menstrual regulation, no pregnancy test is done.

Emergency contraception is available only in the Netherlands and Finland. It is not formally provided in the service delivery points in the other countries studied in this appraisal. The lack of access to emergency contraception is remarkable as international bodies have agreed that combined oral contraceptives can be used as a safe and effective way of preventing pregnancy when taken within seventy-two hours of unprotected sexual intercourse.[8] One problem surrounding their use is that, in most countries, the products are not explicitly labelled as emergency contraceptives with details on the dosages to be taken. In addition, family planning clinic staff are usually not trained to provide emergency contraception.

Who determines method choice?

After reviewing the availability of contraceptives in the eight country settings studied, one cannot help but wonder why certain methods are available in a setting. One must ask: Who defines which methods are available? For example, why do women in Bangladesh have access to menstrual regulation when women in other developing countries where abortion is also legally restricted do not have access to this option? Why are women visiting Thailand's first-line services for a birth-spacing method offered a choice between hormonal injections or hormonal pills, but generally not IUDs? Why are women in Bolivia given a choice between pills and IUDs but are rarely able to choose an injectable? Why are women in all eight countries rarely or never told about diaphragms and the advantages of such non-invasive and non-systemic forms of contraception? Why is emergency contraception so rare in situations where many young people have sex without using proper protection? And why are once-a-month injections and hormonal IUDs not available more generally?

The answers to these questions stem from the fact that family planning administrators define what is good for their clients. Men and women in the diverse settings do not participate in the formulation of family planning programmes and policies. They are clients and as such they are provided with a choice from among the methods that family planning administrators consider suitable to offer. This lack of community participation reflects a top-down implementation of programmes.

In fact, many national family planning administrators in practice are not free to choose the contraceptives either. These depend on the methods that donors are willing to supply. Not much more explicit are the criteria by which donors and family planning administrators decide which methods to offer: ease of supply, cost, client preferences? It is unknown. It is also clear that new recommendations made in international fora based on review of safety and efficacy of methods do not filter down adequately to the programme level in countries. Thus, scientifically approved methods such as LAM and the use of contraceptive pills as a means of emergency contraception are not incorporated in national programmes.

Non-medical restrictions

Even if a method is available in a service delivery point, this does not mean that a client can always obtain it. Non-medical restrictions, such as age and marital status, were found to be widely though not consistently applied in the research settings. If one compares the restrictions applied to women who want to use the contraceptive pill in the eight countries, it is shown that providers in the research areas in Nigeria generally apply a wide range of restrictions. Providers deny young and unmarried girls access to methods and require spousal consent from married women. In Kenya, less attention is paid to marital status, but providers generally deny young girls access through age restrictions. In Bangladesh, these restrictions are also applied, though less often, i.e. by less than half of the service delivery points. In Bolivia and Mexico, age restrictions are a hindrance to access and are applied in approximately one-third of the clinics.

From this, one can conclude that adolescent men and women suffer most from denied access to services. In focus group discussions conducted in some of the countries, the researchers found that adolescents tend to rely on drugstores for their fertility-regulation needs. In Thailand, interestingly young males said that they would go to pharmacies to buy postcoital pills if their girlfriends' menstruation was delayed. In Nigeria, where spousal consent is often required for contraception, the restrictions allow men to deny women access to contraception.

Applying such restrictions is an important violation of reproductive rights. The ICPD *Program of Action* includes the 'right of men and women to have access to safe, effective, affordable and acceptable methods of family planning of their choice'.[9]

It is important to keep in mind that restrictions were not applied consistently in the service delivery points studied. Individual men and women if denied access in one service delivery point could go to another one which might follow different policies. This seems to be especially the case in Bolivia, Thailand and Bangladesh where only a minority of the service delivery points reportedly apply the non-medical restrictions highlighted in this study.

Providing information

Informed choice is further embedded in the provider–client encounter. It is essential that providers treat their clients in a friendly manner and with respect and that they encourage them to discuss their reproductive goals and make a choice out of the presented contraceptive options. In Nigeria, providers told researchers that they would allow clients to choose the method they wanted for birth-spacing. In Kenya, providers were found to promote especially hormonal methods for child-spacing. In fact, an appraisal by Family Health International in Kenya confirms that a bias against IUDs is the single most important factor constraining growth of IUD use in the country. Providers rarely said that they would recommend IUDs or condoms.[10] Indeed, looking at contraceptive-use figures in Kenya, we see that IUDs are used only by 2.8 per cent of reproductive-age women while the pill is used by 7.5 per cent of women (see Table 3.3, Chapter 3). In contrast to the situation in the African countries, providers in Bolivia were found to favour IUDs in their counselling to clients. They reportedly discouraged use of the pill, condoms and injectables because of expected

user-failure with these methods, especially among poorer clients. Contraceptive-use figures reveal that in Bolivia, in line with provider preferences,
the IUD is the most commonly used method. In Mexico, Bangladesh and
Thailand, provider preferences were more difficult to document. Providers
in Mexico indicated that their preference for birth-spacing clients would
be pills, IUDs and injectables. In Bangladesh, most providers at government health centres said that they would recommend condoms, IUDs and
injectables; while among private clinics and pharmacists, combined pills
and condoms were found to be the most popular methods. In Thailand,
some providers indicated that they would rarely recommend diaphragms,
Norplant® or natural family planning, but most providers said that the
client should choose. In the Netherlands, contraceptive pills were recommended most frequently by providers for birth-spacing purposes and
indeed pills are by far the most used contraceptive in the country. Most
doctors considered condoms and IUDs second-choice options. In Finland,
the providers stressed that clients know a lot about methods. When asked
which methods they would recommend, they said the pill and condoms.
For adolescents, they said they would stress the need to use condoms. In
this study, Finland is the country where condoms are most frequently
used with 18 per cent of reproductive-age women mentioning condoms
as a method of contraception (for all contraceptive prevalence figures, see
Table 3.3, Chapter 3).

The data on provider preferences show that providers tend to have
certain methods in mind to recommend to clients. The preferences are
reflected in contraceptive use figures. The congruence between the preference data and the contraceptive prevalence figures is not easy to interpret.
Does this mean that providers influence choice; or does it indicate that
providers tend to consider clients' own preferences in the advice they
give? Although they indicated preferences, the majority of providers said
in interviews that they would inquire about reproductive goals and encourage clients to choose the contraceptive that best fitted their needs.

Observing consultations

In response to hypothetical situations, it is fairly easy for providers to say
that they aim at meeting clients' needs. Observations of consultations,
especially if done unobtrusively, are a good way to assess what providers
do in practice. The number of consultations with new clients observed
has, however, been limited here as, in the majority of the consultations
observed, clients came for resupply of contraceptives or to discuss problems. Therefore, it is difficult to compare the results of the consultation
observations and formulate conclusions on the quality of counselling to
new clients.

The observations made of client consultations do indicate, however, that for the most part providers treat clients with respect and encourage them to make their own choices. In Kenya and Nigeria providers were observed to encourage clients to make their own decisions. This was also found to be the case in Bangladesh and Finland. In Bolivia it was observed that providers inquired about reproductive goals in approximately two-thirds of the cases. When clients came for resupply, providers would generally ask if the client had experienced any problems with the method. In Mexico, the quality of provider counselling was found to be best among clients indicating that they wanted to change methods. New users were very rarely asked about their reproductive goals. Resupply clients were mainly asked about past problems with the method. In the Netherlands, no observations were done.

Patient satisfaction

Another indicator on the quality of the provider–client interaction is the satisfaction that clients expressed in exit interviews. The findings from this study's exit interviews confirm the generally positive assessment of the quality of counselling. For example, in Nigeria, 74 per cent of the eighty-eight interviewed clients said that they were satisfied with the services provided, even though two-thirds of the clients had to wait for more than an hour for the consultation.[11] In Kenya even more clients evaluated their consultation positively. Of forty-five interviewed clients, 98 per cent said the staff was friendly and that they were easy to under-stand. In total, 89 per cent felt that they got what they wanted. In Bolivia, 74 per cent of forty-nine interviewed exit clients said they got what they wanted, though only 59 per cent said that they had received information on various methods.[12]

Informed choice

Being satisfied with the consultation does not mean that the client is informed properly about the advantages, disadvantages and contraindica-tions of the method he or she is using. For clients to make an adequate choice among contraceptive options they need to be informed about the relative risks and benefits of the contraceptives from which they can choose and providers need to screen for contraindications. This is especially important for new users who have not yet received information during earlier consultations.

Information on the choice of methods available, their effectiveness in preventing pregnancy and possible side effects should be given by providers during the consultation. This information should be understood by the client. Informed choice is enhanced if written (or other printed) informa-tion is available at the service delivery point, such as information leaflets

Table 12.2 Provision of information during counselling in service delivery points

	Nigeria	Kenya	Bolivia
Written material available	General	Lacking	General
IEC materials are used	Lacking	Very limited	Lacking
Written guidelines and manual for providers available	General	Very limited	General

Notes: [1] 'General': more than 80 per cent; 'lacking': 50–80 per cent; 'very limited':
Source: Field data; A. Hardon.

with written text and/or with drawings and pictures to clarify points. Even in areas with high illiteracy rates, written information is important as people can go to educated people in the community to have the text explained. In addition, information can take the form of posters, a group lecture, or displays of contraceptives. Aside from the information provided during the consultation, written information should give the client more detailed information on how the method should be used, what to do if side effects occur and when next to visit the clinic.

In all eight participating countries, researchers assessed the provision of written information. As Table 12.2 suggests, the studies indicate that information on methods is often available but rarely used in the surveyed service settings.

In Kenya, only 25 per cent of the clients reported during exit interviews that they had received written information. In the cases where information was provided, the clients indicated that they found it difficult to understand. In Nigeria, only 35 per cent of clients in the exit interviews said they had received information materials and among these respondents only half said that they had understood them. In Bolivia, information materials were found to be generally available but used only in about 20 per cent of observed consultations. Only 45 per cent of clients in exit interviews reported that they had received information. In Mexico, though information materials exist, they are not distributed properly. As a result, around one-fourth of the visited service delivery points had no materials available. Only 29 per cent of the clients questioned in exit interviews said that they had received information at the clinics. In this country, a more elaborate assessment of the provided information was made involving eight elements such as if the client was told how the method worked, how to use it, and possible risks. Using these criteria, only 22 per cent of the clients observed during the consultations received adequate information on the method selected.

In Bangladesh, information leaflets are not used during consultations, and for providers[1]

Mexico	Bangladesh	Thailand	Finland	Netherlands
Lacking	General	General	General	General
Lacking	Lacking	No use	General	Lacking
Lacking	Lacking	Lacking	General	General

less than 50 per cent.

but information leaflets are available in the clinics for clients to take home. In exit interviews, 70 per cent of the clients reported that they were told how the method works and informed about possible side effects. However, only a small percentage of clients were told what to do if side effects occurred. Consultation observations showed that the quality of the information provided was relatively good, with providers discussing how to manage side effects, for example, in 86 per cent of consultations. It should be noted that most of the consultations concern resupply clients. In Thailand, most service delivery points had written material available for clients. However, few providers gave the information directly to them. They would display the material in the waiting room and clients could pick it up. Observing consultations revealed that clients were not well informed. About one-half of the clients participating in exit interviews said that the health providers did not explain how the method worked when they first obtained it. Only one-third of the interviewed clients had been told about side effects.

Researchers in the Netherlands observed that knowledge about contraception is widespread, especially about the contraceptive pill. General practitioners (GPs) generally have information on contraceptives available in their waiting rooms. The researchers were not able to observe consultations in the GP practices but at the visited NGO clinics they found that leaflets were actually used in approximately half of the consultations. In Finland, too, the researchers found that family planning providers tended to assume that their clients already knew a lot about family planning. Still, in Finland, the majority of clients (82 per cent) did receive written materials during the consultation. In most cases, though, they had received brochures produced by pharmaceutical companies manufacturing that contraceptive.

These findings, which highlight the lack of comprehensive information provision in the family planning services, raise a number of issues concerning the quality of care. First, it should be noted that, in general, the availability of contraceptives and the related choice offered to clients is better than the information provided on them. This finding is puzzling. Surely, if clients are not provided with adequate information on the methods they select, one cannot expect them to use the method in a satisfactory way. This is especially true if one considers that most contraceptives have side effects that users need to be aware of.

The studies also indicate that more attention needs to be paid to the ways in which information is provided and the effectiveness of these various strategies in informing clients. Often, clinics display their written information leaflets in the waiting room for people to take home. Such passive information distribution is likely to be less effective than a mixed communication strategy in which the provider actually refers to the materials in his/her counselling effort. Health education theory teaches that method mix is a crucial factor in effective communication. If messages are reinforced through various channels then they are more likely to be internalized and understood. Information provided to men and women through mass media and community channels can encourage clients to demand information from their providers.

The results of this study also reveal that, in many settings, providers, in fact, expect clients to know in advance about contraceptives. They ask clients to make a choice without sufficiently realizing that their knowledge about the risks and benefits of available methods may not be as good as they assume.

In Finland, the researchers found that most of the information leaflets available were produced by pharmaceutical companies. The problem with such industry information is that it may include exaggerated claims of efficacy and/or safety in order to enhance product sales. Providing clients with information on a range of methods and putting forward the advantages and disadvantages of each of them should not be expected from companies who have an interest in the market share of their own product.

Informing providers

A health-care infrastructure that enables safe fertility regulation is not easy to define. It includes a number of elements such as the physical infrastructure of the health facilities, adherence to certain family planning procedures (that may differ between countries), adequate training and supervision of staff and the availability of written guidelines and manuals describing the proper provision of contraceptives.

The country studies did not evaluate the content of existing guidelines, except in Mexico where the researchers noted that national guidelines, developed in 1994 without the participation of women's health advocates, present contraception in a very positive way and provide too little information on risks and contraindications.

In recently published international guidelines, WHO notes that in many parts of the world family planning programmes are still guided by policies and health-care practices based either on studies of contraceptive products that are no longer widely used or on theoretical, method-related risks that have not been substantiated in practice.[13]

The appraisals revealed that in all countries except Nigeria, Finland and the Netherlands, providers lacked access to guidelines in their clinics and that available guidelines are likely to be outdated. In response to the lack of current guidelines, international agencies are now placing much more emphasis on the development of international guidelines. WHO's guidelines are entitled *Medical Eligibility Criteria for Contraceptive Use*. They are based on a review of thousands of studies published on the safety and efficacy of contraceptive methods. On the basis of scientific evidence, experts have classified the use of the methods in the presence of specific health conditions into four categories: (i) no prescribing restrictions required; (ii) advantages of the method generally outweigh the risks; (iii) risks usually outweigh the advantages and therefore the method should not usually be used unless other more appropriate methods are not available or acceptable; and (iv) the method should not be prescribed at all. These criteria can help providers give scientifically sound recommendations to clients depending on their assessment of the client's health status.[14]

The IPPF issued *Medical and Service Delivery Guidelines* in 1992 which it is currently updating.[15] In the USA, the Technical Guidance Working Group consisting of members from various US agencies (Pathfinder International, USAID, Family Health International, and the Program for International Training in Health) have formulated recommendations for updating selected practices in contraceptive use.[16]

While these guidelines can certainly be expected to contribute to better quality procedures at country level, a problem arises as these guidelines are not consistent in layout and content. This is likely to make it extremely difficult for national programme managers to review and compare them. Two specific service delivery issues will now be given as examples to illustrate the conflicting messages a programme manager would receive if he or she intended to draw up national guidelines based upon current international standards.

International guidelines: conflicting messages on two common questions

Case I: pill use in female smokers Can women above age thirty-five who smoke use combined oral contraceptives? The WHO eligibility criteria give the most clear advice.[17] The WHO makes a distinction between light and heavy smoking. If such a woman smokes twenty or fewer cigarettes a day, the risks of pill use usually outweigh the advantages. Therefore, the criteria advise that the method should not usually be used unless other more appropriate methods are not available or acceptable. If the woman smokes more than twenty cigarettes a day, combined oral contraceptives should not be prescribed at all. The IPPF guidelines list smoking above the age of thirty-five as a relative contraindication and do not specify this by how often the woman smokes. Relative contraindications are those conditions which may increase the risks to the client when taking combined oral contraceptives. According to the guidelines: 'Decisions will depend on the circumstances and clinical criteria of each case. The potential risks should be explained to the client and possible alternative methods discussed.'[18]

The *Recommendations for Updating Selected Practices in Contraceptive Use* prepared by the Technical Guidance Working Group mention in the introduction that it is assumed that WHO's medical eligibility criteria for each method's use have been applied. The guide itself deals with service delivery issues, one of which is the question: Is there a minimum or maximum age to receive combined oral contraceptives? In answering this question the guide refers to smoking, but only vaguely, saying: 'Women over age 40 can take COCs, provided other risk factors have been considered (e.g. smoking …)'.[19]

By comparing the advice given in the guidelines concerning use of combined oral contraceptives in women above age thirty-five who smoke, it becomes clear that the WHO guidelines are the most specific and, in fact, strongly discourage prescribing this method to women who smoke heavily. However, the other guidelines are less clear and could cause a family planning programme manager reviewing them to become confused. Statements such as 'Decisions will depend on the circumstances and clinical criteria of each case, other risk factors like smoking should be considered',[20] are a case in point.

Case II: IUDs and STD screening Another example is standard screening for STDs in women who intend to have an IUD inserted. The WHO guidelines indicate that the main restriction for IUD use concerns individual behaviour patterns associated with an increased risk of STDs. It specifically recommends that the presence of an STD or having had an STD within the last three months is an absolute contraindication. This is due to serious concern that IUD use increases the risk of pelvic inflammatory disease in women experiencing STDs. For women who are at increased risk of contracting STDs due to multiple partners or whose partner has multiple partners, the risks usually outweigh the advantages. The guidelines state that IUDs can generally be inserted in women who have only a vaginal infection (vaginitis) without cervical discharge.

The IPPF guidelines advise against IUD insertion in women with 'severe infections of the lower genital tract, including cervicitis, vaginitis' until the infection has been treated and controlled.[21] This advice thus appears to be stricter than that put forward by the WHO. Insertion of IUDs is not recommended when women have a vaginal infection, while according to the WHO this is not a contraindication.

The report of the US-based Technical Guidance Working Group addresses the extremely relevant question: If a woman is at low risk of STDs based on history, may IUDs be inserted without any laboratory tests if there is no cervical discharge containing pus or clinically apparent pelvic inflammatory disease or cervicitis?[22] The answer is *yes*. If pelvic inflammatory disease, mucopurulent endocervical discharge, cervicitis or clinically apparent vaginitis is present, the guidelines advise *not* inserting an IUD and treating the infection.

In this case, the IPPF guidelines and the Technical Guidance Working Group's recommendations are more strict in their recommendations than the WHO guidelines. Again, reviewing the guidelines will not provide clear answers to a family planning programme manager.

Such inconsistency between international standards not only reflects a lack of communication between the agencies involved; it also indicates that areas still exist for which there are insufficient scientific data on which to base clear-cut recommendations. It emphasizes that balancing the risks and benefits of method use is not a value-free process. When scientific evidence is lacking, guidelines are usually made by means of consensus among expert health professionals. This is remarkable, as it is not the experts who will run the risks, but rather contraceptive users.

Involving interested parties in setting standards

Given the arbitrary nature of guidelines, it is advisable to involve women's health advocates in the setting of these standards. For example, they can be involved in making recommendations on screening for STDs in women who want to use an IUD. A number of questions emerge. Should vaginitis be a contraindication or not?[23] What about asymptomatic STDs? Technical guidelines allow insertion if there are no symptoms of infection. Women's health advocates may put forward the risks that women have of contracting chlamydia, an infection which does not cause vaginal or cervical discharge, and therefore often goes unnoticed. If an IUD is inserted in a woman with chlamydia, she runs the risk of developing an infection in her upper reproductive tract. This can lead to infertility. The prevalence rate for chlamydia is estimated to be about 8 per cent among women attending family planning clinics in developing countries.[24] Thus, when formulating national guidelines, women's health advocates may suggest that women be informed about this risk and the possibility of conducting a laboratory test to check for an asymptomatic chlamydia infection.

Alternatively, women's health advocates could call for a policy that discourages the use of IUDs in women who do not have any children and/or want more children, because of the infertility risks, even though international experts tend to agree that this recommendation is no longer justified. This is based on scientific findings that it is not the IUD that increases the risk of pelvic inflammatory disease, but the insertion procedure when women are suffering from an infection. But is this true in practice? Are women aware of the sexual risks they run? Do they know about their partner(s)' sexual behaviour and will they admit to having plural partners to health workers?

Neither women's health advocates nor international experts can in the end take decisions for individual men and women who want to regulate their fertility. Rather than disputing recommendations in policy arenas, perhaps ambiguous decisions such as the testing for STDs in women who seek to use an IUD or the use of the pill by women who smoke should be made by the users. The guidelines then should be changed and made to emphasize ways in which men and women can be assisted in making informed decisions.

Contraceptive-use studies reveal that clients of family planning programmes actively assess the effects of contraception on their health. It has been estimated, for example, that approximately half of the women who start using hormonal pills and injectables stop using them within twelve months, often for health reasons.[25] Health concerns are also found worldwide to be one of the most important reasons for non-use of contraceptives by women who do not want to become pregnant. The main cause of concerns and discontinuance is lack of appropriate counselling on the adverse effects. Providers can encourage clients to make more realistic and informed trade-offs between the benefits and possible adverse effects of available methods, thus taking their health concerns more seriously.

In conclusion: reproductive rights in practice

This book on quality of care and adherence to reproductive rights in family planning services has shown that much still needs to be done to ensure that women and men worldwide can make a free and informed choice about contraceptive methods.

The preceding chapters have shown that, in general, the availability of contraceptives is relatively good but, in many settings, non-medical criteria are used to restrict access. The main group affected by this practice is adolescents.

Method availability and restrictions vary from country to country and even from clinic to clinic. Clearly, some service delivery points are better than others in providing clients with a choice of contraceptives. However, in comparison, there is an apparent lack of access to emergency contraception, abortion services and barrier methods in all of the countries involved.

Contraceptive choice could be tremendously enhanced and consequently unmet need diminished if more attention was paid to these types of family planning services. Further promotion of the LAM method is also a recommendation resulting from the study. Based on such observations, there is a need for more participation by interested parties in determining the method mix available to clients.

This book has demonstrated that the health and development context of a country is often not a determinant of free choice among contraceptives. This is because donors support the family planning programmes operating in poorer countries thus ensuring a relatively good supply of contraceptives. Problems in terms of choice lie in the area of non-medical restrictions and in providers' attitudes towards the available contraceptive options. For example, providers' preferences are reflected in contraceptive-use patterns in Kenya where the IUD is rarely promoted by providers and rarely used, whereas in Bolivia providers prefer the IUD and it is commonly used. In the same way, in the Netherlands both providers and clients prefer the contraceptive pill.

Common to all the involved countries except Finland is the tendency of providers not to promote condoms as a birth-spacing method. The contraceptive prevalence figures subsequently show that in these countries condoms are rarely used. This situation is remarkable given the global impact of STDs and HIV transmission which could be prevented with condom use. It seems that providers still consider the condom to be a second-choice method, probably because it is less effective in preventing pregnancy and because they do not really expect men to use them.

Social marketing programmes have found that publicizing condoms as a dual-purpose device to prevent pregnancy and disease can work. The SOMARCH project of the Futures Group tested this approach in ten African countries where HIV transmission is a particularly severe problem. Baseline data showed that condoms were used mainly outside marriage and that the method had a negative image. A media campaign depicting two men (one uses condoms which result in a small and healthy family and the other doesn't use condoms, becomes ill and has too many children) resulted in increased condom use and positive shifts in attitude.[26] Similarly, a recent operational research study conducted by the Family Planning Association of Kenya and the Population Council involved community-based interventions.[27] Community-based distributors were trained in family planning and HIV/AIDS prevention. These distributors were encouraged to focus their attention on men and to work in places where men routinely met. The project resulted in slightly greater use of condoms by males in response to education activities for the prevention of HIV/AIDS.

The quality of care appraisals conducted for this book found that information for users and providers on the appropriate use of contraceptives is generally lacking. Where written information is available in the clinics it is often left for passive distribution and not actively referred to during consultations. This results in a low percentage of clients leaving the clinics with written information. Guidelines and manuals for providers are often not available in clinics which makes it difficult for them to counsel clients appropriately on the advantages and disadvantages of methods or to apply correctly the medical criteria for each method's eligibility.

The study indicates that there is a need to rethink the capacity of family planning programmes to ensure the appropriate use of contraceptives. If information is lacking and guidelines absent, misuse is likely to occur. Misuse can lead to contraceptive failure, unnecessary adverse effects and discontinuation of use. The inappropriate prescription and administration of a method can have serious health consequences for clients, which have been shown to be an important cause of unmet need for contraception and unwanted pregnancy.

This quality of care appraisal is one of the first efforts of women's health advocacy researchers, to the participants' knowledge, to assess the extent to which reproductive rights are respected in practice in a multi-country study.[28] The results can be used at the local, national and international level in debates on how quality of care and adherence to reproductive rights can be ensured. It is hoped that these debates will lead to the involvement of more women's health advocates in setting international and national standards and greater participation of men and women in the formulation and implementation of family planning services.

It appears that, until this point, the conduct of family planning programmes has been based on international blueprints developed by international and national experts without active participation by the women and men who are supposed to benefit from the programmes or women's health advocates who take clients' health needs and reproductive rights as their point of departure. The time has now come for a reorientation of family planning programmes towards clients' needs and reproductive health, adapted to local realities.

Programme for action   Resulting from this comparative analysis are a number of recommendations towards policy-makers and providers operating in family planning programmes at the international, national or local level. These recommendations are directed to the family planning establishment as it is the adherence to reproductive rights in family planning *services* which has been the focus of this collaborative study and book. More country-specific recommendations have been given in each country chapter.

The recommendations are intended to contribute to women's and men's right to be informed and to have access to a choice of safe, effective, affordable and acceptable methods of family planning.

This book has not dealt with factors such as drastically reduced funding for public services in countries where structural adjustment programmes are implemented or the trend to reduce public spending in industrialized countries, the lack of professional staff in rural areas and the difficulties in the logistics of supply to remote areas. Clearly, in refining further the following recommendations such structural constraints need to be considered. The researchers in the participating countries are initiating dialogues with family planning providers and policy-makers to discuss realistic options for change. These dialogues enable providers also to put forward their needs and views.

The suggestions aim at strengthening the quality of care in family planning. Following the recommendations of the 1994 ICPD *Program of Action*, ideally such care should be integrated within a broader reproductive health programme. If the given suggestions to improve family planning services are ambitious, the recommendations for integrated reproductive health care are even more so. Improving family planning services necessarily implies broadening the approach, as this book has shown. Prevention, diagnosis and treatment of STDs are necessary components and so are emergency contraception and abortion services. Such improvements in existing family planning services can be an excellent stepping stone towards the implementation of appropriate reproductive health care. The participatory approaches that are proposed here, with women and men co-formulating and implementing the programmes, lay the groundwork for future collaboration in the strengthening of other components of reproductive health care, such as infertility diagnosis and treatment.

Recommendations

1. Expand choice

Abolish non-medical restrictions for method use Providers should deny specific contraceptive method types on *only* medical grounds. Other criteria such as spousal consent and marital status should be disregarded.

Break down barriers to contraceptives In many cultures, single women and men are barred from obtaining contraceptive methods in service delivery points. No woman seeking contraception should be turned away because her spouse has not given his permission. Women have the right to decide about their own reproductive plans.

Provide quality contraception to lactating women Breastfeeding women seeking contraception need access to safe alternatives to the combined contraceptive pill as studies have shown that its use when lactating decreases the quality and quantity of breastmilk. Ideally, apart from IUDs, sterilization and barrier methods, lactating women should be informed about the lactational amenorrhoea method (LAM) and offered the choice of progestin-only pills.

Widen choice for pill users For women to use the contraceptive pill in a satisfactory manner, they must be able to select among different combinations and dosages of oestrogens and progestins in order to find a combination which results in the least adverse effects. Such a choice is also important in the light of new evidence of increased deep venous thromboembolism risks related to use of so-called third-generation, progestin pills (pills containing gestodene or desogestrel). Women should be offered a choice between pill brands and told about the relative advantages and disadvantages of the various types of combined pills. A constant supply of the selected brands should be ensured.

Enhance accessibility of emergency contraception In all family planning clinics information should be available on the use of contraceptive pills as emergency contraception.

Promote barrier methods This study has shown that barrier methods, especially those designed for use by women, are vastly under-represented in clinic programmes. Women and providers need to be made more aware of the health benefits of these methods. Methods such as diaphragms should be added to the types of methods offered by programmes. Barrier methods' added benefit of providing protection against STDs should be emphasized.

Improve outreach to adolescents Adolescents have special needs regarding contraception. At the same time, they often lack knowledge and access to contraception because of programme rules or cultural norms. Family planning programmes need to acknowledge the sexual activity of teenagers and find ways to offer them non-judgemental, quality counselling and referral services for STDs, abortion services and reproductive health care. As this group has been found to rely largely on drugstores, a first step could be to provide better information through these outlets. In the family planning services all restrictions on the basis of age and marital status need to be abolished to enhance accessibility of services to adolescents.

Encourage men to take responsibility for contraception Women are still the central figures in contraception today. More efforts need to be made to involve men in contraceptive decision-making with their partner(s). There are not too many contraceptive options available for men. Men should at least be informed about condom use and its benefits in preventing STD transmission as well as preventing pregnancy. Providers should be encouraged to promote condoms in a positive manner, breaking prejudices against the method. They should also be informed about the safety and simplicity of male sterilization procedures as compared to female sterilization.

Redefine how programme methods are chosen Contraceptive users must have a much more central role in deciding which contraceptive methods are available to them. The current emphasis on longer-acting, provider-controlled methods in many countries should be re-examined and discussed with representatives of users. Other interested parties such as women's health activists should be involved in this process as well.

Offer a wide range of contraceptive options Clients can have real choice only when they are given a full range of options from which to choose. Programmes should not unnecessarily limit the types of methods they offer to clients. When particular methods are unavailable at a service delivery point, clients should still be informed about their action, risks and benefits and referred to another delivery point if they are requested.

2. Provide adequate and balanced information and conduct good counselling

Inform clients about all contraceptive methods This study has under-scored that a wide spectrum of contraceptive methods are available, though some may be obtainable only at considerable distance, cost and client effort. Clients should be informed about all contraceptives, even if they are not available from that particular provider so that they can weigh the risks and benefits of each one before selecting a method.

Give clients complete information about methods Adequate client counselling means much more than getting a client to accept a method. All clients should receive full information about how their chosen method works, its risks and contraindications, how to manage possible side effects, its efficacy in preventing pregnancy and STDs and when next to return to the clinic for follow-up. Clients should be encouraged to make informed trade-offs between benefits and disadvantages of the various methods. Providers should not assume that clients already know everything they need to know about a method.

Show respectful treatment to clients The privacy of clients during the consultation and examination should be ensured. Providers should treat patients with respect.

Sensitize providers to reproductive rights Training programmes need to be developed to teach providers how they can contribute to informed decision-making by clients and how they can respect the client's autonomy and bodily integrity. Learning to listen and encouraging clients to ask questions and voice their concerns are elements in such training.

Spread family planning information to the general public Information provision to the general public and providers needs to be improved. This is necessary to strengthen the interactions between providers and clients and to ensure that clients' needs and medical criteria are met. Informed choice for clients should ideally not only include information in clinics. Better use of mass media and community health education strategies can empower men and women to make decisions concerning the regulation of their own fertility. Such information should accurately and responsibly reflect new scientific data and controversies regarding risks and safety to users.

Encourage providers to make better use of available information   This book's data suggest that providers seldom make full use of the information available in the clinic or medical practice. Providers should actively incorporate brochures, booklets, drawings and models of contraceptives into their consultations with clients. It is not enough to have material displayed in waiting rooms. This can lead to better information understanding and method use.

Develop better written information about methods   Ideally, information on contraceptives available at clinics or doctors' practices should be client-oriented, easy-to-understand, objective and developed with the help of programme users. It should also take into consideration cultural factors and gender differences that influence the way people perceive the human body, sexuality, safety, efficacy and reproductive expectations. Inevitably, information about contraception requires some biomedical terms and explanations. Finding the best way to incorporate these into information requires field work among the communities where the information will be given. The depth of the information on safety and efficacy to be included should be explored in a similar participatory fashion. Information should be available in local languages for clients to benefit from it.

Avoid using industry materials   Clients cannot receive an accurate picture of a method if it is explained in material produced by a company selling that method. Providers need to be aware of a possible bias in industry-provided material and should be encouraged to use objective, independent material instead.

3. Develop and improve national guidelines on family planning

Encourage participatory action on national guidelines   In order to develop national guidelines on family planning, it is extremely important that programme managers not only review available guidelines, but also discuss the decisions that need to be made regarding the provision of contraceptives in family planning programmes with all interested parties. It is crucial that women's health advocates concerned with clients' needs and health be involved in this process and that in service delivery contexts clients are enabled to make decisions on the risks they want to take.

Promote use of national guidelines for providers This comparative assessment revealed that written guidelines and manuals are lacking. Sometimes they are clearly available at the national level but are poorly distributed. More coordinated efforts need to be made to place up-to-date, complete method information into the hands of providers so that they can give the highest quality of care possible to family planning clients.

Revise guidelines periodically Guidelines and manuals need to be updated when new scientific data on efficacy and safety appear. The recent consensus on the efficacy of the LAM method, for example, is essential for women to know. Also, new concerns about third-generation contraceptive pills and their increased relative risk for blood clots need to be explained to pill users. Also, the HIV/AIDS epidemic requires a reassessment of the relative advantages and disadvantages of available contraceptives in terms of their relevance for STD prevention. Providers are in the best position to advise women when new scientific data become available. But, for them to do so, they themselves need to be appropriately informed.

4. Broaden family planning services to reproductive health care

Implement integrated reproductive health care Family planning services need to be broadened to incorporate other elements of reproductive health care which enhance quality of care such as the prevention and control of reproductive tract infections, safe menstrual regulation and abortion services and prevention, counselling on sexuality, information on reproductive cancers and the diagnosis and treatment of infertility. Changes towards such improved health care should be based on participatory processes, by which users and non-users of family planning services can put forward their reproductive health needs and suggestions for improved care.

These recommendations are not only directed towards family planning policy-makers and providers; they are also directed at women's health advocates who are increasingly becoming interested in quality of care. In fact, their interest in this subject is relatively new. As highlighted in Part One, during the 1970s and 1980s, the main concern within the women's health movement was the demographic orientation of family planning programmes. Women's health advocates vehemently criticized the setting of targets for contraceptive prevalence as well as policies giving incentives to contraceptive acceptors and placing sanctions on non-acceptors. The provider-dependent and longer-acting nature of new contraceptive technologies such as Norplant® and anti-fertility 'vaccines' was also an issue of concern. Misuse of such technologies by providers in family planning programmes that aim at reducing fertility rates was a recurrent issue in debates and dialogues with researchers and policy-makers. Empirical evidence for the concerns was often anecdotal rather than based on systematic research.

Now an increasing number of organizations within the women's health advocacy movement are examining more closely the way in which family planning programmes operate. They are also describing systematically how such programmes violate reproductive rights and how they could be changed to empower women and men to regulate their fertility in line with their own needs and interests.[29]

New empirical evidence is revealing that women's reproductive rights are violated in different ways. One main issue that became apparent during this study is the way in which providers restrict availability of contraceptives by demanding spousal consent and denying access to unmarried people. These restrictions need to be addressed. They are not related to demographic objectives but to gender bias and cultural norms on sexuality. Another problem that emerged was not so much the provision of disempowering contraceptives such as Norplant®, but the lack of methods that potentially meet the reproductive needs of women. The absence of postcoital and barrier methods requires attention. In this eight-country study, incentives and disincentives turn out to be non-existent, except in Bangladesh. Plus, the longer-acting and provider-dependent methods such as Norplant® are hardly available.

Providers' attitudes need to be changed. Family planning providers should treat women with dignity and empower them by providing balanced and complete information on contraception. They should also listen to their concerns, instead of following their own preferences. Other issues have been addressed in the recommendations. The contributors to this book hope that all of them will be taken up by women's health advocates in their work for change.

As an important tool for future action, a number of those involved in the writing of this book have also written a methodology handbook (*Monitoring Family Planning and Reproductive Rights: A manual for empowerment*) that lists the issues found to be core indicators of quality of care in family planning programmes. These indicators should inspire women's health advocates to conduct their own appraisals and identify the specific ways in which reproductive rights are violated by family planning programmes in the contexts where they live. High quality reproductive and sexual health care are on the agenda in national and international family planning arenas. Concrete suggestions for change based on systematic observation of the actual conduct of family planning programmes can have an immense impact in reorienting family planning programmes so that they meet women's health needs and respect reproductive rights.

Notes

1. United Nations (1994) ICPD *Program of Action* (UN International Conference on Population and Development) (New York: ICPD Secretariat), para. 7.2.

2. Where men do play a role in fertility regulation, it seems to be a negative one of authority, granting or withholding consent on women's reproductive choice.

3. K. Tomaševski (1994) *Human Rights in Population Policies: A Study for SIDA* (Lund, Sweden: SIDA). This particular reproductive right has been highlighted because it is the right that family planning services seek to fulfil. Reproductive rights include more rights, i.e. the defence of women's autonomy, bodily integrity and personhood (see S. Corrêa [1994], *Population and Reproductive Rights: Feminist Perspectives from the South* [London: Zed Books]).

4. J. Bruce (1990) 'Fundamental Elements of Quality of Care: A Simple Framework', *Studies in Family Planning* 21(2): 61–91.

5. In the appraisals, it proved difficult to determine accessibility to male and female sterilization. Service delivery points generally refer clients for these services. The emphasis in this comparative analysis is on the availability of birth-spacing methods, not sterilization.

6. S. Townsend (1992) 'The "New" Contraceptive Method of Breastfeeding', in *Network* (October): 4–8.

7. The logistics of supplying multiple pill brands is demanding. In Kenya, the lack of consistent supplies of various brands causes problems as women are forced to shift from one brand to another, not out of choice but because their own brand is out of stock.

8. WHO (1996) UNDP/UNFPA/WHO/World Bank Special Programme of Research, Development and Research Training in Human Reproduction, *Biennial Report 1994–1995*, 40 (Geneva: WHO). The number of pills to be taken depends on the pill's strength. The total dose to be taken is 100mcg ethinylestradiol and 0.5mg levonorgestrel in the first dose. This dose is repeated twelve hours later.

9. United Nations (1994) ICPD *Program of Action*, para. 7.2.

10. W. R. Finger (1994) 'Method Choice Involves Many Factors', in *Network* 15(2): 14–17. Finger cites John Stanback of Family Health International who directed the analysis and has begun an in-depth study of the issue.

11. This finding suggests that waiting time, which international experts tend to list as a quality of care indicator, is not a good measure from a client's perspective as clients may actually value the time.

12. A disadvantage of exit interviews is that non-clients who may have had bad experiences in the past are not interviewed.

13. World Health Organization (1996) 'Improving Access to Quality Care in Family Planning: Medical Eligibility Criteria for Contraceptive Use', in *Family Planning and Reproductive Health* (Geneva: WHO).

14. Ibid.

15. C. M. Huero and C. Briggs (1992) *Medical and Service Delivery Guidelines* (London: International Planned Parenthood Federation).

16. K. M. Curtis and P. L. Bright (eds) (1994) *Recommendations for Updating Selected Practices in Contraceptive Use. Results of a Technical Meeting*, Vol. 1 (London: IPPF, Technical Guidance Working Group).

17. WHO (1996) 'Improving Access ...'.

18. C. M. Huero and C. Briggs (1992) *Medical and Service Delivery Guidelines*.

19. K. M. Curtis and P. L. Bright (eds) (1994) *Recommendations*.

20. C. M. Huero and C. Briggs (1992) *Medical and Service Delivery Guidelines* .

21. Ibid.

22. K. M. Curtis and P. L. Bright (eds) (1994) *Recommendations.*

23. If the cervix is not affected then hygienic insertion is possible as the speculum would prevent the IUD from coming into contact with the infected vagina. Of course, service providers need to be aware of the special precautions called for in such circumstances.

24. J. N. Wasserheit and K. K. Holmes (1992) 'Reproductive Tract Infections: Challenges for International Health Policy Programs and Research', in A. Germain et al. (eds), *Reproductive Tract Infections: Global Impact and Priorities for Women's Reproductive Health* (New York: Plenum Press).

25. World Health Organization (1995) 'Perspectives on Methods of Fertility Regulation' (background paper) (Geneva: UNDP/UNFPA/WHO/World Bank Special Programme of Research, Development and Research Training in Human Reproduction).

26. R. W. Finger (1994) 'Should Family Planning Include STD Services?', in *Network* 14(4): 4–7.

27. Family Planning Association of Kenya/Population Council (1995) 'Increasing Male Involvement in the Family Planning Association of Kenya (FPAK) Family Planning Program', unpublished document.

28. An extremely interesting study on gender and quality of health care has been conducted in Latin America by the Latin American and Caribbean Women's Health Network. More information can be obtained from Maria Isabel Matamala, Casilla Postal 50610, Santiago 1, Chile. Results of this study are in the process of being published.

29. Examples of such innovative studies, other than the contributions to this book, include work on quality of care from a gender perspective conducted by Maria Isabel Matamala and Maria José Araúgo of the Latin America and Caribbean Women's Health Network (see *Women's Health Journal* 3–4, 1995). In addition, Mala Ramanathan and Sylvia Claudio Estrada are working within the Gender, Reproductive Health and Population Policies project, coordinated by the Health Action Information Network (the Philippines) and the University of Amsterdam (the Netherlands). Publications on this work are starting to appear. See, for example, M. Ramanathan et al. (1995) 'Quality of Care in Laprascopic Sterilization Camps: Observations from Kerala, India', *Reproductive Health Matters* 6: 84–94.

Bibliography

Aitken, I. and Reichenbach, L. (1994) 'Reproductive and Sexual Health Services: Expanding Access and Enhancing Quality', in G. Sen et al. (eds), *Population Policies Reconsidered: Health, Empowerment and Rights*, Harvard Series on Population and International Health (Boston, MA: Harvard University Press).

Alcala, M. (1994) *Action for the 21st Century. Reproductive Health and Rights for All: Summary Report of Recommended Actions on Reproductive Health and Rights in the Cairo ICPD Program of Action* (New York: Family Care International).

Ali, M. S. et al. (1978) *Report on the Legal Aspects of Population Planning* 31 (Dhaka: Bangladesh Institute of Law and International Affairs).

Anon. (1984) 'One-Month Injectables are Popular Choice in Mexico', *Network* 5(3): 4–5.

Anon. (1996) 'Many Poor Condoms for Sale', *Consumentengids* 6: 348–51 (the Netherlands).

Beets, G. and Verloove-Vanhorick, P. (eds) (1992) *A Smart Girl Plans Her Pregnancy Ahead of Time* (Amsterdam: Swets and Zeitlinger).

Bolivian Ministry of Human Development, Ministry of Health (1994) *Plan Vida Bolivia 1994–1997* (La Paz: UNFPA, USAID, UNICEF, OPS/OMS).

Bolivian Ministry of Planning and Coordination (1989) *Two Cases of Family Planning in Bolivia.*

Bolivian Ministry of Public Health (1989) *Seminar on the Struggle Against Abortion* (La Paz: Ministry of Public Health).

Bongaarts, J. and Bruce, J. (1995) 'The Causes of Unmet Need for Contraception and the Social Content of Services', *Studies in Family Planning* 26(2): 57–75.

Browner, C. H. (1985) 'Traditional Techniques for Diagnosis, Treatment and Control of Pregnancy in Cali, Colombia', in L. F. Newman (ed.), *Women's Medicine.*

Bruce, J. (1990) 'Fundamental Elements of the Quality of Care: A Simple Framework', *Studies in Family Planning* 21(2): 61–91.

Buckley, T. and Gottlieb, A. (eds) (1988) *Blood Magic: The Anthropology of Menstruation* (Berkeley, CA: University of California Press).

Cabrera, Y. et al. (1987) *Demographic and Health Survey* (Mexico City: Director General for Family Planning, Subsecretariat for Health Services, Ministry of Health; and Columbia, OH: Institute for Resource Development/Macro Systems, Inc.).

Chao, D. and Allen, K. B. (1984) 'A Cost–Benefit Analysis of Thailand's Family Planning Program', *International Family Planning Perspectives* 10(3): 75–81.

Chayovan, N. et al. (1988) *Thailand Demographic and Health Survey 1987.* Institute for Population Studies, Chulalongkorn University, Bangkok.

Cleland, J. (1985) 'Marital Fertility Decline in Developing Countries: Theories and

Evidence', in J. Cleland and J. Hobcraft (eds), *Reproductive Change in Developing Countries: Insights from the World Fertility Survey* (Oxford: OUP).

Cleland, J. and Parker Mauldin, W. (1990) *The Promotion of Family Planning by Financial Payments: The Case of Bangladesh*, Working paper No. 13 (New York: Research Division, The Population Council).

Cleland, J. et al. (1994) 'The Determinants of Reproductive Changes in Bangladesh', in *A Challenging Environment* (Washington, DC: World Bank).

Corrêa, S. (1994) *Population and Reproductive Rights: Feminist Perspectives from the South* (London: Zed Books).

Curtis, K. M. and Bright, P. L. (eds) (1994) *Recommendations for Updating Selected Practices in Contraceptive Use. Results of a Technical Meeting*, Vol. 1 (London: IPPF, Technical Guidance Working Group).

Delft, M. L. E. (1991) *Social Atlas of Women*, Part I (Rijswijk: Social and Cultural Plan Bureau).

Donabedian, A. (1988) 'The Quality of Care: How Can It Be Assessed?', *Journal of the American Medical Association* 260(12): 1743–8.

Family Planning Association of Kenya/Population Council (1995) 'Increasing Male Involvement in the Family Planning Association of Kenya (FPAK) Family Planning Program', unpublished document.

Federal Republic of Nigeria (1988) *National Policy on Population for Development, Unity, Progress and Self-Reliance.*

Finger, W. R. (1994) 'Should Family Planning Include STD Services?', *Network* 14(4): 4–7.

— (1994) 'Method Choice Involves Many Factors' in *Network* 15(2): 14–17.

Finnish Ministry of Foreign Affairs (1994) *International Conference on Population and Development 1994: Finland's National Report on Population* (Ministry of Foreign Affairs).

Garcia-Morena, C. and Claro, A. (1994) 'Challenges from the Women's Health Movement: Women's Rights Versus Population Control', in G. Sen et al. (eds), *Population Policies Reconsidered: Health, Empowerment and Rights*, Harvard Series on Population and International Health (Boston, MA: Harvard University Press).

Germain, A. and Kyte, R. (1995) *The Cairo Consensus: The Right Agenda at the Right Time* (New York: International Women's Health Coalition).

Gutiérrez, M. et al. (1994) *National Demographic and Health Survey* (La Paz: National Institute of Statistics; and Calverton, MD: Macro International).

Hardon, A. P. (1992) 'The Needs of Women Versus the Interests of Family Planning Personnel, Policy-makers and Researchers: Conflicting Views on Safety and Acceptability of Contraceptives', *Social Science and Medicine* 35(6): 753–66.

Hartmann, B. (1987) *Reproductive Rights and Wrongs: The Global Politics of Population Control and Contraceptive Choice* (New York: Harper and Row).

Hartmann, B. and Standing, H. (1985) *Food, Saris and Sterilization. Population Control in Bangladesh* (London: Bangladesh International Action Group).

Huero, C. M. and Briggs, C. (1992) *Medical and Service Delivery Guidelines* (London: International Planned Parenthood Federation).

International Planned Parenthood Federation (IPPF)/IWRAW (1995) Reproductive Rights Wall Chart (London: IPPF Distribution Unit).

International Reproductive Rights Research Action Group (IRRRAG) (1996) *Negotiating Reproductive Rights: A Seven Country Study of Women's Views and Practices* (New York: IRRRAG).

Jain, A. K. (ed.) (1992) *Managing Quality of Care in Population Programs*, 18 (West Hartford, CT: Kumarian Press).

Kabir, S. et al. (1989) 'Factors Affecting Discontinuation of Injectable Methods in Bangladesh', *Journal of Family Welfare* 35(4): 28–37.

Kay, B. J. et al. (1991) *Quality/Calidad/Qualité – The Bangladesh Women's Health Coalition* (New York: Population Council).

Ketting, E. (1994) 'Is the Dutch Abortion Rate Really That Low?', *Planned Parenthood in Europe* 23(3): 29–32.

Khoo, S. E. (1979) 'Measuring the Family Planning Program's Impact on Fertility Rates: A Comparison of Computer Models', *Studies in Family Planning* 10: 137–45.

Kisekka, M. N. (1990) 'Family Planning Services: Access to Contraceptives', *World Bank Report 1992*.

Kisekka, M. N. et al. (1992) *Niger State Family Planning Situational Analysis Study* (Submitted to the Population Council's African Operations Research and Technical Assistance Project.)

— (1992) 'Women's Organized Health Struggles: The Challenge to Women's Associations', in M. N. Kisekka (ed.), *Women's Health Issues in Nigeria* (Zaria: Tamaza Publishing Co.).

Knodel, J. et al. (1987) *Thailand Reproductive Revolution* (Madison: University of Wisconsin Press).

Koetsawang, S. (1993) 'Illegally Induced Abortion in Thailand'. Paper presented at IPPF SEAO Regional Programme Advisory Panel Meeting on Abortion, 29–30 October, Bali, Indonesia.

Kosunen, E. (1996) *Adolescent Reproductive Health in Finland: Oral Contraception, Pregnancies and Abortions from the 1980s to the 1990s*, Vol. 486 (Tampere: University of Tampere).

Kremer, J. and Haspels, A. A. (1991) *Birth Control*, 8th revised edn (Lochem: De Tijdstroom).

Laderman, C. (1983) *Wives and Midwives: Childbirth and Nutrition in Rural Malaysia* (Berkeley, CA: University of California Press).

Langer, A. and Romero, M. (1995) 'Diagnosis of Reproductive Health in Mexico' *Reflexiones* 1(11).

Mason, K. (1987) 'The Impact of Women's Social Position on Fertility in Developing Countries', *Sociological Forum* 2(4): 718–45.

Mexican Ministry of Health (SSA) (1992) *Report of the Interinstitutional Programme of Family Planning* (Mexico City: SSA).

— (1994) *Official Mexican Standards of Family Planning Services* (Mexico City: SSA).

— (1995) *Profile of Contraceptive Practices* (Mexico City: Cuadernos de Salud. Población y Salud, Secretaría de Salud).

Miller, R. A. et al. (1989) *A Situation Analysis of the Family Planning Program of Kenya: The Availability, Functioning, and Quality of MOH Services.* Population Council.

Mintzes, B. et al. (1993) *Norplant: Under Her Skin* (Delft: Women's Health Action Foundation and Eburon).

Mitra, S. N. et al. (1994) *Demographic and Health Survey 1993–1994,* National Institute of Population Research and Training (NIPORT) (Dhaka: Mitra and Associates; and Calverton, MD: Macro International Inc.).

Monoja, L. (1994) *Mission Report to Nigeria* UNFPA/CSTAA (29 May–26 June).

National Association of General Practitioners (LHV) (Netherlands) (1994) *The General Practitioner in Figures* (Utrecht: LHV).

National Council for Population and Development (NCPD), Central Bureau of Statistics (CBS) (Office of the Vice President and Ministry of Planning and National Development, Kenya) and Macro International Inc. (MI) (1994) *Kenya Demographic and Health Survey, 1993* (Calverton, MD: NCPD, CBS and MI).

Newman, L.F. (ed.) (1985) *Women's Medicine: A Cross-Cultural Study of Indigenous Fertility Regulation* (New Brunswick, NJ: Rutgers University Press).

Ngin, C. (1985) 'Indigenous Fertility Regulating Methods Among Two Chinese Communities in Malaysia', in L. F. Newman (ed.), *Women's Medicine.*

NHG (Dutch Association of General Practitioners) (1989) 'NHG Standard: The IUD', *General Practitioners and Science* 32: 62–5.

— (1991) 'NHG Standard: The IUD', *General Practitioners and Science* 34: 89–94.

— Protocol Commission (1993) 'Disinfection and Sterilization', NHG Protocol Brochure No. P25 (Utrecht: NHG).

Nichter, M. and Nichter, M. (1989) 'Modern Methods of Fertility: When and For Whom are They Appropriate?' in M. Nichter (ed.), *Anthropology and International Health: South Asian Case Studies* (Dordrecht: Kluwer).

Nigerian Federal Ministry of Health (1990) *State Profiles* (Lagos: Department of Population Activities, Family Health Services).

Nigerian Federal Office of Statistics (1992) *Nigeria Demographic and Health Survey 1990* (Lagos: Institute for Resource Development; and Columbia, OH: Macro Systems, Inc.).

Pariani, S. (1989) *Continued Use of Contraceptives Among Clients in East Java, Indonesia.* PhD dissertation. Department of Sociology, University of California, Los Angeles.

Prasartkul, P. et al. (1983) 'The Population Project: Organization and Input', in *Impact, Effectiveness and Efficacy of AFPH Programs on Family Planning Status in 20 Provinces* (Bangkok: Institute for Population and Social Research, Mahidol University), Ch. 1.

PROLAP/UNAM (1993) *Demographic Transition in Latin America and the Caribbean* (Mexico).

J. Rademakers, (1992) *Abortus in Nederland 1991–1992. Jaarverslag van de landelijke abortusregistratie (Abortion in the Netherlands 1991–1992. Annual report of the national registration of abortion)* (Utrecht: Stimezo).

Ramanathan, M. et al. (1995) 'Quality of Care in Laprascopic Sterilization Camps: Observations from Kerala, India', *Reproductive Health Matters* 6: 84–94.

Rance, S. (1995) *Abortion, Money and Reproductive Health* (Summary of Phase I of the Research Project; Bolivia).

Ross, J. A. et al. (1996) 'Country Report on Gender, Sexuality, Reproductive Health'. Paper presented at the Asia and Pacific Regional Network on Gender, Sexuality and Reproductive Health and Fora on the Teaching of Health Social Science Conference. Cebu City, the Philippines.

Saldías, E. and Del Castillo, E. (1981) *Knowledge, Attitudes and Conception and Contraceptive Practices in the City of La Paz.*

Sayavedra-Herrerías, G. (1995) 'Mexico: The Difference Between Policy and Practice', in E. Hayes (ed.), *A Healthy Balance? Women & Pharmaceuticals* (Amsterdam: Women's Health Action Foundation).

Sihvo, S. et al. (1995) *Contraception and Use of Health Services: Results of a Population-based Study 1994*, STAKES series: 27/1995.

Simmons, R. et al. (1986) 'Client Relations in South Asia: Programmatic and Societal Determinants', *Studies in Family Planning* 17(6): 257–68.

Simmons, R. (1991) 'Methodologies for Studying Clients' Interactions'. Paper presented at the seminar on Client Relations and Quality of Care (New York: Population Council).

Thai Division of Epidemiology (1992) 'National HIV Sentinel Surveillance Report'. Unpublished manuscript, Bangkok.

Thai Working Group (1991) 'Estimation and Projection of HIV/AIDS in Thailand'. Unpublished manuscript, Bangkok.

Tomaševski, K.(1994) *Human Rights in Population Policies: A Study for SIDA* (Lund, Sweden: SIDA)

Townsend, S. (1992) 'The "New" Contraceptive Method of Breastfeeding', *Network* (October): 4–8.

United Nations (1974) *Report of the United Nations World Population Conference* (New York: United Nations).

— (1979) *UN Convention on the Elimination of All Forms of Discrimination Against Women* (CEDAW), UN Doc. A/Res/34/180 (New York: UN).

— (1984) *Report of the International Conference on Population* (New York: UN).

— (1992) *Abortion Policies: A Global Review*, Vol. 1 (New York: Department for Economic and Social Information and Policy Analysis).

— (1993) *Abortion Policies: A Global Review*, Vol. 2 (New York: Department for Economic and Social Information and Policy Analysis).

— (1994) ICPD *Program of Action* (UN International Conference on Population and Development) (New York: ICPD Secretariat).

United Nations Children's Fund (UNICEF) (1994) *Kenya Maternal Mortality Baseline Study* (UNICEF).

United Nations Development Program (1993) 'Decentralization for Local Action', *Report on Human Development in Bangladesh*.

United Nations General Assembly (UNGA) (1969) *Teheran Proclamation on Human Rights*, Res.2545 [xxiv], (New York: UN).

United Nations Program on Human Reproduction (UNFPA) (1991) *1991 Program Review and Strategy Development Report* (New York: UN).

Vennix, P. (1990) *The Pill and Its Alternatives* (Delft: Eburon).

Wasserheit, J. N. and Holmes, K. K. (1992) 'Reproductive Tract Infections: Challenges for International Health Policy Programs and Research', in A. Germain et al. (eds), *Reproductive Tract Infections: Global Impact and Priorities for Women's Reproductive Health* (New York: Plenum Press).

Wongboonsin, K. (1995) *Population Policy and Programmes in Thailand 1929–Present.* Institute for Population Studies, Chulalongkorn University, Bangkok.

World Bank (1991) 'Bangladesh Managing Public Resources for Higher Group', *Publication 9379 BD*, p. 2.

— (1992) *Federal Republic of Nigeria: Implementing the National Policy on Population Sector*, Report, Vol. 2.

World Development Report 1995: Workers in an Integrated World (1995) (Oxford: OUP and World Development Indicators).

World Health Organization (1991) *Maternal Mortality: A Global Fact Book* (Geneva: WHO).

— (1993) *Abortion: A Tabulation of Available Data on the Frequency and Mortality of Unsafe Abortions* (Geneva: WHO/Division of Family Health).

— (1995) 'Perspectives on Methods of Fertility Regulation' (background paper) (Geneva: UNDP/UNFPA/WHO/World Bank Special Programme of Research, Development and Research Training in Human Reproduction).

— (1996) 'Improving Access to Quality Care in Family Planning: Medical Eligibility Criteria for Contraceptive Use', in *Family Planning and Reproductive Health* (Geneva: WHO).

— (1996) UNDP/UNFPA/WHO/World Bank Special Programme of Research, Development and Research Training in Human Reproduction, *Biennial Report 1994–1995*, 40 (Geneva: WHO).

Index